Why the Bubble Burst

NEW DIRECTIONS IN MODERN ECONOMICS
Series Editor: Malcolm C. Sawyer,
Professor of Economics, University of Leeds, UK

New Directions in Modern Economics presents a challenge to orthodox economic thinking. It focuses on new ideas emanating from radical traditions including post-Keynesian, Kaleckian, neo-Ricardian and Marxian. The books in the series do not adhere rigidly to any single school of thought but attempt to present a positive alternative to the conventional wisdom.

A list of published titles in this series is printed at the end of this volume.

Why the Bubble Burst

US Stock Market Performance since 1982

Lawrance Lee Evans Jr.

US General Accounting Office

NEW DIRECTIONS IN MODERN ECONOMICS

Edward Elgar
Cheltenham, UK • Northampton, MA, USA

Published by
Edward Elgar Publishing Limited
Glensanda House
Montpellier Parade
Cheltenham
Glos GL50 1UA
UK

Edward Elgar Publishing, Inc.
136 West Street
Suite 202
Northampton
Massachusetts 01060
USA

A catalogue record for this book
is available from the British Library

Library of Congress Cataloguing in Publication Data

Evans, Lawrance Lee, 1970-
  Why the bubble burst : US stock market performance since 1982 / Lawrance Lee
  Evans, Jr.
    p. cm. — (New directions in modern economics series)
  Includes bibliographical references.
    1. Stock exchanges—United States—History. 2. Stocks—United
  States—History. I. Title. II. New directions in modern economics.

HG4910.E93 2003
332.64'273'09048—dc21
                                                                      2003040827
ISBN 1 84376 075 4

Printed and bound in Great Britain by MPG Books Ltd, Bodmin, Cornwall

Contents

List of Figures   *vi*
List of Tables   *vii*
Acknowledgments   *ix*

1. Towards an Understanding of the Stock Market Bubble   1

2. Competing Theories of Stock Price Behavior   12

3. Empirical Approaches to Stock Values   45

4. Theoretical Approaches to the Stock Market Boom   74

5. Empirical Analysis I: The Stylized Facts   108

6. Empirical Analysis II: Formal Econometrics   149

7. Boom, Bubble and Burst   204

Notes   213
Bibliography   218
Index   234

Figures

2.1 Theories of equity price determination — 44

4.1 Stocks versus bonds — 87

5.1 Household net purchases — 113

5.2 Household portfolio composition — 115

5.3 Institutional investor portfolios — 118

5.4 Net purchases of corporate equity by sector (I) — 126

5.5 Net purchases of corporate equity by sector (II) — 133

5.6 Net capital inflow (by instrument) — 135

5.7 Net issues of domestic corporate equity — 138

5.8 Net issues of domestic corporate equity and stock market performance — 140

6.1 Impulse response functions — 168

Tables

4.1	S&P 500 dividend growth	80
4.2	Value estimates for the S&P 500	89
5.1	Equity as a percentage of total financial assets (by sector)	111
5.2a	Household direct and indirect ownership of corporate equity	121
5.2b	Percentages of equity outstanding held by sector 1965–99	122
5.3	Means and standard deviation of net purchases of corporate equity	128
5.4	Correlation coefficients net purchases	130
5.5	ROW impact on US financial markets (correlation coefficients)	136
5.6	Net issues, and stock price, profit and earnings growth	139
5.7	Correlation coefficients for stock performance and potential factors	141
6.1	Glossary of primary variables	151
6.2	Augmented Dickey–Fuller and Phillips–Perron tests for stationarity	156
6.3	Bivariate Granger causality tests	158
6.3c	Summary table for bivariate Granger causality tests	160
6.4	Multivariate Granger causality tests	166

6.5   Variance decompositions   173

6.6   Correlation coefficients   180

6.7a   Bivariate OLS results I   182

6.7b   Bivariate OLS results II   183

6.8   Preliminary multivariate results   187

6.9   Full multivariate results   190

6.10   Instrumental variables results   196

6.11   Summary – OLS results   200

Acknowledgments

First and foremost I would like to thank Robert 'Doc' Pollin for his tireless effort, patience and continued support without which this book would not have been possible. I owe a great intellectual debt to James Crotty whose years of support and guidance are undoubtedly reflected throughout this study. Thanks are also due to Bernard Morzuch for continued econometric training and mentorship. I must also thank Gerald Epstein, Jane D'Arista, Andrew Brimmer and Leonce Ndikumana whose suggestions and comments have contributed to this work in a significant way. Collectively, these individuals have contributed immensely to my professional development and I will be forever indebted.

Alan Sturmer, Alison Stone and Tara Gorvine at Edward Elgar Publishing provided essential editorial and support services that helped to shape the treatise that follows. I must express my appreciation to Carol Angus, Five College, Inc. and the entire Economics Department at Amherst College for accommodating me as a Fellow for the year when the bulk of this research was conducted. Special thanks are due to Walter Nicholson and Frank Westhoff for comments on portions of the project as well as technical support. A collective thank you goes to all my mentors, teachers and all others who have helped make this possible, especially Tom Michl, Don Waldman and Harvey Sindima at Colgate University, Efrain 'Freddy' Medina in Rochester, NY, Tom Palley and Charles Rice.

This work also benefited greatly from feedback I received from Steve Pressman and Ric Holt. I wish to sincerely thank my parents, Lawrance Sr. and Gwendolyn Evans, as well as other family members and friends whose support and kind words helped inspire me to complete this process in a timely fashion. A special thank you goes to my loving, patient wife, Vanessa Evans, for all those things too extensive to be listed here.

This book reflects my own independent work on the US stock market and is not based on any analysis conducted by the US General Accounting Office. As such the opinions and ideas expressed here do not reflect or represent the views of the US General Accounting Office in any way.

1. Towards an Understanding of the Stock Market Bubble

How we value the stock market now and in the future influences major economic and social policy decisions that affect not only investors but also society at large, even the world. If we exaggerate the present value of the stock market, then as a society we may invest too much in business startups and expansions, and too little in infrastructure, education, and other forms of human capital. If we think the market is worth more than it really is, we become complacent in funding our pension plans, in maintaining our savings rate, in legislating an improved Social Security system ... (Shiller, 2000a).

In the late 1990s societal preoccupation with the stock market and its spectacular performance was so pervasive that books like *Dow 36,000* found receptive audiences throughout the US. The authors confidently proclaimed elsewhere that, 'A sensible target date for Dow 36,000 is early 2005, but it could be reached much earlier'.[1] Based primarily on the belief that stocks were indeed destined to provide investors with superior returns going forward, funds flowed into the stock market at an unprecedented rate fueling one of the biggest bubbles in US history. Yet, although they may exist for an undetermined length of time, financial bubbles by their very definition are predestined to burst. The performancè of the US stock market from the second quarter of 2000 through 2002 made this painfully obvious to investors and stock analysts, many of whom believed that market would continually produce the double-digit gains with little to no downside risk. There will be no Dow 36,000 in 2005 – investors should consider themselves lucky if we see a Dow anywhere in the vicinity of 10,000 in 2005.

Why did the bubble burst after appearing seemingly impregnable to global financial crises and internal debacles like the collapse of Long-Term Capital Management? To fully comprehend this we need to understand the evolution of the stock market bubble as the formation itself explains the roots of the collapse. Identifying the forces driving US equity values over the 1982–2000 period take us beyond the standard and popular theories. In short, the unparalleled escalation in stock values was produced by sizeable international and domestic demand flows in the face of a shrinking supply of corporate equity via share repurchases, leveraged buyouts and merger activity. As the insatiable demand chased a diminishing supply, the resulting prices became detached from their more reasonable values. Ultimately, the bubble burst because the stock market had been driven to unsustainable levels by forces unrelated to economic fundamentals and the pace of equity retirements could not be maintained.

The recent proliferation of earnings restatements and recognition of dubious accounting practices, alongside explosive debt to equity ratios, corporate bankruptcies, class action lawsuits and disappearing high-tech companies are the vestiges of a hungover economy confused by unjustified stock market valuations. Companies like Enron, Global Crossing, Adelphia, Critical Path, Qwest, Rite Aid, Kmart, WorldCom, Xerox, ConAgra, AOL Time Warner and Kroger make it abundantly clear that stock prices in the United States by one way or the other produced misleading signals about underlying corporate performance. The meltdown, much like the run-up, has been well chronicled in the business press. Tales of catastrophic losses have replaced the countless narratives of swollen 401(k) accounts. Investors have gone from what Warren Buffet described as 'giddy' to, according to an April 2001 edition of *Business Week*, 'mad as hell'.

While this book does not seriously address the issues of the quality of financial information transmitted to the public, or the role of investment banks and stock analysts in the run-up, the evidence suggests that investors are justified in pointing a collective finger at US corporations and the security industry. (Our focus on the role of corporations in the stock market boom is limited primarily on the retirement of equity on the secondary markets, which served to boost stock prices during the 1980s and late 1990s.) However, investors prone to speculative enthusiasms are unduly susceptible to misrepresentation, corporate fraud and new economy concepts lacking true economic substance. Moreover, it was the exuberant trading activity of investors that was partially responsible for the placing of unrealistic earnings expectations on corporations and the rewarding of high-tech firms without profits, clearly identifiable products, or realistic blueprints for success. Domestic and international shareholders, then, should be equally angry with themselves for providing an environment conducive to dubious corporate practices.

RECAPPING THE PHENOMENON

During the late 1960s and 1970s the stock market in the US performed abysmally. This was exemplified by the performance of the Standard and Poor's (S&P) 500 Index, which increased a mere 1.2 per cent between 1968 and 1980 and actually declined from 1975 to 1981. Yet the stage was being set for one of the most dramatic bull markets in US history. The period 1982 until October 1987 saw the S&P Index rise from 107.8 to 318 (an increase of 171 per cent). Despite the turbulence of 1987 and the bearish climate of 1990, the market continued to record gains and by the end of 1992 the S&P 500 Index stood at 408.27. While the market performance had already surpassed the bull markets of the late

1920s and the mid-1960s, the greatest and most intense run-up in equity values had yet to occur. From 1995 to the end of the first quarter of 2000 the S&P surged from 465 to 1442.12 – another 210 per cent in nominal terms.

By the end of 1999 the S&P 500 Index had risen an extraordinary 1,118 per cent from its 1982 level in nominal terms (644 per cent in real terms). However, over the same period nominal S&P 500 earnings and dividends increased approximately 200 per cent and 150 per cent, respectively (just 40 per cent and 63 per cent in real terms). The total value of US corporate equity was nearly twice the value of gross national income while the key measures of stock market valuation, namely the price multiples, appeared to be at unsustainable levels when juxtaposed to the long-run historical trend. In particular, the price–earnings ratio on S&P 500 stock stood at 44.3 – reminiscent of the 32.6 figure seen just prior to the great crash of 1929. In fact, Robertson and Wright (1998) note that even at the end of 1997 Tobin's q was 'at a historically extreme value, comparable only to that seen this century in late 1929' (p. 20).

Historically, low dividend yields have served as an important indicator of market overvaluation, with market corrections occurring as the yield approaches 2.65 per cent (Standard and Poor's Stock Market Encyclopedia, 1999). However, the new millennium began with a yield on S&P 500 stock of approximately 1.14 per cent, accentuating the fact that equity prices in the United States had reached levels consistent with expected dividend growth rates that were, by historical standards, unprecedented. This implied that either the run-up in equity values was not well anchored by fundamentals, that there had been a significant shift in the risk–return characteristics of the stock market, or that something extraordinary had occurred in the underlying real economy. These possibilities begged questions about the forces underpinning the phenomenal increase in US equity prices and whether the boom was the result of investor euphoria or rational assessments of future prosperity. The popular answers that dominated the academic literature and business press illustrated conflicting visions about equity price movements and more importantly exposed the lacuna in the dominant theory of asset pricing.

Despite the efficient markets hypothesis (EMH), the struggle to understand the forces underpinning equity price movements has been well documented. In 1986, Chen et al. wrote, 'A rather embarrassing gap exists between the theoretically exclusive importance of systematic "state variables" and our complete ignorance to their identity'. In his 1988 address to the American Economic Association, Richard Roll stated, 'The immaturity of our science is illustrated by the conspicuous lack of predictive content about some of its most interesting phenomena, particularly changes in asset prices' (Canova and De Nicolo, 1995). Against the backdrop of the run-up in US equity prices Robert Hall (2001) once again reiterated the perennial struggle to understand equity price dynamics noting, 'Economists are as perplexed as anyone by the behavior of the stock market'. Given this general uncertainty about equity price movements it is to be expected that economists

– especially those attached to the theory of efficient markets – have struggled to understand the recent stock market boom, bubble and burst.

There are two principal views of the 1982–2000 bull market inspired by the EMH: the new economy theory and the falling risk premium theory. The former (in numerous incarnations – some more plausible than others) holds that the revolution in information technology ushered in a high-growth 'new' economic era and thus the appreciation in stock prices was justified primarily on the basis of discounted future dividend payouts. One widely established variant of the latter maintains that the increase in market participation, alongside the push towards portfolio diversification and the proliferation of new financial instruments that help manage risk, resulted in a substantial decline in the risk premium and thus, the required rate of return. Another version of the falling equity risk premium theory argues that investors 'learned' the stock market was inherently less risky relative to alternative investments and were therefore content with a lower expected rate of return going forward. While both theories are consistent with the EMH and justify the stock market boom on fundamental grounds, one portends high earnings growth in the future and the other implicitly assumes that investors will be comfortable with lower returns into the future.

These conclusions are not completely without merit given the robust performance of the underlying real economy and the length of the recent bull market. However, due to the implausibility of the implied dividend growth rates necessary to validate equity values that existed at the end of the first quarter of 2000 coupled with poor profit performance in the late 1990s, especially for the 'new economy' Internet firms, skepticism about the new era theory abounded (Gordon, 2000; Paulre, 2000; Perkins and Perkins, 1999; Browne, 1999). Moreover, from its quarterly peak to the opening of the markets in 2002, the S&P 500 Index declined by 20.4 per cent. Correspondingly, the technology-heavy Nasdaq 5000 Index dropped a whopping 60.8 per cent from its peak value. 2002 proved to be an even worse year for stock market investors as all major market indices in the United States collapsed, erasing the gains attained over the previous five years. Thus, proponents of the new economy theory face a serious challenge to explain the abrupt market downturn of 2000 and the poor performance thereafter. To remain consistent with the EMH, this theory strains credulity as readers are forced to believe the new economy appeared then disappeared over the course of a decade.

The falling risk premium theory also appears deficient in explaining a sizeable portion of price appreciation given the increasing volatility in US equity markets since 1996 and recent econometric evidence suggesting that the risk premium has not significantly trended downwards (see Hayes et al., 1998). Moreover, as we discuss more fully in the later chapters, the theory is premised on developments in the stock market that are at odds with key stylized facts and investor survey data that suggests investors were still expecting near double-digit gains going forward at the market peak. Nevertheless, such theories remind investigators that even though the appreciation in prices was unprecedented, it does not immediately follow that the market valuations were unwarranted by economic fundamentals.

With the significant decline in stock values during 2000–2003 and the implausibility of the theories that trace stock movements completely back to 'fundamentals', other influential theories which break away from the EMH and identify the market conditions as a speculative bubble resulting from 'irrational exuberance' on the part of the investing public appear much more credible. Shiller's (2000a) bubble theory, which builds on his earlier work (1984, 1989), is premised upon social-psychological dynamics that consequently spawn investing fads and fashions, culminating in the under-pricing of risk and a rupturing of prices from their intrinsic values. Others focus on choice under fundamental uncertainty, market psychology and an adaptive expectation process, which facilitates bandwagon and herding behavior, conventionally determined prices and financial euphoria. Central to both, however, is the notion that all flows impart price pressure on market valuations irrespective of economic fundamentals and that the recent boom was not only unprecedented but also unjustifiable. These theories are appealing and, when placed in a historical context, appear to explain why stock prices exhibit excess volatility when juxtaposed to risk-adjusted, discounted future dividends. These diverging views alone make a study of US equity prices during the recent bull market a relevant study.

Beyond the Popular Theories

There are six important stylized facts from the 1982–2000 period that are key to explaining the stock market boom and bubble. One, US corporations experienced strong growth in profitability during the period indicating that some portion of the run-up can be attributed to economic fundamentals. Two, the period corresponded with the significant and unprecedented decline in corporate equity outstanding, initiated in part by SEC Rule 10b-18, which established a safe haven for corporations to repurchase shares. The public has yet to come to grips with the fact that the US corporate sector during the 1980s and 1990s resembled a lizard garnering strength by eating its own tail. Third, the period also saw the United States shift from net lender to net debtor status and the resulting capital flows into the stock market were enormous. Fourth, the most dramatic shift of equity holdings from individual investors to institutional investors as a collective sector had occurred before 1980. In fact, by 1975 institutional investors accounted for 75 per cent of all market trading. Thus, attributing a perceived fall in the risk premium to the rise of institutional investors appears to be an inadequate explanation for the 1982–2000 stock market boom. Fifth, the 1980s and 1990s did coincide with the growth of mutual funds – a sector that is generally held to be myopic,

exhibit noise-trading behavior and serve as a suitable proxy for irrational sentiment. Sixth, more recently, it has been widely acknowledged that corporate profitability was artificially inflated, both by the failure to expense stock options and
the employment of questionable accounting practices by a number of US corporations.

Collectively these facts are more consistent with the speculative bubble hypothesis than those that attribute the run-up entirely to corporate fundamentals.
While the theories stemming from the EMH are untenable, Shiller (2000a) provides an excellent decomposition of the domestic demand side of the equity appreciation puzzle. However, by itself the 'irrational exuberance' hypothesis is an
incomplete postmortem of the stock market bubble as it misses two essential
ingredients, foreign capital inflows into the stock market – stylized fact (3), and
the considerable shrinkage in the supply of corporate equity outstanding –
stylized fact (2). Failure to identify these integral forces precludes a full
understanding of the bubble, that is, why it was so intense, why it was different
from the bubbles of the 1920s and 1960s and more importantly why the downturn
will be intense and protracted. Clearly then, we need to go far beyond the EMH
and augment the domestic irrational exuberance theory to fully explain the 1982–
2000 experience.

OVERVIEW

The book offers an empirical investigation into the 1982–2000 stock market
boom, simultaneously contributing to the literature on equity price dynamics and
shedding light on some of the forces behind the longest and most intense bull
market in US history. The work draws first on the efficient markets literature but
argues that US stock prices reflecting purely rational assessments about the future
growth of corporate profits and changes in discount rates is highly unlikely. The
persistent divergence between stock prices and earnings (price–earnings ratios)
during the 1990s alone is cause for suspicion. As such, we explore alternative
paradigms, including speculative and portfolio allocation theories, many of which
leave room for those important insights emphasized by proponents of the theory
of efficient capital markets. That is, profits and the ability to make cash payouts
to shareholders remain important to interpreting equity price dynamics. However, to the contrary, the speculative theories also emphasize that the flow of
funds into secondary markets which ultimately determine prices are inspired in
part by forces that are independent of economy-wide fundamentals. It is from
here that we frame the investigation, placing supply and demand at the center of
the analysis to identify three main forces behind the run-up in US equity values
during the period.

First, it is argued that the shift in domestic savings towards equity and away
from alternative assets has influenced equity prices in a manner unrelated to the

underlying corporate performance. The important implication here is that the boom can be partially attributed to the manner in which agents have chosen to allocate funds – a choice that is inspired by profit growth, euphoria (unrealistic profit expectations), belief in equity as the superior asset and the poor performance of rival assets. Important to these developments are institutional investors (especially the mutual fund sector) who facilitate this portfolio shift and transform equity markets at the same time. While the theory of efficient capital markets rules out the effect of portfolio behavior, this book holds that the increase in demand is critical to understanding the recent stock market boom.

In the same vein, this book secondly implicates direct international capital flows into the stock market as an important causal force behind the 1982–2000 bull market. This reflects the internationalization of financial markets and has important implications for international policy. These hypotheses, although seemingly obvious, do not have a stronghold in conventional intellectual circles since the dominant theory holds that flows carrying no information about future dividend payments, or that do not spread risk, have no bearing on the equity price determination process. Instead the willingness to buy is balanced by the willingness of lesser enthusiastic investors to sell and thereby unjustifiable price pressure effects net out to zero. However, the portfolio flow theory advanced in Chapter 4 argues that the demand of global investors for equity is a function of the relative risk and return characteristics of domestic and foreign equity markets. Thus, the superior performance of the US market coupled with financial crises occurring during the 1990s in emerging markets served to increase foreign flows into the US stock market. In the same note, the poor equity performance of 2002 reflects in part a global retreat from US stock markets.

A cursory glimpse of the popular theories reveals that the question of what drove the dramatic increase in US equity prices over the last two decades is primarily couched in terms of investor demand. That is, the run-up is attributed to over-exuberant expectations, rational assessments of future prosperity, or the changing risk characteristics inherent in stock market investing. Yet, an important development of the last two decades is that instead of issuing new shares during the period of equity price appreciation, corporations have reduced the volume of equity outstanding on secondary markets. A logical extension of the various flow theories of price determination is that changes in the supply of equity can place upward pressure on market valuations as well. Thus, we maintain that, in addition to domestic and foreign flows, equity retirements from merger, takeover and restructuring activity and share repurchases have contributed to the run-up in US equity values.

Econometric Methodology

The supply and demand theory utilized in this book leads directly to the flow of funds methodology. In this manner we investigate whether institutional investor net purchases, foreign portfolio equity investment and net issues of corporate equity moved stock prices to unjustifiable levels. A similar approach to financial markets can be found in Friedman (1977, 1982), who utilizes a supply and demand model of long-term interest rate determination to examine the effect of financial flow variables (net issues and purchases of corporate bonds) on bond yields.

To explore the tenability of our hypotheses we bring rigorous empirical technique to bear on the subject. Following Lawrence Summers (1991) three main methodological approaches can be readily identified from the empirical literature: (1) the structural model approach, (2) the vector autoregressive approach (VAR) and (3) 'the informal pragmatic empirical approach' (p. 140). The first approach involves beginning with a pre-specified model founded in theory and uses the existing data to determine the orders of magnitude of the structural parameters (Kennedy, 1993, p. 79). To the contrary, the VAR methodology imposes no structure a priori and uncovers the causal relationships that exist through the actual estimation of the model (Sims, 1972, 1980). The 'pragmatic empirical approach' involves the use of various informal methods 'to gauge the strength of associations' among economic variables.

This book employs each of these techniques in the exploration of US stock price dynamics. The exploitation of these econometric methodologies in a complementary manner enables us to better negotiate limitations in the data and prevent the conclusions from becoming unduly sensitive to the method of approach. Utilizing the VAR approach permits an investigation into the interrelationships and dynamic interactions among equity prices, net issues and domestic and international flows. The methodology is appealing since by working with unrestricted reduced forms and treating all variables as potentially endogenous we are more likely to gauge the full effect these variables have on stock prices. The multivariate technique allows for unbiased tests of Granger causality and innovation accounting, all of which enable us to determine whether foreign capital inflow, net issuance, and institutional investor flows influence and explain a statistically significant portion of the variation in stock prices.

The structural model and instrumental variable techniques provide a more robust joint test of the supply and demand-based hypotheses, since we can look directly at the contemporaneous relationship between net flows and stock market performance while controlling for the forward-looking nature of stock prices. Lastly, the pragmatic empirical approach allows us to distinguish between competing theories of the stock market boom, using less sophisticated analyses such as examining descriptive statistics and inspecting trends in the data. Using this more informal approach in a complementary fashion is extremely important since it is often the case that competing theories cannot be dismissed purely on the basis of formal econometrics. Collectively the evidence based on the structural, reduced form and pragmatic empirical approaches indicate generally that the effects of supply and demand should not be omitted from the general assessment of equity price movements and more specifically that US equity prices during the 1982–2000 period were driven largely by forces unrelated to economic fundamentals.

BOOK OUTLINE

The book proceeds as follows. Chapter 2 provides a critical overview of the theoretical literature on general equity price determination and fluctuation. We survey the efficient market literature in great detail alongside noise trading and rational bubble theory. To illustrate the long-established alternative to the conventional theory, we also outline the various speculative theories advanced by Keynes, Veblen, Shiller and Minsky as well as notable others that emphasize fundamental uncertainty in equity pricing. The survey is extensive for three principal reasons. First, since our goal is to explain the explosion in US equity prices each theory could potentially be important in explaining at least some of the movement in prices. Second, the theories surveyed are imperative in placing the book's conjectures and consequent empirical investigation in context. Finally, one must clearly understand the complex joint hypothesis advanced by efficient capital market theorists in order to appreciate the competing supply and demand-based approach advanced here and the empirical work undertaken to illustrate that prices can be moved by flows unrelated to economic fundamentals.

Chapter 3 evaluates the preexisting empirical and econometric literature inspired by the general theories of equity price movements relevant for our purposes. The review fleshes out the various econometric approaches, their successes in evaluating the forces underpinning stock price fluctuation and provides a benchmark model for addressing the relationship between fundamentals along with the caveats that accompany such an investigation. Moreover, while uncovering and evaluating the empirical evidence bearing on the relationship between stock market valuations, fundamentals and flows, we also indirectly review the main empirical investigative techniques as they pertain to the investigation into the forces behind share price fluctuation. The empirical work that attempts to evaluate the claim of a horizontal demand for equity (as well as Friedman, 1977, 1982) serves as a precedent for the flow of funds approach undertaken in Chapters 5 and 6 to evaluate the run-up in US equity prices.

In Chapter 4 we utilize the open-economy Minskian model of financial fragility and the Keynesian-inspired speculative market theories to situate and piece together the supply and demand theory of equity price determination. In short, the model explains how a period of strong profit growth can encourage euphoric expectations that lead to the exaggeration of future profit growth and the underpricing of risk. In this manner we are better able to place the growing demand and shrinking supply in context, explaining not only how these pressures impact prices but also why these developments occurred. From here we use the flow theory directly to explain the run-up in US equity prices during the 1982–1999 period. Chapter 5 juxtaposes the supply and demand explanation for the unprecedented bull market to the stylized facts, establishing a prima facie case for the hypothesis advanced here. We chronicle the domestic growth in the demand of corporate equity, the reduction in supply, and the rise of the mutual fund sector as well as the influx of foreign savings into US financial markets. Additionally, we also discuss why the new economy and falling risk premium stories are untenable and therefore cannot consistently account for escalation in equity valuations.

The formal econometric examination of the hypotheses is conducted in Chapter 6. The evidence from Granger causality tests, innovation accounting techniques and the structural model approach is consistent with the contention that net flows (supply and demand forces) move equity valuations even when controlling for economy-wide fundamentals. More specifically, the hypotheses that negative net issuance, foreign portfolio and mutual fund flows as well as proxies for expected future dividend payouts explain the stock boom are found to be consistent with the data. Based on these theoretical and empirical results we conclude that the bull market, while originating in corporate profitability, was driven to a larger extent by the significant reduction in the supply of equity and the enormous inflow of foreign and domestic flows into the stock market. The most disquieting finding is that among institutional investors it is mutual fund not pension fund flows that are found to explain a significant amount of the run-up in US equity prices. Chapter 7 concludes with a summary of the results and a reconnection with the EMH and speculative theories of asset price determination.

It should be noted that this study is not a test of the theory of efficient capital markets although it bears on the subject and produces evidence contrary to the predictions of the conventional theory. As we detail in the next two chapters the strong version of the hypothesis is elusive and unfalsifiable. The semi-strong version requires event studies, and moreover what actually constitutes violations of the theory in this regard is poorly defined. Similarly, evidence that appears to contradict the weak version of the hypothesis gives rise to fundamental differences in interpretation. Furthermore, the theory is a complex joint hypothesis and thus contradictory evidence can either imply that the model of stock market equilibrium was improperly specified or that the market is truly inefficient. Consequently, it is not our endeavor here to disprove or prove whether markets are efficient, only to investigate the forces which combined to spawn the spectacular

1,000 per cent-plus appreciation in US stock prices and illustrate that supply and demand changes cannot be marginalized in analysis of equity valuation.

The evidence documented in this book suggests that the run-up in US equity prices cannot be traced back singularly to the fundamental factors emphasized by the conventional asset-pricing models and, therefore, more effort should be devoted to the development of alternative theories of speculative price movements. From the analysis it becomes straightforward to understand why the bubble burst and why the fallout has been so dreadful. Nonetheless, astute investors will understand that it will take a protracted period of persistently low or negative returns to generate the historical real rate of return of 7 per cent going forward.

2. Competing Theories of Stock Price Behavior

To their great credit, even the most neo-classical finance theorists accept that financial markets in practice are very imperfect. However, they have not drawn the proper conclusions from this, namely that theory has to start from a consideration of the historical reality of markets, rather than assumptions about how they might work (Toporowski, 1999b).

INTRODUCTION

Asset prices, equity prices in particular, have an important role in the allocation of a society's resources, and therefore understanding their dynamics is crucial to appreciating how economic systems function. Over the last two decades, the stock market's rising size and significance in the global economy, coupled with extraordinary booms and crashes, have forced intensive study of the relationship between stock prices and real economic activity. As a result, the equity price determination literature in the area of macroeconomics, and international and financial economics has become voluminous. Inasmuch as this study is motivated by a general desire to understand the forces underpinning equity price determination and fluctuation, and more specifically, to analyze critically US stock market dynamics during the 1982–2000 period, we draw on much of these works.

While it is conventionally held that asset prices respond principally to fundamental economic news, volatile swings in stock prices, booms and crashes all suggest that other important non-intrinsic elements enter significantly into the determination process as well. Correspondingly, several views have emerged to interpret the function of stock markets as a vehicle for channeling savings and a medium for allocating capital to its best uses. As Barsky and DeLong (1989) note, at one extreme are those who tout the market to be a proper 'social calculating machine' (p. 2). A view of the stock market as the quintessential perfectly competitive market has occupied a space in neoclassical theory since the time of Walras, Marshall and Wicksteed (Raines and Leathers, 2000, p. 3). At the opposite end of the spectrum are cynics who view the stock market as 'no place for widows and orphans – or any other investors with an aversion to risk ... where clandestine investment pools manipulate share prices with impunity' (Kansas, 1996, p. R1).

It seems that ever since active trading began around the buttonwood tree, equity markets have been the center of myth, controversy and competing interpretations regarding its actual function in the real economy. During the 40-year period following 1752, trading in the Wall Street area had been limited to various commodities, ranging from cotton and tobacco to sugar and slaves. It was only on occasion that corporate shares or government securities and scrip were publicly auctioned off, since the former was considered extremely risky and the latter worthless.[1] However, when the government decided to honor its debt obligations in 1790 by repurchasing the $80 million in scrip it had issued during the Revolutionary War, and perhaps more importantly sold $10 million worth of shares in the First Bank of the United States, a vibrant market in securities emerged (Blume et al., 1993, p. 22).

By 1792, the first major stock speculator had gone bankrupt, initiating financial panic in New York City. New York officials viewed the perceived gambling activities as counterproductive and legislated an end to public stock auctions 'to prevent the pernicious practice of stock-jobbing' (Blume et al., 1993, p. 23). Yet the officials underestimated the resolve of at least 24 auctioneers who found a loophole in the legislature and by May 17 of the same year began trading *privately* on Wall Street (Houthakker and Williamson, 1996, p. 111; Blume et al., 1993, p. 23; Bernstein, 1996, p. 88). To achieve these ends, the auctioneers signed the Buttonwood Agreement that circumvented the government intervention, establishing an exclusive trading organization that would later, with the formal constitution of 1817, become the New York Stock Exchange (Johnson and Pazderka, 1995, p. 2).

To some, the New York law mandated against public stock auctions, while not achieving its true purpose was a step in the right direction and at the very least ideologically commendable. Theodore Roosevelt, prior to the Great Depression, claimed that gambling on the stock market was morally equivalent to betting on dice, horses or cards (*The Economist*, October 23, 1999). Keynes, commenting on the speculative nature of stock market activity in the United States over a century after the inception of active equity trading, wrote:

> Americans are apt to be unduly interested in discovering what average opinion believes average opinion to be: and this national weakness finds its nemesis in the stock market (Keynes, 1964, p. 159).

Therefore, to avoid the capital development of countries from becoming the inadequate consequence of casino-like activities, Keynes suggested that either the purchase of equity be made 'permanent and indissoluble, like marriage' or stock markets should be rendered like casinos, 'inaccessible and expensive' to the public (Keynes, 1964, pp. 159–60).

Many contemporary scholars have echoed the themes found in Keynes' *General Theory*. Galbraith (1988), for instance, speaks of equity markets as bacchanalian dens where men and women of ill repute engage in speculative orgies. Strange (1986, 1998) argues that as a result of financial market integration the entire Western financial system has become a large casino containing an assortment of speculative 'games' and the activities therein possess the potential to bankrupt national economies. Special emphasis is placed on stock markets, however, as Strange (1998) observes them to be the most fragile component in the international financial system and harbingers of future crisis. While these works focus on the speculative nature of stock markets, Lewis' (1989) *Liar's Poker* also includes a vision of corporate avarice and financial excess, pointing out internal forces at odds with the attainment of asset prices that solely reflect true corporate fundamentals.

However, economists who envision equity markets as vital intermediaries that pool funds, disseminate information, spread risk, allocate capital, and pressure managers towards efficiency counter these viewpoints. Brealey (1991), for example, takes serious issue with the ideas expressed by Keynes stating that the latter 'did no service to economics with his dismissive quips about stock market investment' (quoted in Pratten, 1993, p. 186). Stigler (1964) espoused a view of stock market speculators as necessary to ensure arbitrage and contended that 'efficient capital markets are the major protection of investors' – a belief that maintains a heavy presence in financial economics (Raines and Leathers, 2000, p. 57). More sympathetically, Johnson and Pazderka (1995) claim that stock markets are misunderstood, vilified and unnecessarily maligned, summing up works analogous to Lewis (1989) as 'scare stories' that 'are easy to write but lack perspective'. In turn, these scholars view stock markets as an ingenious but underappreciated invention, much similar to the Yale lock, zipper or the paper clip (p. ix). Their overview includes an adulation of speculators, hostile takeovers and derivative instruments, all of which enable stock markets to exist as institutions that promote efficiency, capital development and economic growth.

Fischer and Merton (1983) lamented the secondary role the stock market was presumed to perform in investment decisions in the macroeconomic theoretical framework, which traditionally focused attention on bond markets, as it is the interest rate that is taken to be the appropriate measure of the cost of capital. Instead, the authors laud financial economists for properly exalting the stock market as the 'single most important market in finance' (p. 60). In this context, equity prices that emerge from secondary stock markets serve simultaneously as summary statistics regarding expected future corporate earnings and uncompromising graders of past investment decisions. Consequently, stock prices provide key signals to managers regarding the allocation of scarce capital across sectors, and thus become the more apt indicator of the cost of capital. Viewed in this manner, the stock market is simply a 'mirror' that reflects changes in the nation's underlying capital stock (Galbraith, 1988, p. 88). Furthermore, even in the case where stock prices differ from managers' assessments of fundamentals, the authors hold that the stock market should still be exploited whenever these divergences are advantageous. Fischer and Merton (1983) take the financial view of stock markets and equity prices serious enough to advocate the conducting of open market operations in indexed mutual funds rather than in conventional government treasury bills (p. 93).

To be fair, many economists, including some of those aforementioned, would agree that stock markets contain both elements: destabilizing speculative dynamics and beneficial intermediary components (Houthakker and Williamson, 1996; Bernstein, 1996; Shiller, 1989). In many cases the difference between visions of the stock market ultimately come down to which of these elements is most emphasized in describing the evolution of stock prices. In other cases the stock price determination process is stripped bare of any extrinsic influences and married to the rational expectations hypothesis to render stock markets consistent with the theory of perfect competition. Astute scholars of financial markets have acknowledged that:

> Economists and statisticians alike have brought their research tools to bear on this subject, not primarily to find an easy road to fortune (though who is to say that such a thought did not occur) but to establish the relationship of securities markets to the ideal constructs of their theories (Cootner, 1964, p. 1, excerpted in Raines and Leathers, 2000, p. 46).

Nevertheless, the contention between proponents of these differing views has spawned an extensive literature that serves as a rich foundation for any investigation seeking to unpack US equity price movements. For simplicity and brevity we focus only on the literature concerning equity price determination, leaving out many interesting issues that are tangentially related. It is important to underscore that an exhaustive overview is important to flesh out the various theories where they are significant for understanding stock prices since each may be insightful for modeling purposes, and all may help to place our subsequent investigation into the 1982–2000 bull market into perspective.

THEORIES OF EQUITY PRICE DETERMINATION

The Efficient Market Hypothesis (EMH) and Related Literature

Generally there is agreement among economists that the fundamental value of share is the present discounted (and risk-adjusted) value of the expected flow of income emanating from corporate earnings, as reflected in the general present value relation. Although there are several variants, the present value formulation is commonly expressed as 'simple valuation model'. Following Lehmann (1991), this benchmark model, widely held as the 'intellectual centerpiece of financial theory', can be expressed formally as:

$$P_t = \sum_{n=1\ldots\infty} E^*[d_{t+n} Y_{t,n} / I_t],\ Y_{t,n} > 0,\ \forall_{t,n} > 0, \tag{2.1}$$

where P_t is the price of a share, d_{it+n} is the income payments out of corporate profits received at time $t + n$, $Y_{t,n}$ is the pricing kernal, which effectively discounts the income stream by the required rate of return, and $E^*[\cdot / I_t]$ is the expectations operator, reflecting probability beliefs conditioned on relevant information at time t.

There is, however, great dissension over the accuracy with which this stream of cash flows can be approximated by the trading of individuals operating under conditions of fundamental uncertainty, or more importantly how investors behave under such conditions. In the rational markets view, investors trade in a specific stock on the basis of fundamental economic factors (although their information set may be imperfect). Given incomplete information, the current market price that emerges may be dissimilar from the intrinsic value of the share in the short run. Arbitrage possibilities, however, allow astute traders with accurate information to profit from the under- or overvaluation in any specific stock. Consequently, the trading activity of such arbitrageurs eliminates any discrepancy between the market price and intrinsic value. In this lagged manner, market outcomes come to mirror rational assessments of fundamental value (Raines and Leathers, 2000, p. 5).

According to this 'rational market view', equation (2.1) is simply a rough guide to equity valuation. This notion has a longstanding tradition in security analysis dating back to Graham and Dodd (1934), who advised financial advisors to base their investment decision on the intrinsic value of shares, that is, conduct themselves in accordance to 'fundamental value analysis'. In *Security Analysis* (1934), Graham and Dodd contended that actual stock prices fluctuated around their fundamental values, which was approximated by the discounted cash flow accruing to the holder of the security. Gains were then to be had by those investors who traded according to a formula based on fundamental value theory. In short, investors were advised into the role of arbitrageurs, purchasing securities undervalued by the market and selling those overvalued by the market (Leroy, 1989, p. 1586).

It is important to note that Graham and Dodd acknowledged the difficulties inherent in measuring fundamental values such that strict equality was improbable. In fact, they held that:

> The market is not a weighting machine, on which the value of each issue is recorded by an exact and impersonal mechanism, in accordance with its specific qualities. Rather should we say the market is a voting machine, whereon countless individuals register choices, which are the product partly of reason and partly of emotion (Lehmann, 1991, p. 27).

Here, it is evident that Graham and Dodd adhered to the notion that the buying behavior of investors could cause market prices to deviate from their more 'objective' intrinsic values. Yet within their paradigm, rational investors would prevail, resulting in a persistent fluctuation of market prices around their true values as expressed by the standard valuation model.

Alfred Cowles (1933) produced evidence that even the relatively innocent notion of fundamental valuation defied empirical logic. In his view, strict equality between market prices and intrinsic values was not only unlikely but also contrary to expectation. Cowles illustrated that arbitrageur investing based on the fundamental value analysis and prescribed by Graham and Dodd actually underperformed the market, implying that 'investors who paid for these recommendations were wasting their money' (Leroy, 1989, p. 1586). Nevertheless, this and other such evidence, which refuted the weak rational markets view, did not inhibit other scholars from pressing forward with the fundamental value perspective.

For example, J.B. Williams in his *The Theory of Investment Value* (1938) espoused 'rational view' beliefs about the fundamental value of shares dominating the equity price determination process. Williams accentuated the earning power of corporations as the ultimate determinant of equity prices and is accredited with the first formulation of the widely accepted dividend discount model. The model is a slight alteration of equation (2.1) (see equation 3.1), identifying more specifically the source of the income justifying the value of a share – the periodic income payments in the form of dividends to shareholders. It must be emphasized again that these early theorists held the determination of fundamental values to be extremely elusive and, more importantly, made no requirement that individual traders embrace rational expectations. In equation (2.1), the 'early' or 'weak' rational market view implied that 'probability beliefs need only satisfy the general mathematical properties of an expectation' (Lehmann, 1991, p. 487).

Yet, out of this theory, and in the face of contradictory evidence, ultimately surfaced even more radical forms of the rational markets view. Efficient markets theorists separated the new theory from that of its precursors by ordering the probability beliefs fundamental to $E^*[\cdot/I_t]$ in the manner consistent with the rational expectations hypothesis.[2] That is, agents are assumed to know the relevant structural equations and the variables characterizing the equilibrium price of equity, believe that the market clears in a manner consistent with perfect competition, and assume that this information is common knowledge. Ergo, the probability beliefs 'embedded in $E^*[\cdot/I_t]$ represent objective conditional expectations $E[\cdot/I_t]$' (ibid., p. 487). The implication is that in the presence of uncertainty, individuals act as if attaching probabilities density functions to the various potential outcomes '(including the possible future stream of dividends) and act on these probability sets when investing' (Pratten, 1993, p. 4).

This behavior is the sine qua non of the EMH and in its strong version holds that the information set underpinning equity prices contains all that is relevant and available, both public and private. The inevitable outcome is that asset prices purely reflect fundamentals and are independent of extrinsic influences. Consequently, changes in share prices are attributed to new information or 'news' regarding the expected profit stream, discount factors or changes in the risk premium (Fama, 1970, 1991). Thus, for all intents and purposes, the hypothesis is an instantaneous adjustment version of the dividend discount or standard valuation model expressed in equations (2.1) and (3.1), or effectively what Lehmann (1991) terms the 'no-arbitrage' model. There is exact equality between price and objective fundamental value, and thus no grounds for profiting from past price behavior alone. Any portfolio investment strategy employed to beat the market must come at the expense of taking on more risk than the broad market.

Yet, predating efficient market theory, both in terms of intellectual formulation and following as well as empirical work, is the random walk hypothesis. With the standard valuation model pushed to the background, Kendell's (1953) statistical work and Granger and Morgenstern's (1963) econometric study (among a collection of others) demonstrated that stock prices followed a random walk. This meant that the future stock price would equal some random increment added to the price in the preceding period. Early evidence that stock prices exhibited random walk or martingale behavior was taken both as a validation of the efficiency of financial markets and evidence that supply and demand forces were paradoxically absent in stock markets. However, it was quickly recognized that stocks approximated a random walk essentially because new information arrives unpredictably and, in a manner consistent with perfect competition, is impounded in stock prices instantaneously through changes in demand. This empirical finding formed the base for the more developed theory, which held that market prices and objective fundamental values were everywhere equivalent – but not until serious intellectual polishing turned this simple statistical observation into a model of asset market equilibrium.

Leroy (1989) offers one of the most informative and extensive treatments of the history of the theory of efficient capital markets and points out that the random walk hypothesis was by itself an insufficient theory of equity price determination. For one, Cowles (1933) had already produced work that suggested that stock prices exhibited serial correlation. This evidence appeared to be inconsistent with the random walk hypothesis and at odds with theory of perfect competition as it applied to equity markets. However, the research of Working (1960) produced evidence that serial correlation was not necessarily incompatible with the random walk hypothesis, illustrating that if data generated by a unit root process 'were averaged over time spurious correlation between successive changes would result' (p. 1587). Thus, such correlation in stock price behavior was the predictable and uneventful consequence of its random behavior.

However, the apparent discrepancy between stock market dynamics and the theory of perfect competition was a much more damaging blow to the random walk hypothesis. Clearly, patterns in equity prices could exist only if the consequent profit opportunities they signal go unexploited – a clear violation of neoclassical competitive price theory or an indication that investors were irrationally ignoring profit opportunities. Furthermore, even if it were assumed that stock market investors were simply irrational, random walk proponents still had another difficult intellectual pill to swallow. The hypothesis implied that investors were wasting money employing security analysts and their recommendations. That investors were instead procuring substantial income from such advice was a hindrance to the orthodoxy. Both of these points implied that consistency of the random walk hypothesis depended squarely on investor irrationality and a refusal to accept that the large incomes generated by the advice of financial analysts were tangible (Pratten, 1993, p. 19).

Nevertheless, when stripped down to its essentials the random walk theory is merely a statistical observation about price behavior in capital markets with no grounding in the theory of neoclassical economic equilibrium. Even the strongest proponents realized that, in spite of the empirical evidence supporting the random walk thesis, it was still:

> Embarrassing for economists to have to shelve the competitive theory of price when it came to analyzing stock market prices, instead making do with informal qualitative remarks such as if stock prices did not follow a random walk there must exist unexploited profit opportunities. If stock prices had nothing to do with preferences and technology, what about the prices of the machines firms use? What about the wheat the farmer produces and the baker uses, but which is also traded on organized exchanges just like stock? Where does Marshall's *Principles* stop and the random walk start? (Leroy, 1989, p. 1588).

Walras, the founder of general equilibrium analysis, held that stock market activity corresponded most closely to the mechanics of his *tatonnement* process in which equilibrium market prices were established. Marshall, the founder of partial equilibrium concurred, holding that stock markets approximated those markets characterized in his theory of perfect competition and price determination (Raines and Leathers, 2000, pp. 39–42). Consequently, it was an anomaly for competitive equilibrium theory that the quintessential perfectly competitive market failed to yield price outcomes consistent with the stated theory. As the quote above accurately points out, this difficulty with stock price theory potentially extended far beyond stock markets. It is perhaps for this reason that the stock market became subject to intense examination by both neoclassical and heterodox economists. For neoclassical theorists the defense of orderly stock markets and perfect competition systematically required much more than the random walk hypothesis.

Formulating an alternate analytical theory of capital markets within the framework of competitive price theory and economic equilibrium became the explicit task of Paul Samuelson, one of the chief architects of the grand neoclassical synthesis. To these ends, Samuelson (1965) scrapped the random walk hypothesis in lieu of the more tractable martingale model, connecting the latter firmly to capital market efficiency. Although the actual term 'efficient' was not explicitly used in the 1965 paper, 'Proof That Properly Anticipated Prices Fluctuate Randomly' is considered the first analytical formulation of the EMH. To complete this task, Samuelson merged fundamental value analysis with the martingale model to derive the extreme result that market prices were unbiased estimates of intrinsic values.

A stochastic process is said to be a martingale if its dynamics are restricted to random movements about a constant mean. More formally, process x_t is a martingale if the optimal forecast of x_{t+1} given full information is x_t. We can write:

$$E(x_{t+1}|\Phi_t) = x_t$$

where Φ_t is the information set at time t. Correspondingly, x_t is a martingale if $x_{t+1} - x_t$ is a 'fair game', meaning the expectation of this difference, given the information set, is zero (Leroy, 1989, p. 1589). (The term 'fair game' is coined such because it rules out the availability of any abnormal profit opportunity.) The requirement that stock prices follow a martingale is less restrictive than presuming it to follow a random walk, which is deemed by some to be inconsistent with autocorrelation characteristically found in studies of stock price behavior. The relaxation of this constraint was key to Samuelson's development of a model that 'could be linked with traditional assumptions about preferences and returns' (Pratten, 1993, p. 23). It was shown that, on the basis of the fair game assumption, stock prices plus cumulated dividends would be equal to the discounted present value of the expected future prices and dividend payments. Thus, equilibrium in financial markets was properly characterized. At the same time, while the martingale model does not require independence between consecutive price movements, it still captured the basic nature of the random walk proponents' arguments regarding price behavior.

Having characterized stock price equilibrium in a manner consistent with the appropriate economic model, Samuelson couched his remaining analysis of stock market dynamics in terms of an abstract 'shadows' analogy to make the marriage between the martingale model and fundamental value analysis complete. It followed that since future events cast shadows ahead then investors who were self-interested, utility maximizers would 'take account of those elements of future events that in a probability sense may be discerned by casting their shadows before them' (p. 785, excerpted in Raines and Leathers, 2000, p. 46). In more simple terms, the fundamental traders dominate the exchange, trading on the basis of the information set, Φ_t, consequently bidding prices (which reflect the unpredictable 'shadows') to equality with fundamental values. With all profit opportunities extinguished by rational trade, Samuelson bequeathed the martingale model to financial economists, a model which was effectively an extreme version of the standard valuation model (Leroy, 1989, p. 1591).

Samuelson's work ultimately led to the strong version of the theory of efficient markets outlined above where the market price equals the present value of all future dividends. Yet Fama, in his seminal 1970 article that gave life to the term 'efficient capital markets', established two other applicable definitions of efficient markets, identifying them as 'semi-strong' and 'weak'. The semi-strong version requires that the information set used to determine prices contains all publicly held information, omitting that data which is privately held, while the weak form simply holds that future price behavior cannot be predicted on the basis of historical or current prices. Fama (1970) explicitly suggested that the appropriate version of efficiency that characterized capital markets was contingent on the breadth of the relevant information set (or how it was specified). Moreover, three tests were outlined on the basis of these categories: (1) weak form tests, which investigates the relationship between past and future returns, (2) semi-strong form tests, which assess how quickly information is transmitted to market prices and (3) strong form tests, which examines whether or not private information exists that is not impounded in security prices.

Leroy (1989) details the inconsistencies between the fair game model Fama (1970) employs to characterize market efficiency and the actual theory, arguing the mathematical expression, follows tautologously from the definitions presented and assumptions made. That is, the illustration that stock prices approximate a martingale process comes as a direct consequence of the fair game assumption. Consequently, efficient price dynamics are unrestricted and the capital markets theory in this instance is impervious to any empirical evidence that might contradict it (p. 1593). Fama, however, rejected Leroy's criticisms and in his 1976 finance text provides alternative definitions of capital market efficiency.

Here a capital market is defined as efficient if (1) the asset price determination process includes all relevant information, and (2) rational expectations characterize the market. The latter underscores the injection of the rational expectation concept into the theory of capital markets and the subsequent equating of asset prices and fundamental values.

Likewise, the suggested examinations of market efficiency were later abandoned for three alternative tests in Fama's (1991) article, the sequel to his groundbreaking 1970 work. Weak form tests were completely jettisoned in favor of tests for 'return predictability', which broadened the examination to include the investigation into whether specific variables have forecasting power for market returns. According to this article, the finding that returns are predictable is taken to be a powerful violation of the EMH. Regarding the strong and semi-strong from tests, Fama merely changes the labeling, referring to the latter as 'event studies' and the former as 'tests for private information'. If markets are efficient event studies should illustrate that the market processes new information quickly instead of gradually over time. On the other hand, tests for private information would hypothetically show that there exists no undisclosed information, that is information held only by insiders, that is not reflected in current prices.

Nonetheless, Fama's (1970) empirical survey followed Samuelson (1965) in utilizing the martingale model to characterize security prices and interpret market efficiency. As Leroy (1989) notes, 'Fama generally interpreted the near-zero autocorrelations of successive stock price changes as favoring market efficiency, suggesting that he in fact identified efficiency with the characterization or returns as a fair game ...' (p. 1595). In this manner the EMH remained firmly within the framework of economic equilibrium and as such is usually underpinned by the capital asset-pricing model (CAPM), arbitrage pricing theory (APT) or some other appropriate consumption-smoothing model. Pratten (1993) notes it is not surprising then that the theory is in essence a translation of Neo-Walrasian equilibrium theory to financial markets, where the risk-adjusted rates of return are brought into equality by competitive forces. Thus, the 'fundamentals' within the full-fledged efficiency markets framework are taken to be 'the basic parameters defining an economy – such as endowments, preferences and production possibilities' (Pratten, 1993, p. 18 quoting Cass and Shell, 1983). With rational expectations and self-interest, agents are presumed to estimate these 'fundamentals' accurately and trade accordingly.

Fama's market efficiency, then, had become inextricably linked to a model of equilibrium and therefore had metamorphosed into a complex joint hypothesis. The problem here is that once evidence is found that appears to contradict the joint hypothesis it can either be taken to imply that markets are indeed inefficient, or the inconsistency can be attributed simply to an inadequate asset-pricing model. As such one can never be absolutely sure whether the underlying model has been inappropriately specified or if the hypothesis of efficient markets has been truly violated. As Fama (1991) emphasized:

> we can only test whether information is properly reflected in prices in the context of a pricing model that defines the meaning of 'properly'. As a result, when we find anomalous evidence on the behavior of returns, the way it should be split between market inefficiency or a bad model of market equilibrium is ambiguous ... It is a disappointing fact that, because of the joint-hypothesis problem, precise inferences about the degree of market efficiency are likely to remain impossible (p. 1576).

Worse still, the extreme version of the hypothesis cannot be falsified since it is impossible to know the information available to market participants. However, even Fama (1991), the most avid of all early efficient market proponents, proclaimed that the strong version of the efficient market, while not susceptible to testing, 'is surely false' since 'there are surely positive information and trading costs' (1991, p. 1575). Fama suggests that the strong version of the hypothesis is still advantageous to theoreticians since it serves as a good simplifying benchmark model from which to engage in more complex analysis. This notwithstanding, while citing some evidence against, Fama (1970) concluded that the majority of the evidence weighed in favor of general market efficiency. Fama (1991), reevaluating more recent evidence, including the crash of 1987, again concluded that in spite of the occasional indications of inefficiency, the stock price fluctuated in a manner consistent with the hypothesis of efficient capital markets.

Under the craft of Samuelson and Fama, the EMH had come to dominate financial economic theory despite being mathematically 'tautologous' or trivial to some, and its early proponents expressing ambiguity regarding 'what empirical evidence would in principle contradict the theory' (Leroy, 1989, p. 1613). Moreover, it is clear that although the bulk of the discussion is couched in terms of informational efficiency, the far-reaching conclusion is that stock prices are fundamental-value efficient (that is stock prices equal their intrinsic values). Movements in stock prices are attributed solely to changes in discount factors and revised rational expectations about future corporate earnings based on genuine news. In 1978, a noted financial economist, Michael Jensen, wrote, 'the efficient market hypothesis is the best-established fact in all the social science' (Barberis, 1998, p. 163). A decade later, Summers and Summers (1989) wrote that 'prices will always reflect fundamental values' and 'the logic of efficient markets is compelling' (p. 166). Even today some economists, while silent about the market meltdown, maintain that the stock market boom can be attributed exclusively to fundamentals.

The assumption that agents act with full knowledge of the basic economic model that accurately characterizes the economy 'allows economists to construct simple and elegant models which appeal theoretically and require no collection of data pertaining to what really goes on in minds of investors' (Raines and Leathers, 2000, p. 126). For this reason, the EMH is influential and has withstood much of the criticisms launched at its internal logic and inability to explain some of the basic phenomena reflected in equity price movements over and again. Moreover, the incorporation of rational expectations into equity prices transformed the latter from the passive outcome of investor activity to a dynamic entity with a crucial informational role in the allocation of scarce capital. A new theoretical perspective emerged that envisioned stock prices as a leading indicator of economic activity. Further still, the suggested relationship between prices and economic fundamentals is presumed unidirectional. Within this paradigm, equity prices are summary statistics regarding future corporate performance and in general, the stock market is a crystal ball that anticipates changes in the nation's capital stock and productive, earning capacity.

In summation, the EMH makes four significant claims. First, abnormal profits possibilities from arbitrage are absent because equilibrium prices exactly equal fundamental value in an efficient market. The second claim, which extends from the first, maintains that extrinsic forces do not influence asset prices and thus only genuine and new information about discounted present value of expected future dividends (enabled by corporate earnings) initiates fluctuation in stock prices. Third, the stock prices convey valuable information about a particular firm's growth prospects and when aggregated serves as a forward-looking indicator of macroeconomic performance. The fourth claim follows logically from its precursors: In a well-functioning stock market capital is allocated efficiently across sectors. However, when turning to the econometric investigations of equity price fluctuations inspired by the EMH in the subsequent chapter it will become apparent that some of the difficulties encountered in the literature stem directly from the determination to strictly adhere to the latter in earnest. For the most part this is a near impossible task and, ironically, in cases where it is possible the assumptions are detrimental to the quantitative analysis.

Speculative Market and Alternative Theories

One of the most comprehensive and meticulous treatments of speculative market theories is found in Raines and Leathers' (2000) exceptional text, *Economists and the Stock Market: Speculative Theories of Stock Market Fluctuations*. As is noted here, the crux of the speculative market view is that assets are purchased based on the belief of future price appreciation, implying that price movements are based primarily on the balance of public opinion rather than objective fundamentals. While the standard valuation model remains central to most theories of speculative equity price movements it is not utilized to determine the appropriate level of stock prices in a purely mechanistic fashion. Instead, its use is intended to provide a simple framework from which to evaluate the influence of macroeconomic developments on the determination and fluctuation of stock prices.

Stock prices, within this paradigm, while generally tracking the profits of corporations are presumed to be subject to fad, fashion and convention, reflecting their tendency to fluctuate violently and unpredictably. Thus, 'the lack of predictive content about changes in asset prices', noted by Roll in his 1988 address to the American Economic Association (AEA), is the straightforward result of the speculative activities that eventually lead to the determination of these prices themselves (Canova and De Nicolo, 1995, p. 982). Likewise, Hall's (2001) comments to the AEA indicate that economists in general have not paid enough attention to speculative market theory, including the burgeoning field of behavioral finance.

While the efficient market model is characterized by formal mathematics, speculative models 'are usually simple, spontaneous and unsophisticated, consisting of qualitative descriptions of causes, anecdotes suggesting what may happen, and presumed correlations, cycles or other simple patterns of variation of economic variables' (Raines and Leathers, 2000, p. 127 paraphrasing Shiller, 1989). As such, the theory of speculative markets is commonly relegated to the analysis of specific historical incidents, such as the great 'tulipmania', the stock market crash of 1929, the 'South Sea Bubble' or other instances of financial irrationality, and categorically excluded as a systemic theory of capital market behavior in conventional economics. Kindleberger (1989) notes that contributions of speculative theories stemming from the analysis of such episodes in financial history are often minimized, 'taken to amuse, but not to edify' (p. xiii). Correspondingly, the theories emanating from the speculative school of thought are often considered 'unscientific', 'ad hoc' or unnecessarily premised on investor irrationality. The net outcome is a general refusal to acknowledge the potential importance speculative markets theory and the dismissal of evidence supporting such views that has accumulated over time.

Up until recently, mainstream theorists have demonstrated a clear tendency to reassert the basic ideas embedded in the EMH, relying on the theoretically incompatible explanations of 'rational bubbles' and 'noise trading' to conceal the lacuna between the theory of efficient markets and the historical record. To the extent that speculative theories may be important in explaining stock price movements in the United States during the 1980s and 1990s, it is necessary to sketch out some of the major points emphasized by proponents of this dissenting view. To these ends we find a broad conceptual and analytical framework in lieu of the complex, mathematical apparatus put forth by proponents of the dominant paradigm. We include in this survey portfolio theories of stock price fluctuation since shift of funds between assets is codetermined by forces unrelated to the present value of futures dividends.

Most modern treatments of speculative equity price behavior begin with an acknowledgment, citing or reappraisal of John Maynard Keynes' treatment of stock market speculation in Chapter 12 of *The General Theory*. As such, Keynes has been labeled 'the patron saint of the bubble theorists' (Miller, 1991, p. 103; Raines and Leathers, 2000, p. 77). However, prior to *The General Theory*, Keynes sketched out a portfolio or liquidity preference theory of equity price determination in *A Treatise on Money*, which is usually overlooked for his later ideas regarding the speculative nature of stock markets. Here, the price of securities in general is studied in the context of the effect of the former on investment and the implications for overall price stability. While the analysis is to some extent different than that found in Keynes' subsequent writings it still includes the importance of investor psychology in the determination of asset prices.

However, special emphasis is placed on equity as an asset and as an alternative to bank saving deposits. In the long run Keynes viewed the value of equity as dependent on the expected income derived from share ownership, or more explicitly the value of consumption goods the capital assets might purchase. Yet, it is also argued that it is the short run that is more relevant since 'timidity, greed, nervousness or impatience' rendered agents incapable of investment based on a long view (p. 324). Thus, instead of 'fundamentals', equity prices in the *Treatise* are determined primarily by the portfolio preferences of the public. That is, as the public develops a preference for saving deposits (an increased willingness to 'horde'), the amount of wealth stored in securities declines and prices follow accordingly. Fluctuations in security prices then occur as a consequence of portfolio switching generating from changes in opinion or sentiment (p. 228). 'Equilibrium is established as the average opinion changes with prices of securities' (Raines and Leathers, 2000, p. 83).

To the analysis, Keynes adds that price stability can be threatened if a 'bullish' (liquidity preferences excessively low) or 'bearish' (liquidity preferences excessively high) sentiment dominates the economy. It is here that Keynes injects the analysis of investor psychology and its implication for speculative markets found in his later works. It is reasoned that 'the state of speculative sentiment' could trigger unchecked equity price increases:

> If everyone agrees that securities are worth more, and if everyone is a 'bull' in the sense of preferring securities at a rising price to increasing savings deposits, there is no limit to the rise in the price of securities and no effective check arises from the shortage of money (p. 229).

This dynamic, albeit with a more descriptive analysis of the determinants of household portfolio changes, is emphasized in Taylor and O'Connell's (1985) formal model of stock market overvaluation (see Chapter 4), Minsky's (1975, 1982) model of endogenous financial fragility and Veblen's theory of false prosperity (Raines and Leathers, 2000) – all surveyed below.

In *The General Theory*, Keynes shifts gears from portfolio preferences to the absence of probabilistic knowledge with which to form reliable estimates of the income stream emanating from the ownership of a share captured in the right-hand side of equation (2.1). That is, investors 'simply do not know' the likelihood of each of the possible future states of the economy that could prevail. As such the intractable uncertainty cannot 'be reduced or tamed via the calculus of probability' as is the case within the theory of efficient market (Pratten, 1993, p. 11). Consequently, rational investors are assumed to rely on conventions, rules of thumb, adaptive expectations and majority opinion to make reasonable assessments about prospective share values. These aspects make up what is appropriately labeled the 'conventional method of calculation' (Keynes, 1964, p. 152).

The conventionally determined market price implies 'all sorts of considerations enter into the market valuation which are no way relevant to the prospective yield', especially in bull and bear markets (p. 152). Since prices generate from the average opinion of stock traders, this eventuates in a tremendous amount of effort committed to anticipating average opinion. Keynes' likening of the stock market to a 'beauty contest' underscores the fact that even those with information that indicates a particular wave of bullish or bearish sentiment is not rooted in economic fundamentals may not risk betting against the majority. Intrinsic values then get systematically lost along the way. However, the conventional method of estimation also implies that investors accept current stock prices as appropriate summary statistics regarding the present state of affairs and that the pre-existing state can continue indefinitely.

While Keynes held that the long-run view was important in the assessment of intrinsic or 'ultimate' value of equity, it is again short-run expectations that are deemed to dominate the investment process. It is underscored that 'life is not long enough – human nature desires quick results, there is a peculiar zest in making money quickly, and remoter gains are discounted by the average man at a very high rate' (p. 157). What is more important is not what a share is really worth but what value the market will attach to it through conventional valuation. It is these dynamics that are viewed to be central to occasions of both stability and speculative bubbles and crisis. In Keynes' vision, conventions, while a stabilizing force at some times, can change abruptly leading to volatile stock prices and increased uncertainty about the intrinsic value of a share. He writes:

A conventional valuation which is established as the outcome of a large number of ignorant individuals is liable to change violently as the result of a sudden fluctuation of opinion due to factors which do not really make much difference to the prospective yield; since there will be no strong roots to hold it steady (p. 154).

Thus, resting squarely on the pillar of fundamental uncertainty, the theory of speculative stock markets outlined in *The General Theory* holds that prices are inherently volatile and can diverge significantly from their fundamental values. It is from this perspective that Keynes issues one of the most quoted warnings about stock market activity:

> Speculators may do no harm as bubbles on a steady stream of enterprise. But the position is serious when enterprise becomes the bubble on a whirlpool of speculation. When the capital development of a country becomes a by-product of the activities of a casino, the job is likely to be ill-done. The measure of success attained by Wall Street, regarded as an institution of which the proper social purpose is to direct new investment into the most profitable channels in terms of future yields, cannot be claimed as one of the outstanding triumphs of laissez-faire capitalism (Keynes, 1964, p. 159).

This notion of equity markets is, of course, diametrically opposed to the EMH and the associated welfare conclusions that are often drawn but is directly applicable to the Internet bubble, Enron debacle and the inflated corporate profits in the late 1990s exposed by the recent proliferation of earnings restatements.

In juxtaposing the two theories it is important to emphasize that the agents in the Keynesian model are not necessarily irrational. It is true that Keynesian agents do not illustrate 'substantive' rationality as envisioned in the efficient market framework. Substantive rationality presumes that one and only one equilibrium, regarded to be optimal, 'is scientifically relevant' and ultimately uncovered by self-interested agents. However agents in Keynes' broad framework are unquestionably rational in a human or 'procedural' sense, the latter defined as behavior that is the product of 'appropriate deliberation' and contingent on equilibrium process itself (Pratten, 1993, p. 13). In fact, it is explicitly argued that we as economic agents would be irrational if not 'foolish, in forming our expectations to matters which are very uncertain' (Keynes, 1964, p. 148). Instead, in the presence of true uncertainty it is perfectly rational for investors to assume that 'future will look like the relevant past extrapolated' and 'look to average opinion' to circumvent fundamental uncertainty (Crotty, 1993, p. 63). Thus, out of the standard valuation model with a different notion of uncertainty and investor behavior Keynes arrives at a theory of speculative price dynamics.

Cleverly, Anderson (1983/84) argues that in Keynes' speculative market theory prices are informationally efficient and extend directly from the identical assumptions maintained by the EMH. Here, it is maintained that since the reaction of the majority in period t is crucial to the determination of equity prices in period $t + 1$, it is perfectly consistent with rational expectations for agents to attempt to anticipate popular opinion and act on their expectations (p. 285). This is perfectly consistent with the claim that a market which always 'fully reflects' available information is called 'efficient' (Fama, 1970, p. 383). Likewise, Glickman (1994) argues that Keynes' agents, by acting in this manner, are far from irrational and in fact exhibit 'sophisticated rationality' (p. 336). Consequently, informationally efficient prices, stemming from individual rational action, can become irrationally high – the irrational whole is not the sum of its rational parts. Such prices then, on the basis of rational action, are not fundamental value-efficient, and thus informational efficiency does not imply that a rational expectations equilibrium will be attained.

Keynes, nonetheless, never had a complete monopoly on such analysis. Raines and Leathers (1996) point out that Veblen's theory of speculative equity price behavior found in *The Theory of Business Enterprise* (1904) is also rooted in the simple fundamental valuation model yet similar to the Keynesian analysis. In a manner reminiscent of the random-walk view of stock markets, Veblen held that in the long run equity prices would equal their intrinsic values but in the short run price deviations were likely. However, expectations within the Veblenian framework are closely tied to the prospective profits or earning capacity of firms. Consequently, a period of strong fundamentals could encourage over-exuberant expectations about earning capacities ('false' or 'speculative' prosperity), leading to a rupturing of prices from their true values in a speculative manner.

When we consider that Veblen's theory of 'speculative advance' emergent from favorable economic conditions implies a shifting of portfolios towards equity, the analysis closely approximates the ideas expressed in *The Treatise on Money*. While the issue of fundamental uncertainty does not play a role in the analysis, investor psychology does. Consequently, Veblen's conclusions about price fluctuations are not too dissimilar from Keynes' analysis in *The General Theory*. Thus, the two theories are not identical but close enough to be categorized under the same theoretical fraternity of speculative models. Certainly, Veblen asserted that stock price fluctuations were generated by:

> variations of confidence on the part of investors, on current belief as to the probable policy or tactics of business men in control, on forecasts as to the seasons and tactics of the guild of politicians, and on the indeterminable, largely instructive, shifting movements of public sentiment and apprehension. So that under modern conditions the magnitude of the business capital and its mutations from day to day are in great measure a question of folk psychology rather than of material fact (Veblen, 1904, pp. 148–149, excerpted in Raines and Leathers, 1996, p. 141).

Moreover, the deviation of prices from intrinsic values is likely to be severe at times since the false prosperity upon which it is based is perpetuated by a 'habit of buoyancy, or speculative recklessness, which grows up in any business community under such circumstances' (Veblen, 1904, p. 196, excerpted in Raines and Leathers, 2000, p. 73). This observation rooted in psychological phenomena should not be mistaken for 'pure speculation'– the purchasing of equity by investors simply on the anticipation of future price increases irrespective of the earning capacity of firms. Veblen, and Keynes as well, entertain this speculative dynamic but it is neither necessary nor central to the claims of potential under- or overvaluation in the stock market within their respective conceptual frameworks.

Minsky's (1975, 1982) formulation of the theory of endogenous financial fragility builds both on the Keynesian and, although unmentioned, Veblenian traditions. The fundamental idea embodied in the financial instability hypothesis is 'the basic tendency of non-financial companies, deposit intermediaries and other financial companies, encouraged by recent stability and driven to secure enough profits to validate their financial commitments to increase financial leverage' (Gray and Gray, 1994, p. 145). From a condition of normalcy, a period of strong profit growth stimulates firms to take on imprudent levels of debt that eventually outstrips the ability to service it. Thus, the Minskian claim that normal functioning of the economy could culminate in financial vulnerability or that 'stability is destabilizing' is remarkably similar to Veblen's theory of speculative prosperity[3] (Minsky, 1982, p. 68). Both theorists depart from the standard valuation model, which underscores the fact that long-term profit expectations are held relevant for equity market pricing.

Yet, the cornerstone of the financial instability hypothesis is the adaptive expectations hypothesis and the Keynesian notion of fundamental uncertainty, which allows 'financial euphoria' to circulate throughout the economy in a lasting manner. In principle, the theory explicates banking crises triggered by the overextended nature of non-financial firms who were euphoric in their debt financing of investment during a protracted boom. Although essentially about over-indebtedness and banking crises and the focus is not on the stock market, the analysis extends straightforwardly to the general fragility of the entire financial system. The relevance for stock prices appreciation involves the familiar re-shifting of investor portfolios towards equity, placing upward pressure on prices even when unrelated to fundamentals. With investors exhibiting adaptive expectations, a period of strong profit growth (as we had in the United States during the 1980s) can increase the long-term earnings expectations of investors, triggering a stock market boom. Minsky maintained:

> Two immediate consequences follow if the expectation of a normal business cycle is replaced by the expectation of steady growth. First, those [expectations] that reflect continuing expansion replace gross profits in the present-value calculations that had reflected expansion and recessions. Simultaneously there is less uncertainty about the future behavior of the economy. As the belief in the reality of a new era emerges, the decrease in the expected down or short time for plant and equipment raises their present values. The confident expectation of a steady stream of prosperity gross profits makes portfolio plunging more appealing to firm decision-makers (Parenteau and Veneroso, 1999, p. 1).

In this manner, prices become more reflective of the euphoric expectations passed down from corporations and financial intermediaries through the investing public than the actual earning capabilities of the corporate sector. Moreover, within the theory of financial fragility, rising equity prices enable firms to secure more debt, underlining a two-way relationship between debt and equity markets. Nonetheless, it is the speculative environment prompted by a period of strong fundamentals and the psychological response by investors that is central to Minsky's theory of equity price determination as well. It is important to emphasize that the consequent overvaluation in stock markets is endogenously generated.

Kindleberger's (1996) historical work on 'manias, panics and crashes' extends Minsky's single country analysis to speculative asset pricing in an open economy. Kindleberger provides ample evidence which illustrates that 'overtrading has historically tended to spread from one country to another' through various international conduits (p. 14). Hence, exuberant international flows can augment domestic demand forces in placing upward pressure on equity prices. The historical record illustrates that there is no reason to believe that international investors are immune to the domestically bred speculative enthusiasms that lead prices to be ruptured from their more fundamental values. Nor is the case that international investors will dampen the price appreciation by betting against the domestic herd. Instead it is more realistic to place domestic and institutional investors in the same expectational climate and admit that international forces may, at times, significantly fuel the speculative boom.

Kindleberger (1996) also re-emphasizes deeply rooted psychological dynamics that underpin asset price movements. With rational expectations explicitly disregarding from the onset in the descriptive model, psychological propensities such as greed, jealousy (the misfortune of seeing one's neighbors get rich) and mob behavior give way to positive feedback loops between stock prices and expectations of future price appreciation eventually resulting in overtrading and, if unchecked, speculative frenzy. More importantly, it is the euphoric behavior of investors that encourages and ultimately facilitates fraudulent corporate activity. He writes:

> We believe that swindling is demand-determined, following Keynes' law that demand determines its own supply, rather than Say's law that supply creates its own demand. In a boom, fortunes are made, individuals wax greedy, and swindlers come forward to exploit that greed. The position is occasionally expressed elsewhere that sheep to be shorn abound, and need only the emergence of effective swindlers to offer themselves as sacrifices: 'There is a sucker born every minute' (p. 69).

However cruel this might sound in the wake of the Enron, WorldCom, Adelphia and similar debacles, the point Kindleberger attempts to accentuate is that these types of financial schemes are endogenous to the Minsky cycle, largely driven by perverse adaptive expectations. Rationality gives way to irrationality and the underlying corporate structure and monetary system becomes strained to the point that misconduct is to be expected.

Predating Kindleberger, John K. Galbraith's model of speculative stock markets outlined in *The Great Crash* is similarly premised on strong psychological factors driving financial market valuations. His characterization of the conditions of the late 1920s captures the essence of the theoretical framework:

> Far more important than the rate of interest and the supply of credit is the mood. Specu-
> lation on a large scale requires a pervasive sense of confidence and optimism and a con-
> viction that ordinary people were meant to be rich. People must also have faith in the
> good intentions and even in the benevolence of others, for it is by the agency of others
> that they will get rich ... When people are cautious, questioning, misanthropic, suspi-
> cious, or mean, they are immune to speculative enthusiasms (Galbraith, 1988, pp. 169–
> 170).

However, Galbraith's theory is institutionalist at its core, as he viewed the organization of businesses and markets as well as the underlying economic structure as central to the occasional speculative run-up in equity values. Such an
analysis is important in unraveling equity prices movements over the 1980s and
1990s since the rise of institutional investors and relaxation of financial regulation have radically altered both the stock market and the corporate structure of
US enterprises. It should be noted that Galbraith actually predates Kindleberger
in acknowledging that opportunity for financial felony is advanced by the over-
exuberant expectations of investors and their blind trust in the benevolence of
others.

Although Galbraith (1988, 1994) is thorough and methodical in his approach to
speculative markets, Raines and Leathers (2000) accurately note that his analysis
of popular incidents of financial crisis is precisely the type of work considered
'anecdotal by conventional theorists' (p. 104). Furthermore, the agents represented in the model, like those in Kindleberger's, must be considered irrational
since it is never explained how they become subject to the intense waves of mass
speculative psychology that result in financial imprudence.[4] The theory, rooted
as it is in assessments of actual historical episodes, is edifying but at the same
time begs important questions as to how individual rational action can culminate
in irrational collective behavior and/or how rational are stock market investors in
reality. The analysis of Veblen and Minsky appear to address this lacuna rather
well, as does theory advanced by Robert J. Shiller.

Shiller's explanation for fluctuation in stock prices encountered in his 1989
treatise, *Market Volatility*, and his 2000 publication, *Irrational Exuberance*,
maintains attributes of both Galbraith's and Keynes' speculative theories of market behavior. Shiller identified stock market investing as a social activity and,
therefore, the central contention within this paradigm is that equity prices are
greatly influenced by 'social dynamics', such as social movements, fads and fashion ('Stock Prices and Social Dynamics', 1984, reprinted in 1989). Here it is argued that the ambiguity of stock value and the absence of accepted theory of asset
price determination render prices 'relatively vulnerable to purely social movements' (Shiller, 1989, p. 12). Thus, a conscientious use of investor surveys is

substituted for complex quantitative methods to investigate the forces driving equity price movements. In this manner, Shiller blends financial economics with aspects of human behavior to explain the elements of price dynamics ignored by conventional theorists. In fact, Shiller can be considered one of the early pioneers of the behavioral finance school of thought.

Shiller first draws on literature in the field of social psychology to justify the claim that individuals respond to popular opinion and societal pressures when making portfolio allocation decisions. Second, he invokes the theory of 'epidemics' advanced by mathematical sociologists to illustrate how fads can infect the behavior of a critical segment of the population of investors, which culminates in asset price bubbles or 'irrational exuberance'. As an example of a fad that infected a critical mass of investors, Shiller (2000a) notes the role of portfolio insurance (implemented by individual and institutional investors) in the crash of 1987 (pp. 93–5). With respect to wide-scale social movements, it is argued that the expansion in media reporting of stock market news, societal preoccupation with stock market investing and the expansion of defined contribution pension plans resulted in an increased demand for stock and intense upward pressure on prices during the 1990s (Shiller, 2000a, pp. 28–34). While Shiller credits the news media with encouraging the demand for stock, he holds that informal communication between individuals to be of greater importance in the diffusion of over-exuberance about the stock valuations.

This conceptual framework differs from Galbraith's theory (which Shiller, 1989 labels the 'old view of fads'), only in the sense that the behavior of investors that yields irrational high equity prices is attributed to social dynamics and not left unspecified. The conclusions reached by the social psychology theory of equity price fluctuation are also quite reminiscent of the Keynesian, *General Theory* point of view in several ways. Firstly, Shiller reaches a conclusion consistent with the latter, maintaining that daily stock prices fluctuate because among other things, 'the investing public en masse capriciously changes its mind' (1989, p. 1). Second, emphasis is placed also on the possibility of undervaluation in equity prices resulting from mass psychology or social conventions biased towards market retreat. Third, Shiller's theory is premised on the assumption that all flows into the equity market impact returns, that is, the market is not a 'weighting' but a 'voting machine'. Regarding this point Shiller (2000a) emphasizes:

> At its root, the efficient markets theory holds that differing abilities do not produce differing investment performance. The theory claims that the smartest people will not be able to do better than the least intelligent people in terms of investment performance. They can do no better because their superior understanding is already incorporated into share prices. If we accept the premise of efficient markets, not only is being smart no advantage, but it also follows immediately that being *not so smart* is not a *disadvantage* either ... Thus, according to this theory, effort and intelligence mean nothing in investing ... But why should the smartest people set all prices? Many apparently less-

intelligent or less well-informed people are buying and selling – why should they not have an impact on prices? (pp. 173–4).

The implication here is that even those flows unrelated to fundamentals, stemming instead from 'excessively enthusiastic' investors, have equal opportunity to determine the course of equity price movements. This voting view of stock markets advocated by Shiller is the sine qua non of the various theories rooted in the Keynesian tradition and justifies the rupturing of prices from their fundamental values.

Shiller further reasoned that the random-walk behavior of stock prices and, thus, lack of profit opportunities, generates from the unpredictability of changes in fads and fashions in response to important events or developments. This underscores the fact that unit root behavior and the absence of systematic profit opportunities in equity markets is consistent not only with EMH but also with Shiller's model of speculative markets. Yet, the speculative theory appears more persuasive, since it can also explain why stock prices are characterized by a great deal of inertia, and thus predictability, without appealing to ad hoc justifications.

Indeed, Shiller has become one of the most avid critics of efficient capital market theorists, arguing that their refusal to consider alternative theories, especially those emphasizing market psychology is 'one of the most remarkable errors in the history of economic thought' (1989, p. 2). However, Shiller makes it explicitly clear that his model of speculative markets 'is, in fact heavily influenced by the efficient markets literature' viewing the latter in the manner suggested by Fama (1990) – an extreme example, which is edifying in an introductory sense (1989, p. 49). This suggests a fundamental belief in at least some of the ideas embedded in the competing theory. In fact, Shiller maintains that in the unlikely case that 'smart flows' – those flows related to expected profitability of corporations alone – should dominate the market, the outcome would more approximate that one envisioned by the EMH (1989, p. 130). Nonetheless, the model should not be mistaken for an adaptation of the EMH; it is clearly an alternative. The reluctance by efficient market proponents to take seriously the fad model proposed in Shiller (1984, 1989) and the supporting empirical evidence documented by Shiller (1981) and Campbell and Shiller (1988) makes this evident.

Even so, the ideas put forth by Galbraith, Minsky, Veblen and Keynes do not give the impression that fundamentals are never a factor in equity market outcomes. Each theory emphasizes the possible divergence of equity prices from their intrinsic values, thus implying the existence of some apposite value, however elusive and loosely defined. In principle, the very fundamentals that have a tenuous role in equity price fluctuations constrain the market in the end (however distant that might be), justifying market declines. We are led to believe that profits and earnings do not necessarily drive the market but instead are a constraint on speculative price movements. Again, Veblen and Minsky also note that profits have an important role in triggering the speculative forces, which come to dominate the market for a period of time before ultimately reining them in. This underscores the fact that the standard valuation model is not the exclusive domain of the EMH, and drastically different results can be deduced from the implementation of different assumptions about how agents behave under uncertainty.

Yet, not every speculative theory of equity price fluctuation leaves room for the fundamental valuation model, even in the long run. Davidson (1972) who noticeably combines both Keynesian treatments of equity price dynamics found in *The Treatise* and *The General Theory*, en route to a 'liquidity preference theory' of financial markets is one example. Emphasis is placed on equity as an asset, that is, 'a store of value, or mode of transferring purchasing power' (1972, p. 254). The central conclusion eventually reached within Davidson's (1999) conceptual framework is that the fundamental purpose of stock markets and financial markets in general is 'to provide liquidity to asset holders' who seek to transfer purchasing power over time (Davidson, 1999, p. 5). As such the price of equity is determined by the portfolio balance decisions of the wealth-holding public. Thus, the idea that the fundamental value of a share (or the standard valuation model) is relevant for market-pricing outcomes is given little credence.

Davidson (1972) holds the demand for equity to be a function of wealth, current market prices, dividend payments, expectations about future security price changes as well as agents' degrees of confidence and risk aversion. Here, the Keynesian ideas of liquidity preference and uncertainty meet. Davidson suggests that uncertainty leaves the actual estimation of the fundamental value of a share an intractable or even fruitless exercise. He writes:

> If today's market price is to reflect 'fundamentals', then the market must use existing data to make a statistically reliable forecast of the entire future stream of quasi-rents associated with each underlying illiquid investment project. Strictly speaking, to make such a prediction requires one to draw samples from the future and calculate statistical moments about the mean. Since this is impossible, theorists invoke (usually implicitly) the ergodic axiom (Davidson, 1999, p. 12).

But, Davidson notes that the world is not a roulette table where the outcomes are pre-specified and unchanging, and therefore the ergodic axiom is in his view a perverse abstraction from reality. The future rather than a 'statistical shadow of the past' is instead a state characterized by true uncertainty. Given this 'non-ergodicity' and conventional expectation formation, stock price dynamics respond to portfolio allocation decisions of the public and proceed without concern for the economic fundamentals. Accordingly, efficient market prices, semi-strong or weak, have very little opportunity to take form.

Bernstein (1998a, 1998b, 1996) also expresses skepticism about attaining an 'efficient' price equilibrium as well, reiterating Keynes' ideas about the relevancy of the short run. He maintains:

Keynes was really arguing that, in a system naturally volatile and characterized by uncertainty, most of us simply do not have the time required for economic and financial
variables to regress to their long-run means. We are inevitably trapped in the short run
(1998b, p. 183).

Again, on the basis of the short horizon of investors and a Keynesian expectation
formation process, it is concluded that volatility and overvaluation is to be expected in equity markets. In short, stock prices are reflective of extrinsic forces
since they reflect basically 'nothing more than bets on the future, which is ultimately full of surprises' (1996, p. 300). Asset prices determined by market trading by these accounts are the antithesis of those hypothesized in the mainstream
view. Bernstein maintains, as does Glickman (1994) that, 'the fatal flaw in the
efficient market hypothesis is that there is no such thing as an equilibrium price
... a market can never be efficient unless equilibrium prices exist and are known'
(Bernstein, 1998a quoted in Davidson, 1999, p. 5). The equilibrium price Bernstein refers to here is, of course, the 'efficient' or 'rational' market price envisioned in Fama's (1970) framework.

If we are to take the conjectures offered by Bernstein, Glickman and Davidson
that fundamentals simply do not matter and equilibria in equity markets are non-
existent, the stock market crash is implicitly conceived correspondingly as unrelated to fundamental overvaluation. By this standard a market crash could occur
at any time, most likely when the market is incapable of performing its liquidity
providing duty. This prospect is implicit in the theory of capital market inflation
advanced by Toporowski (1999a, 1999b), who jettisons fundamental value analysis in favor of a disequilibrium approach to equity markets and asset-pricing in
general.[5] The theory is an extreme version of the voting (supply and demand)
approach to equity price determination, the essence of which is that net flows into
the market ultimately determine stock prices irrespective of economic fundamentals. Toporowski (1999a) writes:

The theory of capital market inflation is a non-equilibrium theory of capital markets. It
argues that the actual value of capital markets ... is determined by the inflow of funds
into that market ... A large part of the inflow is taken out by securities issued by corporations. The balance is a net excess inflow which forms the liquidity of the market, circulating around until it is 'taken' out by an additional stock issue ... When this inflow
increases, brokers faced with rising purchase orders raise prices to induce stockholders
to sell and maintain broker's stock balances. In this situation, turnover and prices rise in
the market (pp. 2–3).

This vision differs radically from the conventional view of capital markets that
theorizes an efficient mechanism through which equilibrium is ultimately
achieved between the demand for finance (entrepreneurs' need to finance capital)
and the supply of finance (household savings). Toporowski argues that financial
intermediation does not support such a well-organized outcome since inflows of

funds into the stock market (from the purchases of stock) do not necessarily end up with those intending to finance capital accumulation. Instead, the bulk of the inflow is transferred into the hands of other investors and therefore reappears as an additional demand for stock. Hence, the initial inflow is multiplied, circulating around until it is 'taken out' by investors wishing to use the funds to purchase assets other than stock (or commodities) or by corporations issuing new shares to finance investment. As such there is no equilibrium, stock markets are inherently unstable, fluctuating between liquidity and illiquidity in association with the business cycle (Toporowski, 1999b, pp. 22–4).

In this view, equity prices can deviate substantially from their fundamental values (that suggested by the EMH) for long periods of time, giving the stock market a Ponzi-like character. Moreover, stock markets crash not necessarily because prices are detached from their fundamental values (out of equilibrium) but simply because the market is unable to encourage the excess inflow of funds necessary to negotiate the existing sell demands and therefore maintain the current levels of valuation. While specialists can provide temporary liquidity, the bulk of the sell demands must be satisfied by other investors who 'must be concerned about the motives for the trade of investors who have, on net, placed orders so large as to outstrip the specialists' risk bearing capacity' (Lehmann, 1991, p. 31). Thus, as the capital market inflation theory holds, it is ultimately investors' willingness to buy stock which provides liquidity to the market and when those flows are no longer forthcoming, price declines (yet not necessarily crashes) are inevitable. After all, the demand for stocks and, thus, the speculative bubble cannot be expected to grow forever.

Yet, stopping here would underplay Toporowski's contribution to the theory of speculative markets. While most theories focus on the demand side of equity price determination, the theory of capital market inflation, by concentrating attention on inflows, moves supply-side considerations to the fore. Here, not only are the portfolio allocation decisions of the public imperative to market valuations but changes in the supply of equity through new issuances or retirements impact equity prices as well. The latter, of course, can be unrelated to the expected profitability of firms, therefore placing additional 'liquidity at the service of further capital market inflation' (1999a, p. 4). Thus while Shiller (1989, 2000a) focuses on 'smart' and 'ordinary' flows alone, the theory of capital market inflation takes additional account of negative net issuance of shares. Toporowski's theory indicates that the shrinking supply of equity during the 1980s and late 1990s may have been an important causal force behind the dramatic run-up in US equity prices.

Toporowski, Davidson and Bernstein postulate rich theories of non-equilibrium, speculative stock markets that contribute important insights to the literature on equity price dynamics. However, there is more of a profit-based science to equity markets than that attributed by such theories. The problem with scrapping the standard valuation model and denying a role to market fundamentals is that such theories omit an important reason why the public demands shares in the first place and what ultimately reigns in speculative enthusiasms. In fact, it is because shares represent a claim on the future profits of respective corporations that the public deems them valuable. For this reason, the fortunes of corporations must play some role in equity price determination and most certainly the notion of stock market overvaluation must entail some assessment of corporate profitability and ability of firms to disburse dividends. While it is important to stress the speculative nature of equity markets, clearly some concept of intrinsic value is necessary as well (even if true intrinsic values can never be known).

Moreover, conventional wisdom teaches that serious market declines or collapses occur after a time of substantial stock price appreciation, not necessarily at times of illiquidity. This is arguably more consistent with the notion of speculative bubbles ultimately coming to terms with more pragmatic values rather than an inability of markets to remain sufficiently liquid, as Toporowski would suggest. It is fair to conclude that market prices may not be the product of an efficient and precise machine, as is implied by proponents of the theory of market efficiency, but they are not the arbitrary products of a pure speculative market either. Nevertheless, while the flow theory may go to the extreme by completely disregarding fundamental value theory, it remains insightful because it emphasizes supply issues, which are completely abstracted from in both conventional and Keynesian theories of equity price determination.

Theories of Rational Bubbles and Noise Trading

Without a doubt the EMH and its proponents have stimulated much intellectual development and progress in the general understanding of financial markets and asset price dynamics. Samuelson, Fama, Modigliani and Miller, among others, injected mathematical tools into the study of finance and helped transform it from a field that was closer to accounting than economics to a field that blends financial with economic theory. Unfortunately, the negative aspect of this revolution was that it stripped human conduct from the analysis of financial markets (Thaler, 1998). It is this human element that many Keynesian theorists attempt to reinstate into the field of financial economics – indicative of their significant contribution to the understanding of asset price movements.[6] Nevertheless, in 1988, Richard Roll, expressed uneasiness over the lack of progress made in the area of financial markets stating, 'the immaturity of our science is illustrated by the conspicuous lack of predictive content about some of its most interesting phenomena, particularly changes in asset prices' (Canova and De Nicolo, 1995, p. 982). This statement suggested both that previous mainstream theorists on the subject of share price determination had been deficient and perhaps that alternative theorists had been ignored, engendering a substantial number of studies that added significantly to the already voluminous literature on the content of stock prices.

Lehmann (1991) observes that the first 'empirical cracks in the efficient markets edifice' came courtesy of the documentation of the many stock market anomalies observed in US stock markets (p. 493). For example, there is the 'P–E anomaly' uncovered as early as 1968, which reveals that stocks with high price–earnings ratios underperform those with low price–earnings ratios as well the seldom acknowledged 'high volume of trade anomaly' (Thaler, 1998, p. 193; Leroy, 1989, p. 1609; Pratten, 1993, p. 25). The latter refers to the fact that although traders are assumed to be rational and assume others to be rational, agents are still willing to buy what another sells and vice versa – in fact millions of shares are traded daily. Among others, there are also the calendar anomalies such as the 'January effect', the 'weekend effect', the 'Friday-the-thirteenth effect' and the 'holiday effect', all indicative of a pattern in stock prices incompatible with the basic tenets efficient markets model (Aggarwal and Schirm, 1995, p. 201). Additionally, there is 'small firm anomaly': stock returns of small firms dominate those for large firms, particularly in January. Moreover, Aggarwal and Schirm (1995) find that the 'January effect' is present in several other countries.[7] Even more anomalous is the significant relationship found between New York City weather and daily security returns chronicled by Saunders (1993). At best, the 'anomalies' imply that the theory of efficient markets is too restrictive to explain price movements at all times.

Leroy (1989) notes that these findings left two unattractive choices for conventional financial theorists; either consider the contradictory findings inconsequential or incorporate 'irrationality' into their models of equity price determination.[8] The response, however, was to choose neither alternatives. Instead Blanchard and Watson (1982) and Black (1986) advanced theories of 'rational bubbles' and 'noise trading', respectively while attempting to maintain the basic premise and tenets of the EMH. Blanchard and Watson (1982) illustrated in a highly technical manner that there can be rational deviations from the fundamental values of assets without creating the possibility for arbitrage by including a concept of risk compensation.[9] According to 'rational bubble' theory, as prices overshoot their fundamental values there is an increase in the probability the bubble will burst. In turn, the possibility of financial loss increases the risk associated with the ownership of bubbling stock, thereby justifying the acceleration of its price (Pratten, 1993, p. 29). Thus, the increased price appropriately reflects the associated risks of riding a speculative bubble and speculators cannot make profits off the existence of the bubble since all relevant information is still contained in current prices. Certainly, the bubble term in Blanchard and Watson's (1982) formulation satisfies the fair game property.

However, Blanchard and Watson (1982) argue that the case for efficient markets has been exaggerated without abandoning its foundations, writing, 'Rationality of both behavior and also of expectation often does not imply that a price of an asset be equal to its fundamental value. In other words, there can be a rational deviation from this value' (p. 295). Here the stock price is equal to its fundamental value plus a rational bubble term. In any one period, the probability that the 'Blanchard–Watson bubble' will burst is constant but increases if the bubble is uninterrupted by a market correction. The use of the word 'rational' emphasizes the fact the existence of the bubble is held to be consistent with rational expectations and constant expected returns (independent of past information) (Campbell et al., 1997, p. 258). Clearly, Blanchard and Watson (1982) wish to maintain the central assumptions of the theory of efficient capital markets while retreating from the strong conclusions it draws. In doing so the theory of rational bubbles is more of an ad hoc justification than a hypothesis since it cannot explain how bubbles are formed in the first place nor how they are maintained for an extended period of time. Furthermore, the rational bubble theory advanced here cannot explain undervaluation since the bubble term cannot be negative.

Bubbles imply a self-fulfilling prophecy where the existence of abnormally high prices, unwarranted by fundamentals, is justified purely on the basis that investors believe prices will continually increase. Rationality implies that investors know that prices are overvalued and therefore that there will be a reversion to more pragmatic values. More importantly they know this information is common knowledge. This reasoning would constrain the ability of the rational bubble to form in the first place as no rational investor would be willing to pay the 'bubble premium' (Cuthbertson, 1996, p. 159). Therefore, it is not possible to unite substantive rational expectations and bubble behavior in a consistent manner, as the two are antithetical. That traders are compensated for the increased risk is no justification for why a rational trader would purchase overvalued stock in the first place. Thus, the 'rational irrationality' theory cannot be considered a reliable vindication of the conventional approach to financial markets.

Blanchard and Watson (1982) acknowledge that investor irrationality most likely factors into stock price fluctuations but hold that while 'it is hard to analyze rational bubbles, it would be much harder to deal with irrational bubbles' (p. 296). Thus, for simplicity the authors opt for the highly technical, abstract treatment financial markets with the theory of rational bubbles. Yet, the rational bubble theory does a service to the theory of asset price fluctuation since it admits the overly restrictive nature of EMH and attempts to address it. However, it is not clear that the rational bubble, although relatively easier to model, provides enough insight about financial markets to justify circumnavigating the irrational approach (that is invoking Occam's Razor only makes sense if the phenomena to be explained is done so satisfactorily). Glickman (1994), rejecting such theories on the basis that they offer little practical value and no suggestion as to how bubbles actually form, sums up the literature here as 'exercises in empty elegance' (p. 339). While this may be too strong a statement, from the point of view of speculative market theorists, it is an example of what Shiller deems one of the most serious errors in the history of economic thought. He notes, 'My own attitude toward the rational bubble models is that they are too narrow a class of models to focus much attention on ...' (Shiller, 1989, p. 96).

Theories of noise trading appear to go further in the analysis of how speculative bubbles form in financial markets. In the seminal 1986 article, *Noise,* Black presumes that on the fringe of the rational market are noise traders who pursue irrational strategies, basing investment decisions purely on past price movements. This activity causes stock prices to overshoot their fundamental values with noise traders becoming more aggressive as the speculative bubble becomes more intense. Moreover, the longer the duration of an upward trend, the more likely the positive feedback dynamics will continue, owing to the increased confidence of irrational traders. Within Black's conceptual framework irrational flows move prices with impunity because arbitrage is no longer without risk. Consequently, the arbitrageurs whose activity would ordinarily move prices back in line with intrinsic values are reluctant to sell overpriced assets short for fear of noise traders initiating further price increases. Thus, the strength of the noise traders leads to speculative bubbles in asset pricing even though rational traders exist.

Arguably the noise trading concept attracted conventional theorists where heterodox theories of speculative behavior did not because the equating of noise (irrational behavior) with a random error term appeared consistent with the martingale model of stock price behavior. Heterodox theories, one the other hand, appeared to appeal wholesale to a theory of irrationality.[10] Leroy (1989) appropriately notes:

> Given the traditional hostility toward irrationality as manifested, for example in Shiller's fad variable, neither alternative is attractive. Fortunately, Fischer Black (1986) came to the rescue. By renaming irrational trading 'noise trading' Black avoided the I-word, thereby sanitizing irrationality and rendering it palatable to many analysts who in other settings would not be receptive to such a specification (p. 1612).

Yet, in subsuming noise traders in the error term of a model, which otherwise presumes rational behavior, contradicts the notion that noise traders transform the market, a perquisite for the existence of bubbles. Noise trading is not a rational investment strategy, and therefore the fact that it leads to speculative bubbling implies that all flows impact equity returns. To the contrary, the EMH asserts that only fundamental traders determine market outcomes and more importantly differences of opinion are ultimately settled in favor of rational traders. Thus, Black's theory, by holding noise traders responsible for the deviation of market prices from fundamental values, cannot recover the theory efficient markets from its inability to explain speculative phenomenon. Instead it presents a clear alternative.

In short the noise trading theory implicitly proposes that irrational traders are in an amount small enough so that the collective market can be deemed rational but large enough to codetermine the course of equity prices. This is an immediate rejection of the rational expectations hypothesis, which presumes that all agents know the correct equilibrium model of expected returns and know that the information is common knowledge. Moreover, by simply changing the wording in Black's noise trading model reveals a closer association to Shiller's fad model than the efficient markets model it attempts to reclaim. If we label noise traders as 'ordinary money' and rational flows as 'smart' money, the difference between Shiller (1989) and Black (1986) is one of scope – the assumptions about what drives the 'ordinary flows' and skepticism about how cleanly the division can be made between smart and irrational traders.

Shleifer and Summers (1990) make the similarities between noise traders and speculative market theory more overt in their representation of the noise trader approach to financial markets. Here the market is familiarly characterized by the activity of both rational arbitrageurs and noise traders. The existence of market participants whose trades are not fully reflective of fundamental news imposes two types of risk, the first being the risk stemming from the uncertainty about future prices at which current holdings can be resold. The second is the additional price risk described previously by Black (1986), that is 'noise trader risk'. Because of the latter type of risk, arbitrageurs cannot discern whether price increase is generated by genuine information about future dividend payments not already incorporated in the current price or the result of the irrational activities of noise traders. Thus, rather than selling the overpriced stock, would-be arbitrageurs may elect to hold them in anticipation that noise traders will further push up prices. Clearly, central to the noise trading theory is the notion that rational traders must endeavor to anticipate the flows of noise traders when devising their own rational trading strategy, creating a bandwagon effect. This, of course, is directly in the spirit of Keynes.

With the stock market crash of 1987, during which the Dow Jones Industrial Average declined 30 per cent in six days, more literature appeared which sought to maintain the basic ideas found in Samuelson (1965) and Fama (1970) by further advancing 'rational' theories to explain excessive share price fluctuation. Among the most notable are the noise trading or feedback trading models of Cutler et al. (1990) and DeLong et al. (1990b) and the rational bubble models of Froot et al. (1992), Romer (1993) and Bulow and Klemperer (1994). These works maintain the essential flavor of Black (1986), Shleifer and Summers (1990) and Blanchard and Watson (1982) while emphasizing the inefficiency of financial markets. Romer (1993) attempts to forge a middle ground between the rational and irrational views. To these ends Romer argues that stock markets are imperfect in an informational sense, resulting in investors attempting to evaluate the beliefs of others rather than forming sensible estimates of the economic fundamentals. Here, the market approximates the 'beauty contest' described by Keynes (1964, p. 1113) and is more rigorously analyzed within a psychological context by behavioral finance theorists.

SUMMARY

It is clear from our overview that theories of noise trading and rational bubbles or frenzies at the very least make assumptions that are diametrically opposed to the efficient markets framework that they wish to salvage. It is also evident that despite the reluctance to accept the theories advanced by Shiller and Keynes, the theory of noise trading, when stripped of the contradictory assumption related to the EMH, is consistent with heterodox theories of speculative markets. Nevertheless, it is best to look at the various theories of equity price fluctuation that have been surveyed here along a continuum. Figure 2.1 plots the various theories and where they stand in relationship to one another. At one end of the spectrum are the disequilibrium approaches such as Toporowski's theory of capital market inflation, Glickman (1994) and Davidson's (1999) liquidity preference theory, all of which hold that that the fundamental value of a share is inconsequential in asset pricing. At the other end and diametrically opposed, we have the EMH, which holds that only fundamentals matter.

Where theories exhibit consistency we strategically place them in an overlapping manner in Figure 2.1. The diagram underscores the fact that the theories of Shiller, Galbraith, Veblen, Minsky, Kindleberger, Davidson and, to a smaller extent, the theory of noise trading share some of the basic elements found in Keynes' theory of equity price movements. The relationship between the different speculative theories of the stock market is carefully developed in Raines and Leathers (2000), who note the similarities in their treatments of expectations and the placing of investor psychology at the center of financial market behavior.[11] The horizontal positioning of the speculative theories in Figure 2.1 also reflects the fact that they all attempt, in some manner, to inject human behavior into the asset pricing and bubble formation process. In turn, Veblen, Minsky, Shiller and Keynes emphasize stock prices as the discounted present value of expected cash flow but formulate internally consistent theories as to why prices deviate from fundamentals. In contradistinction, the EMH is incompatible with all other theories including the rational bubbles and noise trading approaches, even though such theories attempt to render efficient markets theory consistent with excess volatility in equity markets.

In a sense all of these theories are enlightening. The EMH, while overly restrictive, attributing *all* price changes to shocks to fundamentals, provides a benchmark to assess actual price movements. In short, it informs us of how markets would operate if they were indeed efficient. Even the theory of capital market inflation, which completely disregards fundamentals, informs an investigator that changes in the supply of equity should be considered when addressing equity price dynamics. By default rational bubble theory cautions against remaining rooted to the theory of efficient markets and leads one to consider seriously the alternative theories of price fluctuation that follow the legacy of Keynes and Veblen. In the following chapter we review the econometric literature inspired by these theories in order to place our ensuing investigation of the 1982–99 US stock market boom in perspective.

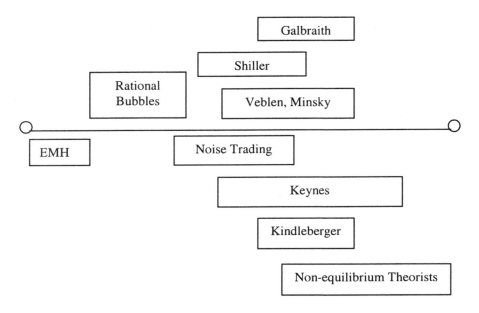

Figure 2.1   Theories of equity price determination

3. Empirical Approaches to Stock Values

A rather embarrassing gap exists between the theoretically exclusive importance of systematic 'state variables' and our complete ignorance to their identity. The co-movements of asset prices suggest the presence of underlying exogenous influences, but we have not yet determined which economic variables, if any, are responsible (Chen et al., 1986).

INTRODUCTION

A cursory glimpse of the quantitative literature reveals that the majority of the investigators in this area are more concerned with illustrating the irrationality or rationality of stock markets than identifying the actual forces determining fluctuations in equity prices. This eventuates in the preponderance of articles inquiring into whether equity prices are, among other things, predictable on an ex ante basis; unduly serially correlated; characterized by mean reversion; quickly reflective of new information; or in violation of variance-bounds criteria. This work, while often important and insightful, seldom overlaps with an investigation into whether equity prices are explainable ex post by fundamentals. Likewise, in the attempt to provide evidence for the contention that speculation and liquidity concerns are the prime movers of equity prices, empirical researchers generally aim to illustrate market inefficiency and leave the actual forces causing inefficiency unidentified. Being that we are interested primarily in the forces influencing US equity price dynamics, the issues surrounding the actual efficiency or inefficiency of financial markets are useful only in the sense that they identify those potential forces and suggest theories that might be consistent with the stylized facts from the 1980s and 1990s.

EMPIRICAL LITERATURE EMPHASIZING FUNDAMENTAL FORCES

The basic framework for financial economists interested in explaining equity prices is the discounted cash flow model, also known as the dividend discount or standard valuation model. The model expresses stock prices as the present value of all future expected dividend payments (cash flows). More formally, the model is commonly expressed:

$$P_t = E_t \Sigma_{k=1...N}[D_{t+k}/(1 + r_t)^k] \qquad\qquad (3.1)$$

where E_t is the expectation operator and D_t and r_t are the dividend and risk- adjusted discount rate (the required rate of return) in period t. From here mainstream theorists identify shocks to expectations of future income flows, the share of income accruing to corporations and discount rates as the driving forces behind equity price fluctuation. Effectively, any systemic force that affects the economy's pricing kernel or dividend payments to shareholders can impact stock prices or returns. The literature here closely follows the directives of the efficient market hypothesis (EMH) such that only those ingredients deemed to be fundamental to share prices are investigated.

Yet, in the attempts to evaluate stock market efficiency, or explain expected returns by way of regression analysis, econometricians immediately confront a serious dilemma. While inclined to demonstrate that equity prices purely reflect future fundamentals, the fundamentals are, of course, unobservable. As a result there is no direct measure for intrinsic values and thus no straightforward test of whether factors related to future corporate profitability alone drive prices. Therefore, ex ante observable variables must be identified which might adequately proxy for the ex post, unobservable fundamentals in the formal econometric work. The downside is that the attempt to control for market fundamentals via alternative measures may introduce measurement error with the results extremely sensitive to the choice of proxy, possibly under- or overstating the efficiency of the pricing mechanism. Thus, one should be skeptical about the ability to adequately proxy or control for ex post fundamentals and the possibility of omitting variables vital to the characterization of stock market equilibrium.

Characterizing Fundamentals

The most influential econometric works representative of this genre (Fama, 1981, 1990; Fama and French, 1988, 1989; Schwert, 1990; Chen et al., 1986; Geske and Roll, 1983; Keim and Stambaugh, 1986; Kaul, 1987; Shah, 1989) employ variables that are deemed appropriate proxies for shocks to expected cash flows to explain stock returns. Holding them to be generally consistent with the standard valuation model, macroeconomic variables such as industrial production indices, gross national product (GNP), bond yields, as well as aggregated dividend yields and inflation are typically exploited in econometric literature. Moreover, since these profit-related variables are presumably linked to national corporations and internal activity, domestic variables are generally investigated exclusively in the published literature on US equity prices.[1] More recently works on small open economies have expanded the variables under consideration to include measures of foreign activity.

The most logical and consistent variable included in studies of stock market valuations in this strand of literature is interest rates (bond yields). Clearly the risk-free interest rate is directly related to market prices through the standard valuation model expressed in equations (2.1) and (3.1). As the relevant interest falls the rate at which future cash flows are discounted decreases justifying an increase in stock prices. Additionally, interest rates are pro-cyclical and thus sensitive measures of business cycle changes. Mainstream financial theorists typically ignore the fact that bonds and equity are competing assets and consequently poor bond performance relative to the stock market stimulates the demand for equity. In this light, conditions may not augur well for the earning capacity of corporations yet equity prices may rise due to the underperformance of alternative assets. However, the theory of efficient capital markets holds that a change in the demand for equity unrelated to fundamentals does not enter into the stock pricing calculus. Thus, the lack of emphasis placed on equity as an asset.

While the use of bond yields is straightforward, it is not evident that the use of the aggregate dividend yield to explain returns is entirely consistent with the theory of efficient capital markets which provides the foundation for the literature here. Fama (1990) notes that the use of dividend yields in forecasting returns dates back to Dow (1920) and justifies its use accordingly:

> The intuition of the efficient markets version of the hypothesis is that stock prices are low relative to dividend when discount rates and expected returns are high and vice versa, so $D(t)/V(t)$ varies with expected returns (p. 1091).

Indeed, Fama (1990), Schwert (1990), Fama and French (1988, 1989), Campbell and Shiller (1988), and Shiller (1984) all document the forecasting power of dividend yields. However, it can be argued that dividend yield's forecasting power necessarily implies the inefficiency of stock markets. According to Standard and Poor's Stock Market Encyclopedia (1999), the yield on the S&P 500 measures how properly or improperly the market has valued current investments. They hold, 'Traditionally, a market decline has always occurred when the yield of the "500" reaches about 2.65 per cent' (p. 4). Thus, given the relevant misalignment of market prices with intrinsic values, low yields generate expectations of a price decline while high yields anticipate future price increases.

Seen in this light, the explanatory power of the dividend yield in forecasting returns implies that markets can experience periods of under- or overvaluation, contrary to the insights of the theory of efficient markets. This 'irrational bubble' theory explaining the association between the dividend yield and stock returns is in fact acknowledged by Fama and French (1989). Moreover, the relationship between the dividend yield and market price emphasizes the tendency of the market to correct itself and therefore infers the predictability of stock returns. Granger and Escribano (1987) and Granger (1986) hold that error correction models, fit to the stock market, should produce insignificant error correction terms if markets are efficient since significance would imply predictability. Therefore, it could be argued that the use of the dividend yield, in its capacity to measure overvaluation and, hence, market disequilibrium, approximates the role of an error correction term. In this circumstance, exploiting the dividend yield in an investigation of equity price movements appears antithetical to the spirit of the EMH and its power in forecasting stock returns damaging to the letter.[2]

Since all future dividends enter into the pricing calculus any investigation of stock prices requires a long-horizon approach, that is the utilization of forward looking, and leads of cash-flow-related variables. The most logical manner in which to proceed in explaining stock market fluctuations would appear to be the utilization of leads of profits or earnings in stock return regressions. Since stock market activity is assumed to be the well-organized consequence of investors attempting to estimate the potential profit streams of corporations, equity prices should ideally reflect future movements in such firm-performance variables. This would formally allow an investigation into how informative past stock prices were in predicting future developments on the real side of the economy. Unfortunately, since a high premium is placed on large samples and the comparison of results at different frequencies, the unavailability of profits on a monthly basis often provides justification for the standard use of industrial production as a proxy in the literature.

Fama (1981) notes that, 'the stock market is concerned with the capital investment process and uses the earliest information from the process to forecast its evolution' as a justification for using industrial production in lieu of corporate profits (p. 555). Chen et al. (1986) also regress expected stock returns on industrial production not necessarily because it is a proxy for corporate profitability but simply because 'the equity market is related to changes in industrial activity in the long run' (p. 387). Other works such as Fama (1981), and Canova and De Nicolo (1995) employ GNP or gross domestic product (GDP) to summarize the fundamental forces influencing expected profits and, thus, the stock market. Since stock prices are understood to capture *future* developments in the real economy, the econometric work that estimates the relationship by way of classical linear regression models lead these variables (industrial production and GNP) by one year. Nevertheless, the articles aforementioned along with Balvers et al. (1990), and Barro (1989, 1990) all document a positive relation between real stock returns and changes in expectations of future real activity.

The use of such proxy variables is not as straightforward as it might appear. Using surrogates for corporate profitability instead of actual profits invites additional measurement error to that already existent due to the necessity to proxy for unobserved, expected cash flows accruing to shareholders. Additionally, Fama (1990) notes that it is also probable that the portion of the fluctuation in industrial production that is inconsequential for equity returns 'acts like measurement error to smear the relevant information in production about returns' (p. 1107). Furthermore, the information impounded in stock prices sends noisy signals about future developments in the real economy, especially at the monthly frequency. Fama (1981, 1990), Kaul (1987), Schwert (1990), for example, document that industrial production (or other measures of economic activity) explains more of the variation in stock returns at longer horizons. Typically the adjusted R^2 statistics from regressions on annual data are larger than those from exploiting quarterly data and significantly larger than those documented at the monthly frequency.

It is argued in the literature that this stylized fact – the disparity in variation explained across time frequencies – generates from the fact that any given monthly (quarterly) stock returns contains information pertinent to *many* future production growth rates and, thus, adjacent monthly (quarterly) returns also have information pertinent to production growth in a given period (Fama, 1990, p. 1090). Thus, the information impounded in stock prices sends noisy signals about future developments in the real economy. Another equally reasonable line of reasoning is that stock prices under- and overreact to corporate fundamentals and therefore the shorter the time horizon the less likely industrial production (and like variables) will be able to explain a fair portion of the variance in stock returns. Over longer time frequencies the variation explained will be greater due to mean reversion in stock prices. This explanation is, of course, unfavorable to the conventional theory and consequently given no forum in the literature.

Nevertheless, the net result is that the explanatory power of industrial production in regressions on quarterly and monthly data and, therefore, the role of fundamentals in equity pricing, will be underestimated by the coefficient of determination. Hence, if longer horizons, that is, quarterly and annual frequencies, are more accommodating to the investigation, it would seem more precise to utilize actual future profits or earnings to proxy the unobserved fundamental forces driving stock prices. This would also be consistent with the rational expectation hypothesis (implemented in conventional macroeconomic models) that forms the cornerstone of the EMH. However, the literature illustrates a predisposition to employ leads of industrial production over profits or earnings since fixed capital investment creates the capacity to generate future cash flows. That is, industrial production is considered more 'fundamental'.

In addition to industrial production and bond yields, the spreads between both short- and long-term interest rates (term spread) and between high- and low-grade bonds (default spread) are employed in the determination of whether fundamentals rule the market. It has been suggested that term and default spreads among other financial variables are informative business cycle variables that lead turning points in real activity and capture information on the evolution of the real side of the economy (Canova and De Nicolo, 1995; Balvers et al., 1990). Bernanke (1990) demonstrates empirically that the default spread has predictive power for several real economy variables such as industrial production, durable orders, unemployment rate, personal income, capacity utilization and consumption. However, during the 1980s it is reported that the predictive power of this interest rate spread waned significantly.

Chen et al. (1986) argue that the default spread proxies for changes in the expected risk premium and documents a positive relationship between the contemporaneous default spread and expected stock returns. That is, when spreads are high, financial markets conditions are poor and inherently more risky, warranting a higher rate of return. Keim and Stambaugh's (1986) study provides evidence that substantiates the claim that bond spreads proxy for changes in the risk premium and demonstrate that the relationship extends to bond returns as well. On the basis of work by Fama and French (1989) and Fama (1990) the literature concurs that default spread is a leading indicator of business cycle conditions and track similar variations in expected stock returns as dividend yields, also used to predict returns.

Likewise, the term structure or yield curve is reported to 'capture cyclical variation in expected returns' or the term premium on stock returns (Fama, 1990; Fama and French, 1989). Estrella and Mishkin (1998) show that the slope of the yield curve impounds important business cycle information, leaving commonly accepted indicators like past levels of real GDP and monetary aggregates with little forecasting power when included. Lower than average spreads are found to be associated with a higher possibility of recession while higher than average spreads indicate a lower than average probability of a recession. Correspondingly, Keim and Stambaugh (1986) demonstrate that the term structure of interest rates has a shallow slope around business cycle peaks and a steeper slope around business troughs. Thus, both default and term spreads are pro-cyclical and capture future developments of the real side of the economy and are consequently able to serve as proxies for macroeconomic shocks to expected cash flows in the econometric literature.

Others such as Chen et al. (1986) suggest that the shape of the yield curve measures the unanticipated return on long-term bonds. In this regard, the higher the spread between long- and short-term bonds the more likely an increase in yield to long-term bonds, effectively raising the rate at which expected cash flows are discounted. This notion went against the conventional wisdom at the time, which held that a steep yield curve indicated not that higher returns on long bonds were expected but that short-term rates were expected to rise. After the evidence has been weighed, however, it is now acknowledged that while the expectations theory of interest rates holds in the long run, a steep yield does indicate the domination of long over short bonds (Cochrane, 1999, pp. 59–60). In this manner the term structure also proxies for macroeconomic shocks to discount rates. Thus, the inclusion of the default spread and term spread in stock return regressions effectively incorporates future movements in required rate of return for the stock market.

From Identification to Estimation

Utilizing the set of macroeconomic and financial variables identified by proponents of the EMH described above, econometricians have investigated the role of fundamentals on stock market valuations. The emphasis is placed on explaining stock returns rather than prices since it is returns, prices and reinvested dividends that are deemed to exhibit the martingale behavior necessary for consistency with the theory of efficient asset markets (Leroy, 1989, p. 1590).[3] Even with forecasting variables such as the dividend yield and interest rate spreads, a disquieting portion of the actual fluctuations in aggregate stock returns is explained by the factors on an ex post basis. On the whole, the investigators are rarely successful in explaining little more that 50 per cent of the yearly variation in real stock returns. The lone exception is Fama (1981), who estimates several separate specifications and finds that the regression that utilizes the lead of real GNP growth and the contemporaneous rate of capital expenditure as explanatory variables explains 70 per cent of the yearly variation in stock prices. Formally, Fama estimates:

$$RS_t = \beta_0 + \beta_1 \Delta GNP_{t+1} + \beta_2 \Delta \text{Capital Expenditure}_t \qquad (3.2)$$

where RS denotes aggregate stock returns (New York Stock Exchange (NYSE) value-weighted). Fama concludes that these results 'suggest a "rational expectations" or "efficient market" view in which the stock market is concerned with the capital investment process and uses the earliest information from the process to forecast its evolution' (p. 555).

However, the models estimated in the seminal works of Chen et al. (1986) and Fama (1990) provide the standard which many other articles follow in the published empirical literature. The former article models share returns as a function of leads of monthly and yearly industrial production (IP), unanticipated inflation (UI), change in expected inflation (DEI), unexpected changes in the risk premia (UPR), proxied by the default spread, and the change in the term structure (TERM). More formally the authors estimate:

$$RS_t = \beta_0 + \beta_1 \Delta IP_{t+1} + \beta_2 DEI_t + \beta_3 UI_t + \beta_4 \Delta UPR_t + \beta_5 \Delta TERM + \varepsilon_t \quad (3.3)$$

where RS_t is the return on a given portfolio of stock. A sample of US stocks was selected and grouped into twenty different portfolios based on firm size. For the model fitted to cross-sectional data during the 1958–84 period, the authors document a positive coefficient on monthly and yearly industrial production as well as the default spread. The 'state variables' on term spread, changes in expected inflation, and unanticipated inflation, however, indicate a negative relationship with stock returns. In point of fact, Chen et al. (1986) develop no 'theoretical foundation for the state variables' but suggest that their signs are plausible (p. 395).

Fama (1990) offers two sets of regressions. In one, Fama regresses NYSE share returns (RS) on the dividend yield (D/V), leads of industrial production, the term structure (TERM), and shocks to both the yield curve and default spread (TSH and DSH). The latter variables are the simply residuals from a first-order autoregression fit to the term and default spread.[4] The other model regresses share returns on all the variables indicated previously, except the default spread (DEF) is substituted for the dividend yield. The model attempts to illustrate that the default spread and dividend yield explain an overlapping portion of the variation in expected stock returns. The conclusion drawn is that both variables are related to business conditions and impact the value of equity correspondingly. Thus, if the default spread is a true measure of expectations about future income streams given business cycle conditions, the dividend yield by association may be an adequate proxy.

Formally, the two models are:

$$RS_t = \beta_0 + \beta_1 D/V + \beta_2 TERM_t + \beta_3 DSH + \beta_4 TSH + \beta_5 \Delta IP_{t+i} + \varepsilon \quad (3.4)$$

$$RS_t = \beta_0 + \beta_1 DEF + \beta_2 TERM_t + \beta_3 DSH + \beta_4 TSH + \beta_5 \Delta IP_{t+i} + \varepsilon \quad (3.5)$$

For the 1953–87 period Fama documents a positive relationship between stock returns and the dividend yield, industrial production, and both bond spreads, while the coefficient on shocks to both spreads (DSH and TSH) are negative. In turn, the model explains 56 per cent to 59 per cent of the variation in annual stock returns. The combined explanatory power of the variables declines to 27 per cent when the model is fit to data at the quarterly frequency and just 9 per cent for the monthly frequency. This again reflects the 'horizons puzzle' discussed above.

The proxy variables for expected dividend payments employed beg questions as to how they are selected and their consistency with the theory of efficient capital markets. Do interest rate spreads accurately anticipate future corporate fundamentals? If investigators elect not to use actual corporate earnings or profits in regression analysis, why is industrial production the variable of choice? Why not durable orders, employment, investment or inflation, which measures the economy's growth potential in the face of counter-cyclical monetary policy? Fama (1990), moreover, concedes the lack of rigorous theoretical foundation for the choice of variables. He writes, 'One can also argue that the regressions overstate the explanatory power. The variables used to explain returns are chosen largely on the basis of goodness-of-fit rather than the directives of a well developed theory' (p. 1107). Schwert (1990) responded by employing a version of Fama's model on an expanded sample, the 1918–88 period, and documenting similar results. Despite finding that the model explains less than 40 per cent of the variation in annual stock returns, it is concluded that the results suggest Fama's findings are robust.

One of the explicit goals of Fama (1990) is to evaluate market efficiency, but in explaining only 59 per cent of the variation in returns it is ultimately 'left for the reader to judge' how well stock prices reflect information about corporate profitability (p. 1089). To be fair, one must acknowledge that measurement error could bias the result in an unfavorable manner, thus underestimating the true explanatory power of the model. This of course must be balanced against the selection of explanatory variables on the basis of goodness-of-fit. However, supposing that it is true that the results are understated it does not alter the fact that Fama starts out to judge rationality but concludes in establishing that stock returns are partially predictable by several forecasting variables.

Some interpret predictability illustrated in Fama (1990), Schwert (1990), Fama and French (1988) and Campbell and Shiller (1988) as indicative of market inefficiency or irrationality, fads and speculative bubbles since it conflicts with the EMH which implies that stock returns fluctuate unpredictably. While it can be construed as such, Fama and French (1988) and Fama (1991) argue that neither predictability of, nor autocorrelations in, stock prices imply market inefficiency, only that expected returns vary over time. Consequently variables like the dividend yield capture the time variation in expected returns and should therefore be capable of forecasting future returns on that basis.

Furthermore, another potential explanation for predictability is that the correct general equilibrium model of asset returns is consistent with the variation of returns over time (Balvers et al., 1990; Canova and De Nicolo, 1995). Balvers et al. (1990) characterize market equilibrium as one achieved by individual investors who maximize expected utility by way of consumption smoothing. The substance of the model is that in order to maximize utility:

> investors attempt to smooth consumption by adjusting their required rate of return for financial assets. For example, investors anticipating lower output in the next period will attempt to transfer wealth to this anticipated period of scarcity and therefore will accept a lower rate of return in order to smooth consumption (p. 1110).

This rationalizes the positive relationship between output and stock returns that has been well documented in the empirical literature. More importantly, the consumption patterns suggested here are closely associated with aggregate output. Given the well-known stylized fact, backed by conventional theory, that output is characterized by serial correlation, implies that a significant portion of consumption is predictable. Therefore, the linkage between stock returns and output by way of consumption smoothing implies the former is expected to have a predictable component as well.

The key, however, is that no excess profit opportunities present themselves in the market. This is essentially because in the model the exploitation of profit opportunities, by increasing variation in consumption and introducing more uncertainty, leads to a decline in expected utility. Thus, the basic premise of market efficiency is retained even in the presence of predictability. From theory to empirical tests, Balvers et al. (1990) estimate a simple model for the 1947–87 sample where stock returns are regressed on rational forecasts of output growth (calculated by running a regression of industrial production on one lag of itself plus a time trend). The authors find the model to predict 22 per cent of the variation in stock returns. Finally, in adding the dividend yield as an explanatory variable the variation of stock returns explained actually declines to 20 per cent.

A Critical Look at the Proxies for Economy-wide Fundamentals

Qualitatively, it is not clear that the variables exploited in this branch of the literature such as the dividend yield and bond spreads are consistent with the theory of efficient markets even considering that returns vary over time. Chen, et al. (1986) would argue that bond spreads are among those variables essential to the description of the macroeconomic environment in which the expectation of future cash flows are formed (p. 384). Even so, they cannot be considered variables that describe unobserved market fundamentals exclusively. To be sure, the default spread could very well proxy for influences other than changes in the pure risk premium. For example the spread between low- and high-grade bonds could proxy for lax credit market conditions and general financial euphoria that gives rise to 'irrational exuberance'. To the extent that the dividend yield and default spread are highly correlated, the role of the latter again raises questions as to its consistency with the theory of efficient markets. The same may not apply to spread between long- and short-term bonds, but it should be noted that the coefficient on the term structure is insignificant for monthly, quarterly and yearly horizons in both Schwert (1990) and Fama (1990).[5] Moreover, as indicated above, Chen et al. (1986) find the term premium to impact stock returns negatively.

Shiller (1989) warns that the slope of the yield curve could give misleading information about future changes in interest rates and business cycle developments due to 'extraneous fashions and fads' in bond markets (p. 227). In other words, fundamentals may not rule the bond market and thus bond prices can respond to extrinsic forces. The point to be emphasized here is that it is presumed the bond market is efficient in order to assess stock market efficiency and examine the fundamental forces underpinning equity price movements. If, however, bond spreads give false signals their role as a proxy for shocks to cash flows and discount rates is immediately called into question. Certainly, economy-wide speculation which impacts the stock market may also influence the shape of the yield curve and induce a correlation between the two variables which is unrelated to fundamentals.

Clearly, the relationship between the variables deemed 'fundamental' and stock returns is more convoluted than first anticipated, and the literature is not unanimous. At best, Fama (1990) can be interpreted as an illustration of the same long-run rationality in stock prices posited by early theorists such as Graham and Dodd (1934) that later scholars sought to defend by injecting rational expectations into stock market phenomenon *à la* Samuelson (1965) and Fama (1970). (Recall Graham and Dodd understood equity prices to fluctuate randomly about their fundamental values, not that price equals fundamental value as suggested by EMH proponents.) At worse, Fama's model is an eclectic one and, along with Chen et al. (1986), demonstrates that other extrinsic elements, outside of those thought to be fundamental to the equity price determination process, move markets as well.

Quantitatively, one of the problems with estimating models such as those characterized in (3.2)–(3.5) and interpreting the results as suggestive of the rationality or efficiency of markets is that it disregards the potential simultaneity between returns and the various proxies for real activity. The possible simultaneous equations bias that arises from taking real economy variables as wholly exogenous with respect to stock prices suggests that a relationship found to be indicative of market efficiency could be overstated. As Barro (1990) and Bosworth (1975) note, the relations between developments on the real side of the economy and stock prices could generate from two other potential sources other than the market predicting the evolution of future production and cash payouts. First, stock prices and industrial production may simply respond simultaneously to interest rates or other important causal variables. Second, and more importantly to our argument here, stock prices may cause real activity.

There are three well-documented channels through which stock price fluctuations can transmit to real activity. First, changes in stock returns are synonymous with changes in wealth, which in turn can influence the demand for consumption goods (Poterba, 2000; Poterba and Samwick, 1995; Barro, 1990; Bosworth, 1975). Second, changes in stock returns alter the cost of capital, which may influence future investment demand (Morck et al., 1990; Barro, 1990; Fischer and Merton, 1983; Ciccolo, 1978; Ciccolo and Fromm, 1980; Tobin, 1969).[6] Keynes (1964) provides a line of theoretical justification for the relationship between share prices and investment in *The General Theory*, writing:

> But the daily revaluations [sic] of the Stock Exchange, though they are primarily made to facilitate transfers of old investments between one individual and another, inevitably exert a decisive influence on the state of current investment. For there is no sense in building up a new enterprise at a cost greater than that at which a similar existing enterprise can be purchased; whilst there is an inducement to spend on a new project what

may seem an extravagant sum, if it can be floated off on the Stock Exchange at immediate profit (1964, p. 151).

Furthermore, in a footnote subsequent to the above quotation Keynes notes:

> In my *Treatise on Money* (vol. ii., p. 195) I pointed out that when a company's shares are quoted very high so that it can raise more capital by issuing more shares on favorable terms, this has the same effect as if it could borrow at a low rate of interest.

Third, changes in stock returns signal balance sheet changes, impacting corporations' ability to acquire bank loans with which to finance future investment (Parenteau and Veneroso, 1999; Goodhart and Hoffman, 1999; Bernanke and Gertler, 1995; Minsky, 1982, 1995; Tease, 1993; Morck et al., 1990).[7] Additionally, all three channels may be reinforced by an expectation effect, whereby agents take the stock market as a leading economic indicator and adjust their activity accordingly (Poterba, 2000; Otoo, 1999; Minsky, 1982, 1995; Morck et al., 1990; Mishkin, 1977).

The work of Chamberlain and Gordon (1989) suggest that investment models based on Tobin's q and other profitability variables outperform the neoclassical capital theory models pioneered by Jorgenson (1963). Sensenbrenner (1991) provides evidence that stock prices help explain investment and that dynamic-q investment models are robust across six OECD countries, including the United States. To the contrary, on the basis of both firm-level data and aggregate data, Morck et al. (1990) conclude that with respect to investment 'the market may not be a sideshow, but nor is it very central' (p. 199). Blanchard et al. (1993), Mullins and Wadhwani (1989), Summers (1981), Clark (1979) and Von Furstenberg (1977) present empirical evidence that indicates that Tobin's q has limited predictive power for US investment.

While the evidence on q-theory is clearly mixed, it should be noted that q is a reduced form expression for the complex of many forces of which the stock market is merely one. Barro (1990), in introducing stock returns directly into the investment equation in lieu of the standard q-variable, illustrated that stock prices have significant explanatory power for US investment. These results suggest, 'the stock market variable outperforms the q-variable because the market-equity component of this variable is only a rough proxy for stock market value' (p. 115). Thus, Barro (1990), in decomposing q, captures the direct effect of stock price on investment, including the influences brought about by motivating changes in household and business expectations.

The evidence of the effect of stock price changes on consumption is less subject to controversy. Econometric work generally finds that the impact of a dollar change in stock market wealth on consumption ranges from three to approximately seven cents (Poterba, 2000; Ludvigson and Steindel, 1999; Starr-McCluer,

1998; Poterba and Samwick, 1995; Mankiw and Zeldes, 1991). This is important to note since the real net worth of US households increased by fifteen trillion dollars during the 1990s – a good portion of it stock market-related (Poterba, 2000). Further still, Otoo (1999), exploiting both the Conference Board and Michigan Survey Center's measures of consumer confidence, documents evidence that changes in equity prices have consequences for consumer sentiment. The results were consistent with the notions that individuals view stock price changes as leading indicators of macroeconomic activity and that the stock market influences the real economy via an expectations conduit.

Collectively then, theory and empirics suggest that the stock market is much more than the sideshow implied by the strict neoclassical characterization of finance as a 'veil' over the macroeconomic process. Therefore, in modeling share prices an investigator should at least be concerned with the possibility of reverse impact or feedback and, accordingly, simultaneous equations bias. Yet, many investigators of the efficient markets perspective often discount these issues when modeling stock price behavior, either for simplicity or theoretical essentiality. Even Fama (1983, 1990), perhaps the leading empirical researcher in this field, proceeds as if the real economic variables impact stock returns without feedback. This makes the small fraction of the variation in stock returns explained by the 'fundamental' macroeconomic factors considered important in this branch of literature problematic for the EMH.

That the real economy might be influenced by fluctuations in stock prices is not completely ignored in the literature, however. For example Chen et al. (1986) acknowledge that:

> No satisfactory theory would argue that the relation between financial markets and the macroeconomy is entirely in one direction. However, stock prices are usually considered as responding to external forces (even though they may have feedback on the other variables). It is apparent that all economic variables are endogenous in some ultimate sense ... our present goal is merely to model equity returns as functions of macro variables and non-equity asset returns. Hence this paper will take the stock market as endogenous, relative to all markets (p. 384).

Fama (1990), before proceeding to model stock returns under the assumption that the explanatory variables are exogenous, also addresses the issue of causality. He writes:

> Disentangling cause and effect in the relations between stock returns and real activity is an interesting and formidable challenge, not addressed here. For present purposes, as long as the return variation that results from the relations between stock returns and real activity is rational, it is a legitimate part of the story for rational variation in returns (p. 1092).

In neither piece are the possible negative implications for taking such an approach addressed. We are led to believe that the choice is innocuous as far as the econometric analysis and interpretation of the results are concerned.

Correspondingly, in the work utilizing OLS or GLS estimating techniques, measures of economic activity are considered exogenous with respect to share prices and even standard Hausman tests are not conducted to gauge the strength of the contemporaneous correlation. Fama (1981) acknowledges that the exogeneity proposition could be tested and concludes that, while failure is expected, it would not necessarily invalidate the EMH. He writes:

> Unfortunately, the model is likely to flunk these exogeneity tests when in fact it is true and when markets are characterized by rational expectations. Since we are not likely to find the exact form of the true structural model or all the exogenous variables which are relevant in explaining the growth of real activity, current and past inflation rates or stock return set by rational markets are likely to have marginal explanatory power in the Sims–Gewke tests; that is, the tests are likely to lead to the false conclusion that future activity is caused by past inflation rates and stock returns (p. 556).

While Fama could possibly be correct about not identifying the correct specification for a true test of simultaneity and thus market rationality, this statement is likely to be true for many of the tests conducted in econometrics. For example, we know Dickey–Fuller tests for unit roots have low power in rejecting the null hypothesis; nevertheless we conduct them anyway and leave it to the reader to judge the results and their significance for the modeling procedure.

Indeed, Fama (1990) is apt in noting that the resolution of the cause and effect issue in the relations between real activity and the stock market is an intricate task. This reflects the important fact that stock prices are pro-cyclical, leading variables. This difficulty appears even more extreme for econometricians theoretically linked to the efficient markets paradigm. Here, in their attempt to identify the determinants of equity price fluctuation, leads of presumably exogenous macroeconomic variables are employed as proxies for future movements in unobservable fundamentals. Yet, the endogeneity of real variables would suggest that stock market under- or overvaluation could have a self-fulfilling impact on the real economy. This eventuality renders tests of the validity of the EMH less reliable. Thus, for consistency, stock prices, in impounding information about future real activity, are presumed not to cause but signal or anticipate economic activity. In this manner the issues of causality, that is, causal relations running from prices to real economic variables, are circumvented. This includes not testing for endogenous right-hand-side variables, failure of which would be a clear violation of the classical linear regression model with implications worthy of mention.[8] In assuming a unidirectional relationship it could be argued that many econometricians often defer to the theory they are attempting to test.

Moreover, the quote from Fama (1981) reads like the standard critique of structural models by proponents of the vector autoregression (VAR) methodology. It is argued that in order to impose structure on the data heroic assumptions must be made and, furthermore, the structural evidence is only as good as the model upon which it is based (Sims, 1980; Summers, 1991, p. 137). While it is noted that the test for exogeneity might fail as a result of the misspecification of the structural parameters, Fama (1981) pauses short of suggesting that the results (which he concludes argue in favor of market efficiency) may be based on an incomplete model. Nor is the recommendation favoring reduced form econometrics to augment the ordinary least squares (OLS) results forthcoming. Instead, reminiscent of the manner in which failure of the EMH is taken as possibly indicative of an incorrect model of market equilibrium, failure of a test for exogeneity is taken as a failure to identify the correct structural parameters. Thus, given the difficulty of testing the joint hypothesis and the propensity to presume its validity beforehand, it is unlikely that the question of market efficiency will ever be settled in an empirical court.

In some cases, investigators have analyzed the two-way causality between stock returns and real variables in an attempt to resolve the exogeneity–endogeneity issue. Ciccolo (1978) finds that stock price influences economic activity without feedback for both the 1919–39 and 1953–74 periods on the basis of a Granger–Sims test for exogeneity (p. 54). Gjerde and Saettem (1999), Gallinger (1994) and Lee (1992) acknowledge that the relations between the stock market and the macroeconomy are not unidirectional, addressing the endogenous nature of the variables by employing the multivariate vector autogregression methodology. The use of the multivariate technique supports unbiased tests for Granger causality, producing generally more credible results than those based on the bivariate procedure (Sims, 1980; Granger, 1969).

Gallinger (1994), investigating with co-integration models, finds that stock returns Granger-cause industrial production for the 1953:1–1987:12 period and the degree of causality is found to be particularly strong during the 1980:1–1990:9 interval. Full evidence, of course, points towards contemporaneous correlation. Gallinger also documents that stock returns Granger-cause the spread between yields on six-month commercial paper and the six-month treasury bill (that is, the default spread) for the 1972:1–1990:9 period. Likewise, Gjerde and Saettem (1999) in their study of the Norwegian economy find that domestic economic activity impacts real stock returns significantly and industrial production explains 8 per cent of the forecast error variance in stock returns. However, real stock returns explain only 1 per cent of the variance in the first difference of industrial production. This relationship between lagged stock returns and real activity suggests the stock price transmission mechanism is weak or that stock prices contain little predictive content for the macroeconomy in Norway. These results are not surprising given the small size of the stock market in Norway and its small contribution of stock to total wealth (p. 69).

Lee (1992) finds that stock returns appear Granger-prior to, and enhances the predictability of, measures of real activity for the periods 1947–87 in the United States. Furthermore, variance decompositions (innovation accounting) show that real stock returns explain a significant portion of the variance in industrial production. However, true to the sprit of the EMH, a causal relationship is not asserted. Instead Lee (1992) concludes that the results are 'consistent with the view that the stock market rationally signals (or leads) changes in real activity, and that the relation between stock returns and real activity is positive' (p. 1597). This again appears to underscore the propensity of investigators to place faith in the theory of efficient markets before empirical evidence. Ironically, the *raison d'être* of the VAR analysis is that it imposes no causal structure on the data a priori, treating all variables as potentially endogenous and allowing whatever relations that exist to emerge from the data (see Chapter 6).

James et al. (1985) employ a vector autoregressive moving average model (VARMA) to examine the causal links between stock returns, real activity, money supply and inflation. The authors also document evidence suggestive of a two-way causal linkage between real activity and stock returns. However, the results of the VARMA model are not taken as an indication of the explanatory power of stock return on the relevant variables in a causal sense. Instead they write, 'stock returns can be considered an indicator of expected real activity' and, thus, we are inclined to conclude that the former simply aids in the predictability of the latter.

Domian and Louton (1997) on the basis of an asymmetric autoregressive approach uncover results consistent with the literature on business cycles (Neftci, 1984; Rothman, 1991; Hussey, 1992). Just as business cycles 'exhibit pronounced asymmetries', Domian and Louton (1997) find evidence that stock price declines are associated with abrupt decreases in growth rates of industrial production and that increases are correspondingly associated with mild increases in industrial production (p. 168). The authors conclude that the information about real activity conveyed by a stock market boom is considerably smaller than that relayed by market busts. These findings run parallel to Zandi (1999) who maintains that consumers respond differently to wealth contractions than expansions. Others have also addressed the potential asymmetry exhibited by the wealth effect (see Poterba, 2000). Thus, the stock market transmission mechanism may indeed be more potent during market downturns than upswings in the United States.

Notwithstanding the fact that reduced form evidence precludes a query into the actual stock price transmission channels and that the impact on the economy may be asymmetric, these works clearly establish that variables which proxy real activity should be presumed endogenous unless tests indicate otherwise. In our view, premised on an objective view of how financial markets operate, the conclusion to be drawn is clear. Econometric work, which uses leads of real variables in explaining equity price movements, may produce misleading results and should therefore be interpreted carefully to avoid any grand claims of market efficiency where such are not warranted. The very possibility of causation running from stock prices to changes in investment and consumption implies that stock price appreciation can be self-justifying, thereby maintaining a reasonable relationship with real activity.

It should be acknowledged that VAR models rely crucially on timing to resolve the causation issue. This implies that if they are indeed forward-looking variables, stock prices should always appear Granger-prior to the real macroeconomic variables and thus it is reasonable to interpret the results in the manner suggested by proponents of the theory of efficient markets. In-sample estimation techniques can only positively gauge association and therefore any theory that surmises a relationship between stock returns and real activity cannot be dismissed purely on the basis of Granger causality tests. Consequently, the issue of whether stock prices are truly exogenous will not be decisively resolved even with a reduced form approach. It must be emphasized again, however, that it is the a priori economic theory and reasoning, not the econometrics, from which the conclusions of market efficiency or inefficiency are drawn.

It is for such reasons that Summers (1991) maintains that substantive advance can rarely be reached via formal econometric work and that empirical researchers who believe so suffer from 'scientific illusion' (p. 129). Instead, 'The Scientific Illusion in Empirical Macroeconomics' argues that it is 'pragmatic empirical work' which has answered meaningful questions and influenced academic opinion. That is, work that assesses 'the strength of associations rather than estimate structural parameters 'coupled with 'verbal characterizations of how causal relations might operate rather than explicit mathematical models' and the 'skillful use of carefully chosen natural experiments rather than sophisticated statistical technique to achieve identification' (p. 130).

Summers (1991) argues on one hand that the work employing the average economic regression methodology is 'unenlightening' for two principal reasons. First, failure of a hypothesis based on identifying 'deep structural parameters' can be taken either as falsification of the central theory or 'instead a consequence of auxiliary assumptions made in testing it'. The example used is the work of Hansen and Singleton (1983) where inconsistency of their results with the model of asset pricing is taken to be not a failure of the model but the inability to identify the precise structural parameters (Summers, 1991, p. 135). This is not too dissimilar from the work on the EMH, surveyed above. Second, Summers notes that the rejection of a theory on the basis of structural models gives no indication of how future investigators should proceed. In the case of Hansen and Singleton (1983) the direction in the modification of the consumption-based theory of asset pricing is left unclear. These issues are problematic since, as it is duly noted, 'science proceeds by falsifying theories and constructing better ones' (ibid., p. 135).

On the other hand, Summers (1991) holds that the VAR approach championed by Sims (1972) suffers from the inability to enlighten economic theory as well, noting that it is unlikely that substantive progression can result from empirical work that economizes on identifying assumptions and structure. It is not surprising that economic theory is ultimately necessary to interpret causal relationships and associations estimated by the technique. Even the variance decompositions and impulse response functions, auxiliary to the VAR technique and necessary when the reduced form evidence is uninterpretable, requires ordering the variables according to some economic theory. Thus, Summers argues that works such as Bernanke's (1986) attempt to unravel the relationship between money and output 'without introducing information beyond that contained in times series ... are shadow boxing with reality' (p. 139).

While Summers is accurate in addressing the limitations of formal econometric work and advocating the importance of 'pragmatic empirical approach', it could be argued that he pushes his argument too far. Substantive advance with formal econometrics can be made if econometricians are thorough in their examinations, including clearly stating the identifying assumptions central to the particular theory to be tested, and genuine in the interpretation of the results. In our case, we are concerned with explaining the forces underpinning the dramatic rise in equity prices, and to that extent both VAR and OLS approaches can be extremely useful. Upon using sophisticated quantitative tools to identify these forces we can show consistency or inconsistency of the data with the various theories of equity price determination and fluctuation during the 1982–2000 period. Nevertheless, this book does not attempt to test 'deep structural parameters' nor does it rely heavily on a single methodology.

Fundamentals and International Forces

It is essential to note that rapid financial market internationalization has left the literature surveyed above somewhat dated in its exclusive considering of domestic variables. While a few works on European economies have included and explored the role of international variables (Asprem, 1989; Wasserfallen, 1989; Gjerde and Saettem, 1999), the standard empirical treatments of US share price dynamics proceed with little regard to foreign influences and as if the United States is immune to the consequences of financial market integration and globalization. One notable exception is Canova and De Nicolo (1995) who investigates the relationship between equity returns, foreign and domestic output growth and foreign stock returns for Europe and the United States within the context of a general equilibrium, multi-country model. Technology and government expenditure shocks are assumed to be transmitted internationally while consumption and production interdependencies link domestic economies in the model.

This approach both characterizes behavioral equilibrium in asset markets in a manner consistent with the joint hypothesis and expands the investigation to include the impact of foreign dynamics on domestic stock returns. Canova and De Nicolo (1995) find some rather interesting results. First, it is reported that lagged European stock returns explain GNP growth in both Europe and the United States while lagged US stock returns are significant in explaining European GNP growth but insignificant in explaining US GNP growth. Second, it is found that, in including foreign influences, the relationship between real activity and the stock market intensifies. On the basis of the general equilibrium model it is reasoned that, 'future foreign output growth will help to predict domestic stock returns if it carries information about future domestic output growth which is not entirely incorporated in domestic variables' (p. 995). Yet, it is important to acknowledge the possibility that the US stock market impacts international production through a wealth effect channel and the marginal propensity to import.

In the literature on small open economies, typified by Gjerde and Saettem (1999), Asprem (1989) and Wasserfallen (1989), investigators are compelled to investigate the role of international variables on domestic equity price changes given their sensitivity to foreign shocks. Gjerde and Saettem (1999) investigates Norwegian equity price dynamics, including exchange rates, oil prices and international industrial production among the standard explanatory variables to capture the openness of the economy to foreign economic activity. Asprem (1989) investigates the importance of foreign news in ten European countries and finds that in several countries stock prices are sensitive to the S&P 400 index as well as the changes in the US term spread (yield curve). With the exception of the United Kingdom and Sweden, which were highly correlated with US markets, Asprem finds domestic stock prices are more strongly correlated with a weighted portfolio containing UK, German and Swedish stock market indices. The explanatory power of exchange rates was generally weak, while that of imports were mixed – the relationship between imports and stock returns proved to be the most significant for France and the United Kingdom.

Wasserfallen (1989), recognizing that firms positioned in global capital markets and engaged in international trade are responsive to 'demand conditions in foreign markets, prices of imported goods and raw materials as well as on exchange rates', expands the set of explanatory variables in a study of Germany, the United Kingdom and Switzerland (p. 618). The empirical results, even though measures of international economic activity are omitted, are not encouraging. Exchange rates, real exports and import prices are found to be insignificant explainers of price fluctuation and thus, the author concludes, 'no effects of macroeconomic developments occurring on the international goods and capital market can be found ...' (p. 621).

Aggarwal and Schirm (1995) examine the effects of economic integration on the sensitivity of US asset prices, interest rates and exchange rates to the current account. The authors find that in the years prior to the 'Plaza Agreement' for international economic cooperation only interest rates were sensitive to news regarding the trade balance. However, in the post-'Plaza' years, 1986–88, information in the US trade balance influenced interest rates, exchange rates and equity values. These results suggest that asset-pricing modeler should utilize a more comprehensive set of explanatory variables, reflective of the increased openness of domestic goods and capital markets and the consequent interdependencies between national economies that result. Even from the perspective of the EMH, the growth of the foreign companies listed on US exchanges suggests that foreign 'fundamentals' should factor into the equity price determination process.

Summary

In summary the econometric literature identifies several domestic macroeconomic and financial variables deemed to determine the equilibrium value of aggregate stock market indices. In turn, these proxies for changes in expected future dividend payouts and discount rates have traditionally explained a good portion of the variation in annual stock returns. However, a sizeable amount of the variation is still unexplained by industrial production, the term structure, risk premium and short-term interest rate, even though they are primarily selected on the basis of goodness-of-fit and the potential endogeneity of the variables is ignored. This partially reflects the fact that the determination of the fundamental value of stock, even on an ex post basis, is an extremely difficult task. However, these results may also be indicative of the fact that other elements enter into the equity price determination process than those deemed 'fundamental' by proponents of the theory of efficient capital markets.

EMPIRICAL WORK CONSIDERING SPECULATIVE FORCES

Most proponents of the speculative market theories of equity price determination identify shocks to expectations of future income flows and discount rates as important to understanding stock market fluctuations. However, as was illustrated in the previous chapter, the fundamental value of a share is seen as elusive in the environment of true uncertainty. Accordingly, all the speculative market theories hold that extrinsic elements (forces not related to economic fundamentals) are consequential and at times become the main impetus behind equity price movements. According to such theories we need to know more than the ex post rational price to understand stock market price dynamics. Yet the central problem is that identifying those speculative forces for quantification is nearly impossible.

Thus, the literature here, with a few exceptions, basically serves to corroborate alternative theory by invalidating the claims of market efficiency through formal analysis. Here we find some penetrating examples of what Summers (1991) would label pragmatic empirical work, using 'skillful use of carefully chosen natural experiments rather than sophisticated statistical technique to achieve identification' (p. 130) and casual empiricism. Ironically, this would also includes the work of Galbraith (1988, 1994), popularly categorized as unscientific, and Shiller (1984, 2000a), which finds a reluctant academic audience.

Shiller (1981) and Leroy and Porter (1981) illustrated that share prices fluctuated much more excessively than could be justified by their underlying fundamentals, the discounted stream of dividends, thereby initiating a body of empirical literature consistent with Keynesian views of equity price dynamics. The seminal articles were couched in terms of variance-bounds analysis. In essence two basic facts about the martingale model are exploited to test whether stock prices fluctuations are consistent with the notion of efficient markets. Noting (1) that the sum of the variance of price and returns equal the variance of the 'ex post rational price', denoted p^* in both articles, and (2) that p^* is independent of the breadth of the information set agents possess, bounds on the volatility of stock prices consistent with the martingale model are set. The variance is bounded from above by assuming agents have near perfect information, which implies high volatility in prices and bounded from below by the low information situation, which implies low volatility in prices. Both Shiller (1981) and Leroy and Porter (1981) reject the martingale model on the basis of bivariate autoregression model for prices and dividends, finding the prices to violate the variance-bounds criteria. The former finds prices to be 'far too high – five to thirteen times too high – to be attributed to new information about future dividends ...' (p. 434).

Shiller (1981) concludes that 'the failure of the efficient markets model is thus so dramatic that it would seem impossible to attribute the failure to such things as data errors, price index problems, or changes in tax laws'. Moreover, since it is unlikely that the degree of uncertainty was underestimated in the formal investigation, it would appear that rational elements were insufficient to fully explain fluctuations in equity prices. However, as is pointed out in Leroy's (1989) extensive survey, troublesome econometric problems that biased the test against the martingale model were noted by Flavin (1983) among others (pp. 1599–1600). This ushered in a second generation of variance-bounds or ratio tests, most notably Campbell and Shiller (1988), Jegadeesh (1990) and more recently Pesaran and Timmermann (1995) and Campbell and Shiller (1998). All find that stock prices are excessively volatile with respect to those prices implied by the EMH. This evidence was taken by some as concrete evidence of the irrationality of investors (fads, fashion and market psychology) or more simply to others, the speculative nature of stock markets designed primarily to provide liquidity to asset holders.

Although successful in calling into question the validity of EMH, dissenting work, which has emphasized the speculative nature of stock markets, has used formal empirical work primarily to disprove the EMH. Therefore, there are few attempts to explain stock price movements empirically, rather only to show that they cannot be justified on the basis of economic fundamentals. Consistent with Keynes' analysis, Pratten (1993) develops a theory of share price volatility in terms of intractable uncertainty and conventionally based expectations, but no empirical investigation follows. The intuitively appealing theory of capital market inflation identifies mismatches in supply and demand of long-term securities as the major force in share price fluctuations (Toporowski, 1999a, 1999b). However, the empirical work in this case is non-existent. However, by emphasizing flows, it does provide a manner for the indirect quantification of speculative elements in stock markets. That is, it is possible to show that flows unrelated to news about discount factors and future real dividends significantly impact equity prices. (It is this type of approach that we adopt in Chapter 6 to investigate the 1982–2000 bull market.)

The absence of econometric work again reflects the fact that speculative dynamics are difficult to formalize in terms of econometric tests. However, it also reflects the reality that financial economists have not taken the pre-existing empirical work as a significant enough challenge to the EMH so as to warrant its modification or rejection. If so, the seminal works employing the variance-bounds analysis would have surely initiated a large body of quantitative work on speculative markets. As science proceeds by falsifying unsuitable theories and modifying or scrapping them for alternatives, this tendency may imply that resources will continually be devoted to showing inefficiency rather than developing and testing alternative theories.

A few works go a little further than illustrating inefficiency to more formally estimating the speculative elements underpinning stock price movements. For example, Tease (1993) documents empirical evidence that supports the view that both fundamental and speculative dynamics influence equity prices in G–7 countries. Tease (1993) estimates an unrestricted error correction model that provides a joint test of both the speculative view and the question of whether price 'gradually reverts to equilibrium over time' (p. 44). With S, PY and i denoting share prices, nominal GDP and the interest rate, respectively, the model is expressed:

$$\Delta S_t = \alpha + \Sigma \Phi_i \Delta S_{t-i} + \Sigma \Psi \Delta PY_{t-j} + \Sigma \rho \Delta \, i_{t-j} + AS_{t-1} + BPY_{t-1} + Ci_{t-1} + \xi_t \quad (3.6)$$

The model is specified such that short-run fluctuations in equity prices are a product of changes in nominal GDP, interest rates and stock prices while in long run 'fundamentals' (GDP and interest rates) rule the market. The error correction terms, B and C, reflect the cointegrating relationship between stock prices and the present value of expected nominal income flows. Correspondingly, the coefficient, A, captures the potential reversion to equilibrium if stock prices under- or overshoot the value justified by PY and i.

For the 1960:1–1991:4 interval, lag changes in stock returns enter significantly into the regressions for the United States and all other G7 countries with the exception of France. This is consistent with the extrinsic value theories that maintain that share price dynamics are codetermined by speculative forces (Veblen, Keynes, Minsky and Shiller). In turn, Tease (1993) documents a negative and significant error correction term on lagged stock prices, A, for all countries except Germany, and the coefficients B and C are noted to exhibit the right signs across the board (positive and negative, respectively). These results are consistent with improperly valued stock price moving towards equilibrium over time. As was noted in the previous chapter the significance of the error term implies the forecastability of stock prices and a rejection of the EMH.

Similarly Choi et al. (1999) finds evidence of a co-integrating relationship between industrial production and lagged market returns and significant error correction coefficients for all the G7 countries, except Italy. Poterba and Summers (1988) document evidence of mean reversion but like Fama and French (1988) and Fama (1990) conclude that the finding is consistent not with fads, fashions or speculative dynamics drive stock prices but with the time-varying nature of expected returns. Here predictability is understood as generated by rational changes in business conditions and investor perceptions of risk. This gives rise to prices slowly adjusting in a manner that characterizes a mean reverting process.

Shaikh (1995) contends that stock price movements can be traced directly to fundamentals, here taken to be the 'real incremental rate of profit' (p. 12). According to Shaikh, the problem with analysis based on the standard valuation model is that it improperly assumes a constant rate of return and constant dividend growth rates (p. 6).[9] On the basis of a developed theory of 'turbulent arbitrage' and analysis of means and standard deviations of the rate of return on investment and the S&P 500 return, it is maintained that ultimately interest rates and earnings drive market returns. Shaikh notes that, 'this does not exclude the possibility of fads and fashion. Rather, it affirms the fact that in the end fundamentals do rule' (p. 9).

Nevertheless, the findings of Tease (1990) are supported by the related empirical work of Cutler et al. (1990). Instead of an error correction model, the latter illustrates that the deviation between a proxy for intrinsic value (P_e), estimated as a constant multiple of real dividends and the actual market stock price (P_a), predicts future fluctuations in stock prices positively. That is when the P_a is greater than P_e ($P_e - P_a < 0$), future prices will decline and if P_a is less than P_e ($P_e - P_a > 0$) the market price will rise. The variable, $P_e - P_a$ is not too dissimilar from the dividend yield used in Fama (1990) to forecast stock returns.[10] Moreover, Cutler et al. (1990) counters the claim that time variation in returns explains the relationship between $P_e - P_a$ (or the dividend yield) and future stock prices (Fama and

French, 1988; Fama, 1990) since it exists in other financial markets with weak correlation to the stock market. Further, the relationship is also found across countries. Thus, the evidence weighs against market efficiency and substantiates the assertion that speculative elements do indeed factor into the equity price determination process.

Stock Prices and Flows

A few works attempt to illustrate the presence of non-fundamental forces in asset pricing by analyzing whether flows into the stock market, unrelated to news about future dividends and discount factors, impact stock market valuations. Such a finding would militate against the theory of capital market efficiency, which effectively holds that only information-carrying flows determine market prices. An important prediction (or corollary) of the EMH is that the demand for equity is perfectly (nearly) horizontal at the full information price. This outcome again derives directly from the rational expectations hypothesis, which guarantees that trade is objectively based on the conditional expectations of fundamentals, and perfect markets, which ensures that the market processes information promptly and in a manner consistent with the absence of any arbitrage opportunities.

Furthermore, the high substitutability of stock is assumed to render market prices independent of supply changes. Thus, not only is the demand curve elastic, but with supply considered irrelevant for equity price fluctuation, the de facto excess demand function for equity is perfectly (or nearly) horizontal as well (Shleifer, 1986). Consequently, price pressure effects stemming from supply and demand changes should net out to zero, and only flows that carry genuine information about future movements in the discounted value of real dividends can influence return behavior. Therefore, through an attempt to show that flows explain returns even after controlling for information about fundamentals, it is possible to capture the speculative dynamics in equity pricing. Simultaneously, such investigations test whether the demand curve for equity is truly perfectly elastic as predicted by the EMH.

The 'horizontalist' perspective (the idea that the demand for equity is horizontal at the full information price) dates back to Scholes (1972). Scholes (1972) demonstrated that the selling of large blocks of stocks had 'a negligible impact on the stock price when these trades are made for pure liquidity reasons', that is, when trades convey no private information (Stulz, 1999a, p. 281). The familiar justification is that arbitrageurs will profit from any deviations of price from fundamental value, moving the market price back in line with its true underlying value. Consequently, it is only new information about securities, conveyed by rational investor flows, that alters market prices. The direct implication is that uninformed flows, no matter how large, in leaving the fundamental value of equity unchanged, have negligible influences on equity price dynamics. This clearly underscores the inconsistency between the theory of noise trading and the theory of efficient capital markets since noise traders move returns with non-fundamental (information-free) purchases of equity.

Several studies have scrutinized the demand side of the EMH corollary and successfully challenged the evidence documented by Scholes (1972). Shleifer (1986) and Harris and Gurel (1986) document evidence, based on event studies of new inclusions of stock into the S&P 500 Index, that increased demand for stock purely for liquidity reasons cause permanent price changes. That is, flows unrelated to fundamentals directly influence stock price behavior. When a new firm is added to the S&P 500, demand is created since indexers, in attempting to mirror the return on the broad S&P 500, must purchase the stock for their portfolio regardless of its price (Shleifer, p. 580). Since no new information is revealed by the purchases of the stock, in accordance with Scholes (1972) the share prices of the new S&P 500 corporation should remain unaffected. However, both Shleifer (1986) and Harris and Gurel (1986) estimate that the increased demand causes price to permanently increase by 3 per cent to 4 per cent, respectively. This evidence is not only consistent with theories which hold fundamentals alone are inadequate for explaining price fluctuation but also with the idea that fundamentals do not necessarily rule in the long run.

More recently, the assumption of horizontal demand curves for stock has been tested indirectly by analyzing mutual fund flows into the stock market. Warther (1995) uncovers evidence that concurrent flows from mutual funds in the United States influence equity price behavior using a two-step regression of stock returns on unexpected net sales of mutual fund shares. Using monthly data for the 1984:1–1992:10 period, the coefficient on net sales is found to be positive and highly significant (with an R^2 of 0.53) indicating that a 1 per cent increase in mutual fund stock assets, or an inflow of $4.57 billion in the stock markets, instigates a permanent 5.7 per cent increase in stock prices (p. 235). Since mutual investors are popularly considered to be less-informed investors, Warther's results suggest that not only is the market a 'voting machine' but it is an absolute democracy with 'sophisticated' and 'unsophisticated' flows having an equal opportunity to decide the course of equity prices.

Wermers' (1999) rigorous empirical study corroborates these results, finding evidence of herding behavior among equity mutual funds. This herding activity in small stocks is found to generate permanent changes in market prices. For the 1975–94 period, abnormal returns are found to be highest (lowest) for stocks purchased (sold) in herds by mutual funds (pp. 610–11). Dennis and Strickland (2000) similarly find that the size of the change in a particular firm's stock price is positively related to the percentage of institutional ownership in the firm. Moreover, abnormal turnover in a firm's shares is found to be more closely correlated with the proportion of those shares held by mutual fund investors. Adding in the evidence documented by Ippolito (1992), Hendricks et al. (1994) and Sirri and Tufano (1993) that mutual funds with the best annual performance attract excess inflows from individual investors, it would appear that Warther's (1995) findings suggest that theories of speculative price movements should be taken seriously. Furthermore, the results also suggest that mutual funds are a 'logical place to look for indicators of unsophisticated investor sentiment' (p. 213).

However, Warther (1995) does not appropriately account for economic fundamentals, therefore the strong conclusions drawn are critically dependent on the assumption that mutual funds flows are more reflective of investor sentiment than new information about the earning capacity of corporations. On the other hand, Edwards and Zhang (1998) do control for fundamentals, investigating contemporaneous causality between flows and stock returns during the 1961:1–1996:2 interval with the instrumental variable methodology (two-stage least squares) to account for the potential simultanety. The fundamentals are proxied for in a manner consistent with the financial economics literature surveyed in the previous chapter, following closely Chen et al. (1986). The results, however, are not straightforward.

On the basis of Granger causality analysis it is found that mutual fund net sales (sales less redemptions) do not Granger-cause stock returns with the exception of the 1971–81 sub-period. Moving to the two-equation structural model, with the term spread, risk premium, t-bill rate and the growth rate of monthly industrial production included as proxies for market fundamentals, unexpected net sales of mutual fund shares are significant at the 10 per cent level in explaining stock returns. However, once the 1971–81 interval is excluded (the only period which suggests a Granger causal relationship), the null hypothesis cannot be rejected for any reasonable level of significance. Thus, Edwards and Zhang (1998) conclude 'the recent run-up in stock prices cannot be attributed to the rapid growth of equity mutual funds during the 1980s and 1990s ...' (p. 279). However, what these results suggest for speculative market theory is less obvious.[11] Given that mutual funds still make a small segment of the stock market (pension funds are a significantly larger player in equity markets), illustrating that mutual fund flows are not significant by themselves to explain equity price appreciation, seemingly says nothing about whether 'speculative' flows in general can.

International Capital Flows and Stock Price Movements

One of the implications of the various theories of speculative asset pricing is that foreign capital flows can aid in or even initiate asset price bubbles. Since the efficient market literature is exclusive in its consideration of domestic factors, the literature here, in attempting to evaluate efficiency or use statistical techniques to illustrate inefficiency, omits open economy considerations by default. As a result the impact of foreign activity on domestic equity price dynamics has not been given the examination it warrants. This is a potentially significant omission given that financial market integration has resulted in an increase in the amount of international funds that make their way into and out of US capital markets.

As both Stulz (1999a) and Froot et al. (1998) duly note, the work on international capital flows and domestic asset returns is generally sparse and, in the case of developed countries, economists have neglected the potential relationship altogether. There only exists a minute amount of literature most of which documents a positive, contemporaneous correlation between capital inflow and equity returns in developing countries and an even smaller literature on developed countries, in which the relationship is typically insignificant. It is not clear what is to be taken away from these few studies since most verify association but not causality. Even where they do, they do not attempt to account for economic fundamentals that may induce the correlation.

Froot et al. (1998) employ both bivariate vector autoregression and structural models on daily data for 49 countries obtained through State Street Bank and Trust and finds that portfolio flows are positively and significantly related to contemporaneous returns for developing countries but no relationship was found for developed countries. Because flows quickly impound information into stock prices, Froot et al.'s (1998) use of high-frequency data grants statistical precision unparalleled in the remaining studies. (It should be noted that such studies using high-frequency data could possibly pick up a good deal of noise as well.) Brennan and Cao (1997) and Tesar and Werner (1995), on the strength of structural models, document a positive contemporaneous correlation between foreign net purchases of equity and equity returns using quarterly data. The evidence of the former suggests that the United States is in a unique position – US purchases of equity in foreign developing markets are positively associated with returns while foreign purchases of US equity are not related to the US market index.

Studying developing countries, Tesar and Werner (1993) document a positive relationship between equity inflows for the majority of Latin American and Asian countries through correlation coefficients alone. Clark and Berko (1996), Bekaert and Harvey (1998a) and Bohn and Tesar (1996) utilize monthly data to formulate an econometric model and uncover a positive contemporaneous relationship in developing countries as well. In the former study, it is found that a 1 per cent increase in unexpected inflows as a percentage of stock market capitalization leads to a 13 per cent appreciation in equity prices with no evidence of price reversals. Bohn and Tesar (1996) document evidence of positive feedback trading in a significant amount of the countries included in the study.

However, these notable studies, as do the remaining few on developing countries, focus wholly on international equity portfolio flows and as such ignore the other channels through which global capital flows in general can transmit shocks to share prices. The lone exception is Sokalska (1997), who, although addressing only developing economies, does takes into consideration foreign purchases of local bonds in addition to portfolio equity flows when assessing the impact of capital flows on share prices. Sokalska (1997) investigates the co-movement of equity prices in the Czech Republic, Hungary and Poland and concludes that group's equity prices are strongly influenced by the inflow and outflow of foreign capital. This phenomenon, however, is attributed to the 'thinness' of the markets in question, the implicit assumption being that any relationship between international capital movements and stock prices is most adequately reserved for immature markets.

Nevertheless, the potential relationship between capital flow and equity returns, according to Stulz (1999a), could either reflect a spreading of risk across more investors, or simply that international flows lead to a rupturing of prices away from fundamentals even in developed countries. The same of course can be said of the domestic flows (institutional investors). For the most part, economists have not been compelled to investigate the influence of international capital flows on securities in mature economies because trading is presumed to be undertaken by fully informed individuals, local and foreign, who trade based on their accurate assessment of the 'underlying fundamentals' (Froot et al., 1998). In this view, the level of equity prices, determined through trading by fully informed agents, can be properly gauged by way of the tools of standard valuation analysis, leaving no room for capital flows to impact equity prices. Here, the demand for securities is again perfectly horizontal at the 'fundamental' price, holding information constant.

There have been several attempts at explaining the positive correlation between capital flows and returns in mature and developing countries. The Dornbusch and Park (1995) inflow price theory mitigates in favor of the correlation being a product of less-informed international investors engaging in feedback or noise trading. Furthermore, the authors express concern over excessive volatility, holding that foreign investors establish a more liquid market aiding and abetting speculative trade.[12] Brennan and Cao (1997) provide supporting evidence for Dornbusch and Park's (1995) claim and argue that the positive contemporaneous relationship stems from the positive feedback trading of the lesser-informed foreign investors. However, no evidence is presented suggestive of causality running from returns to capital inflow necessary to support the hypothesis (Stulz, 1999a). Froot et al. (1998) find positive correlation in international flows but reject Brennan and Cao's hypothesis, challenging instead that the majority of the of the correlation derives from returns predicting future inflows. Stulz (1999b) argues that international investors are better diversified and thus demand a lower risk premium. Here the risk–return profile of the domestic market is transformed by the influx of foreign capital and in this sense the impact of flows of prices can be deemed 'fundamental' rather than a matter of speculation. Again, the same can be maintained for domestic institutional investors.

SUMMARY

The empirical evidence, while not unimpeachable, lends credence to the claim that speculative and extrinsic forces enter into the formation of equity prices. To this extent prices reflect more than rational assessments of future cash flows discounted by the required rate of return or, more simply, the present value of future dividend payments. A few works have illustrated that flows unrelated to corporate fundamentals move US equity prices. In principal, the supply and demand forces that are given no direct causal role within the efficient markets paradigm are re-established as the ultimate governors of equity markets. These empirical pieces provide a methodological blueprint for the indirect quantification of extrinsic forces underpinning equity price fluctuation and an entry point into a thorough investigation into the unprecedented run-up in US equity values in the 1980s and 1990s. Using the proxies for genuine information carved out of conventional empirical finance literature we illustrate that with qualified analysis of the growing demand and shrinking supply of corporate equity much of the stock market boom puzzle can be explained.

4. Theoretical Approaches to the Stock Market Boom

A little understood facet of how financial and real values are linked centers around the effect of stock market values. The value of real capital rises when the expectation that a recession will occur diminishes and this rise will be reflected in equity prices. The increased ratio of debt financing can also raise expected returns on equities. Inasmuch as owners of wealth live in the same expectational climate as corporate officers, portfolio preferences shift toward equities as the belief in the possibility of a recession or depression diminishes. Thus, a stock market boom feeds upon and feeds an investment boom ... (Minsky, 1982).

INTRODUCTION

The recent bull market in the United States extended from 1982 to the first quarter of 2000 with its superior performance dominating those markets in all other G15 countries. While stock markets in other countries have witnessed larger increases in stock prices at some time, it is the duration of the bull market that placed the United States in a historically unique situation and presented a puzzle for financial analysts.[1] Broadly speaking, the unprecedented nature of the run-up in equity values has given rise to three competing (although not equally plausible) hypotheses to explain the phenomenon: the 'new economy' concept, the falling risk premium hypothesis and the theory of irrational exuberance. The first two remain consistent with the theory of efficient capital markets while the theory of irrational exuberance is diametrically opposed. The supply and demand theory, which we develop later in this chapter, is consistent with the notion of irrational exuberance yet maintains that all three theories are inadequate by themselves in explaining US equity dynamics over the 1990s.

From the dividend discount model (DDM) introduced in Chapter 3 (equation (3.1)), we can readily identify the three competing theories and illustrate what they imply about the parameters of the model. Recall that DDM model equates the price of a share (or the value of a aggregate index) with the discounted present value of the stream of expected dividend payments adjusted appropriately for risk. Assuming that the expected dividend growth rate is constant from the DDM the price of share (P_t) can be written:

$$P_t = (r - g)^{-1} D_t (1 + g) \qquad (4.1a)$$

or more commonly expressed:

$$D_t / P_t = (r - g)/(1 + g) \qquad (4.1b)$$

where g is the constant dividend growth rate and D_t represents dividends per share and D_t/P_t the dividend yield. In turn, r denotes the required rate of return and equals the risk-free interest rate, i, plus a risk premium, ρ ($r = i + \rho$). The equation is appropriately labeled the Gordon growth equation (or the Gordon valuation model), after Myron J. Gordon (1962) and is widely used to value shares or aggregate stock market indices. The formula implies that in an efficient market, high stock prices will correspond to high future dividend payouts, low future returns or some combination of the two (Campbell et al., 1997, p. 261).

While g and r are presumed constant for analytical tractability, Campbell and Shiller (1988) present a dynamic generalization of the model with variable dividend growth and discount rates. Working from equation (4.1b) in logarithmic form, solving for the required rate of return and expanding with Taylor's formula around the average dividend yield gives:

$$r_{t+1} \cong k + bp_{t+1} + (1 - b)d_{t+1} - p_t \qquad (4.1c)$$

where the lowercase letters denote the natural logarithms of the relevant variables introduced earlier. The terms b and k are the 'parameters of linearization' where $b = -\log(b) - (1 - b)\log(1/b - 1)$ and $k = 1/(1 + \exp(d - p)$ with $(d - p)$ denoting the average log dividend–price ratio (Campbell et al., 1997, p. 261). Assuming prices are formed in efficient markets, solving recursively[2], and taking expectations yields:

$$p_t = k/1 - b + E_t \{\Sigma_{j=0\ldots\infty} b^j [(1 - b)d_{t+1+j} - r_{t+1+j}]\} \qquad (4.1d)$$

Equation (4.1d) is the dynamic Gordon growth model, where the price is a function of a weighted average of expected future growth rates of dividends and risk-adjusted discount rates. In the case where the dividend growth and discount rate are constant, equation (4.1d) reduces to the original Gordon growth model (ibid., p. 263). From the dynamic model, Campbell and Shiller (1988) show that temporary movements in the relevant parameters have a much smaller impact on current prices than persistent movements. Thus, increases in 'rational' asset prices must generate from a persistent increase in the growth rate of dividends, a persistently lower required rate of return or, again, a combination of the two (Carlson and Sargent, 1997, p. 4; Campbell et al., 1997, p. 263). The key word here is 'persistent' implying that the market should be able to discern the difference between payouts that are transitory and those that represent steady increases in corporate earnings. This remains accurate even in the case where share repurchases are substituted for dividend payments (see Chapter 5). Therefore, if the proponents of the efficient markets hypothesis (EMH) are to put forth a consistent explanation for the stock market boom, it must be done utilizing the parameters r and g.

Indeed, the 'new economy' theory of the bull market maintains that high dividend growth rates will prevail permanently into the future (a permanent increase in g), thus predicting double-digit stock returns going forward. As we discuss in more detail below, the new economy concept does not have a strong hold in the academic literature in the area of financial economics but has instead surfaced in the business press as an ex post theory to explain the boom. On the other hand, the falling risk premium theories, which find popularity with proponents of the efficient capital markets theory (for example Fama, French, Sharpe), holds that for a variety of reasons the risk premium and, therefore, the required rate of return has significantly declined (ρ and r have fallen). Accordingly, this theory predicts lower future stock market returns going forward. It must be underscored that although these theories make drastically different predictions about the future performance of the stock market, both maintain that the run-up in equity prices is justifiable purely on the basis of economic fundamentals, thus remaining true to the spirit of the EMH.

Shiller's (2000a) theory of irrational exuberance departs from the above theories by identifying the primary force behind the escalation in equity values as unrelated to either the ability of corporations to make profits and consequently disburse dividends or changes in the risk inherent in stock market investing. Instead, Shiller argues that g has been overestimated and ρ underestimated by a euphoric investing public, encouraged by word of mouth communication and the mass media. Returning to the original formulation of the DDM, the irrational exuberance theory implies that expectations about future discounted and risk-adjusted dividends are formed in such a manner that leads to a separation of market prices from fundamental values. Shiller's general theory of equity price determination was laid out in greater detail in Chapter 2 with the other theories of speculative price behavior. Moreover, the flow theory laid out below encompasses many of the points Shiller emphasizes in his analysis of the US stock boom but provides for a more general understanding of equity price dynamics. Thus, we focus on the two competing theories, which can be explicitly linked to stock market efficiency and rational behavior.

THE NEW ECONOMY THEORY AND US STOCK VALUES

Interpretations of the 'new economy' concept have ranged from relatively modest claims that computer systems would smooth inventory adjustments and that profits would continue to grow rapidly into the future to grander assertions that the traditional business cycle was defunct and the old methods of valuing shares had become obsolete. In fact, due to the variety of definitions that have emerged to describe the US economy during the 1990s, the precise meaning of the term new economy is elusive, requiring intensive research beyond the scope of this study. Paulre (2000), who provides an excellent survey on the evolution of the concept, notes:

> Depending on who is using it, the term can designate: (i) a subset of those economic activities that encompass information and communication technologies, (ii) the US economy's recent performances, and several characteristic features of its current situation – whose surprising or original nature we recognize even though we are not willing to affirm that these new attributes necessary translate into any definitive structural change in the economy, (iii) the technological and economic revolution that the US is currently experiencing, of which these surprising economic performances are but the first but not the only symptoms (with many people feeling that these performances will continue for the foreseeable future) (p. 4).

The 'new economy' concept initially surfaced in the business press (*Business Week*) in 1994 as a response to the historically unprecedented economic growth and stellar stock market performance of the early 1990s.[3] Here, the third definition suggested by Paulre (2000) was evoked as part of the more complete explanation. It held explicitly that digital technologies, informational advances and the Internet had fundamentally altered the economy such that the United States could grow at a faster, non-inflationary rate, renegotiating its past relationship within the business cycle. This original meaning was complemented with an acknowledgment of the broad trend towards globalization, which was held to stimulate greater competition, efficiency and entrepreneurial innovation (Paulre, 2000, p. 6).

From here the story becomes convoluted, but suffice it to say that this original idea metamorphosed into various definitions as time progressed, each one making more radical and heroic claims than its precursor. Nevertheless, regardless of the definition employed, the term is generally invoked to express an optimistic view of future performance of the US economy stemming from the revolution in information and communication technologies and globalization, which have permanently boosted productivity growth in a manner that enables faster, low-inflationary and sustainable economic growth. Consequently, extraordinary future increases in earnings and dividend growth rates (g in equation (4.1)) would eventually validate the explosion in stock prices over the 1990s. Here, forward-looking US stock prices appropriately reflect the ability of listed corporations to make profits in a manner unachievable prior to the 1990s.

Few academic economists concur with even the most conservative claims about the impact of information and communication technologies on economic growth, the business cycle on stock prices. Among those who champion the idea that stock values appropriately reflected higher future growth rate in dividends are Hobijn and Jovanovic (2000), Hall (2000) and Jovanovic and Rousseau (2000). The latter argue that the 'new era' has resulted in high productivity growth, analogous to the post-industrial revolution period. Hobijn and Jovanovic (2000) go further, suggesting that the information and communication technology revolution was anticipated as early as 1973 but was resisted by incumbents, which resulted in a decline in their market value (p. 4). Thus, not only was information-technology-induced profit growth driving the stock values of the 1990s but also was indirectly behind the undervaluation of the 1970s bear market. Accordingly, both, like those proponents found in the business press, maintain that high productivity growth will translate into higher output growth and, eventually, sustainable earnings and dividend growth.

Hall (2000), in attempting to justify the stock valuations on efficient market grounds, ironically provides an indication of how ill-equipped the theory actually is in explaining the 1990 bull market. Hall argues that the emergence of a large quantity of intangible 'e-capital' – that is, the intellectual capital unique to this highly technological time period explains the high returns reaped by investors over the 1990s. The problem with this miraculous theory is threefold: (1) Where did it come from (2) Why wasn't it captured at least partially in the aggregate statistics and more importantly (3) Where did it go?[4] The most damning evidence against the theory is the steep drop in equity valuations over 2000 and 2001, suggesting that the e-capital hypothesized by Hall all but completely disappeared in two years. One is hard pressed to explain how intangible (intellectual) capital contracts, especially at such a rapid rate. Nevertheless, Hall (2000) illustrates the extreme length one must travel in order to validate the EMH and deny stock market overvaluation.

Shapiro and Varian (1999) acknowledge the manner in which technologies have reshaped business enterprise but maintain that basic economic laws have not been altered. Instead they argue that the notion of a 'new economy' 'should be referred to in explaining the changing nature of certain goods or economic activities, and correlatively, of jobs and profits' (Paulre, 2000, p. 9). This more skeptical view can also be found in the business press although not as apparent or popular as the radical 'new economy' theories (see *Red Herring Magazine*, September 1997). Note well that this definition of the new economy does not deny the role information and communication technologies may have played in the increase in US corporate profitability. However, it maintains that permanently high non-inflationary growth rates of output do not constitute a new economic normalcy such that stock prices at the end of 1999 were indeed overvalued.

In 'Does the "New Economy" Measure up to the Great Inventions of the Past?', Robert Gordon (2000) attempts to debunk the notion that information, Internet and telecommunication technology matches the great inventions of the Industrial or Second Industrial Revolution. In a systematic manner, Gordon shows that although productivity growth during the 1995–99 period eclipsed that of the 'golden age' (1913–72) there are important differences that disqualify the recent 'Internet' era as a period of revolutionary proportions. First, when productivity growth is decomposed into two parts, an unsustainable 'cyclical effect' and a sustainable 'structural effect', the sustainable portion of labor productivity growth is found to be modest. Moreover, the growth is confined to the durable manufacturing sector, outside of which no gains have occurred after adjusting for cyclicality. Second, Gordon argues that, among other things it has not done, the rise of the Internet has not: (1) increased the demand for computers, (2) led to a replacement of older technology, nor (3) resulted in a substantial net increase in investment outside that undertaken for the defense of existing market share. Hence, it is concluded that 'the internet fails the hurdle test as a Great Invention ...' (p. 1).

The globalization theme running through the new economy concept has advocates both inside and outside academic circles. However, instead of attributing the low-inflationary economic growth to global competition, others have noted that financial crises around the world have led to a weakening of world demand that can help explain the lack of inflationary pressure on goods traded globally (Browne, 1999, pp. 8–9). Consequently, the ability of the United States to experience non-inflationary economic growth has come courtesy of the temporary and unfortunate experiences of financially fragile countries, not a restructuring of the conventional relationship between inflation and employment. Thus, the argument goes, as the Asian countries rebound so too will downward pressure on prices.

Furthermore, to the extent that the United States has used foreign capital to help support the economic boom of the 1990s, a rebounding foreign sector or a weakening financial markets in the United States may result in a repatriation of capital as those assets become attractive again vis-à-vis dollar-denominated assets. Skeptics have also pointed towards the fact that the phenomenal growth of the 1990s has been balanced by significant negative aspects of the US economy ignored by 'new economy' proponents including a sizeable current account deficit, rising private debt (corporations and households), growing economic inequality[5] and job quality deterioration (Paulre, 2000).

Generally speaking, financial economists who are proponents of the EMH have not argued that high dividend growth rates generating from a 'new economy' would validate the run-up in US equity prices. This is not surprising since it has been well documented that dividend growth has not measured up to the expecta-

Why the Bubble Burst

tions of 'new economy' theorists (Fama and French, 2001; Jagannathan et al., 2001; Carlson and Sargent, 1997; Blanchard, 1993).

Table 4.1 S&P 500 dividend growth

	Dividend	Real Dividend	Growth (%)	Real Growth (%)
1980	$6.16	$12.04	9.03	− 3.10
1981	$6.63	$11.90	7.63	− 1.19
1982	$6.87	$11.87	3.62	− 0.20
1983	$7.09	$11.81	3.20	− 0.57
1984	$7.53	$12.06	6.21	2.17
1985	$7.90	$12.19	4.91	1.07
1986	$8.28	$12.64	4.81	3.67
1987	$8.81	$12.88	6.40	1.88
1988	$9.73	$13.62	10.44	5.77
1989	$11.05	$14.78	13.57	8.52
1990	$12.10	$15.26	9.50	3.20
1991	$12.20	$14.92	0.83	− 2.17
1992	$12.38	$14.72	1.48	− 1.39
1993	$12.58	$14.56	1.62	− 1.10
1994	$13.18	$14.85	4.77	2.04
1995	$13.79	$15.16	4.63	2.04
1996	$14.90	$15.85	8.05	4.57
1997	$15.50	$16.21	4.03	2.29
1998	$16.20	$16.67	4.52	2.86
1999	$16.69	$16.73	3.02	0.33
Average 1953–99			5.46	1.42
Average 1982–99			5.31	1.94
Average 1960–69			5.64	3.08
Average 1970–79			6.11	− 1.19
Average 1980–89			6.98	1.80
Average 1990–99			3.66	1.27
Average 1995–99			4.85	2.42

Notes: Dividend denotes the actual annual dividend value of the S&P Index.

Source: Shiller (2000a).

Fama and French (2001) calculate the growth rate of real S&P 500 dividends and find that the average growth rate for the first two decades of the 1950–99 period are actually higher than those for the remaining three (p. 10). Moreover, predictive regressions reveal that historical average growth rates provide the best forecast of future dividend growth rates (a year or more ahead). In turn, the authors also find that although real earnings growth is highest during the 1990–99 interval it is not 'unusually high' and furthermore, the real earnings series shows excessive volatility. Thus, regarding the notion of 'new era' dividend growth rates, they conclude, '... such optimism is difficult to justify, given our evidence that historical average growth rates of dividends and earnings do not seem to be near optimal forecasts of future growth rates' (pp. 14–15).

Table 4.1, which reports the real and nominal growth of dividends on S&P 500 stocks, confirms these findings. Over the entire 1953–99 sample the average yearly growth in real S&P dividends is approximately 1.42 per cent.[6] The growth rate for the 1990s was roughly 1.27 per cent (below the historical average), with the greatest increase occurring between 1995 and 1996 when real dividends grew roughly 4.57 per cent. For the 1980s we calculate a growth rate of 1.8 per cent, which is slightly higher than the growth rate for the 1953–99 period. However, if we look at five-year periods, real dividends grew 2.42 per cent on average per annum (1 per cent over the historical average) during the 1995–99 period, although real dividend growth was just 0.33 per cent for 1999. Yet, even here the growth rate is not unprecedented, since the average growth rate of real dividends was approximately 3.1 per cent during the 1960s. Given this evidence, most economists adhering to the theory of efficient capital markets hold that the unprecedented bull market can be attributed not to explosive dividend growth rates but to a decline in the risk premium or, more formally, the required rate of return.

FALLING RISK PREMIUM HYPOTHESIS AND US STOCK VALUES

Historically, investors have demanded a premium for holding stocks over less risky government securities whose expected returns are more predictable. In fact, the standard deviation on treasury bill returns was close to zero during the 1926–96 period while that number was 16 per cent for stock returns. Hence, the required risk premium stems from the greater volatility of the return on stock vis-à-vis the return on bonds and is intuitively, 'a function of the inherent riskiness of the [stock] market portfolio and the risk aversion of market participants' (Claus and Thomas, 1999, p. 6). Correspondingly, the equity risk premium is often defined as the 'difference between the expected return on market portfolio of common stocks and the risk-free interest rate' (Fama and French, 2001, p. 1).

The dividend discount and Gordon growth models assume an arbitrage condition between the risk-adjusted expected rate of return on equity and the risk-free interest rate. Thus, measuring the risk premium (necessary to risk-adjust expected returns) is critical to understanding stock price dynamics. Yet, despite its importance to financial economics, there is a lack of consensus about the appropriate value of the required risk premium (Welch, 2000). Even prior to the stock market boom, some economists maintained that the assumed equity premium was larger than could be accounted for by standard asset-pricing models. While empirical literature suggested a risk premium between 7 per cent and 9 per cent, Mehra and Prescott (1985) argued that aggregate consumption patterns were not volatile enough to justify a risk premium even as large as 2 per cent, thus initiating a body of literature, which sought to unravel the 'equity premium puzzle'. Given this history, not all versions of the falling risk premium theory should be considered ex-post justifications for the stock market boom. Nevertheless, suggested values for the historical equity risk premium range from overly optimistic values of 13 per cent to overly pessimistic values of 2 per cent (Welch, 2000).

Clearly then, there are alternative ways to estimate empirically the risk premium required by investors. One rudimentary method to calculate the implicit risk premium is to employ the Gordon growth model, making assumptions about future dividend growth rates. However, this measure is a tautological one, as there is always some value of the required rate of return that equates the market price to the discounted income stream (Ritter and Warr, 2001, p. 29). The standard approach is to calculate the historical difference between realized stock returns and returns on bonds, that is, estimate the historically realized equity premium. Ibbotson Associates (2000), whose measures of the risk premium have traditionally dominated the empirical literature, follow this methodology, arriving at values between 7 per cent and 9 per cent. Although considered the most reliable estimate, it has been debated whether the ex post (implicit) measure of the equity risk premium is the ex ante one expected (or required) by investors. Furthermore, it is argued that historical averages may not provide an accurate approximation of the future expectations of investors. This notwithstanding, Cochrane (1997) illustrates that a mean equity premium of 8 per cent has a standard deviation of just 2.4 per cent and consequently with 95 per cent confidence we can reject a historical risk premium lower than 3 per cent or higher than 13 per cent.

Although the ex post (implicit) measure is widely referred to in both academia and on Wall Street, some hold ex ante measures of the equity premium to be more precise since they do not rely on the 'noisy' data on actual market returns (Blanchard, 1993). This approach involves forecasting dividend yields, employing econometric technique, and then utilizing some version of the Gordon growth model (equations (4.1a)–(4.1d)) to estimate the expected stock yield. Subsequently, subtracting the yield on government bonds gives the ex ante risk premium. Using this modus operandi, Fama and French (2001) estimate a risk premium of 4.83 per cent for the 1950–99 period and Wadhwani (1999) arrives at estimates for the risk premium of roughly 4.5 per cent over the long-term government bond. Mayfield (1999), who follows Merton's (1980) methodology, estimating the risk premium as a function of observed market volatility, calculates a risk premium of approximately 4.1 per cent. These estimates deviate significantly from the long horizon estimates, found in corporate finance textbooks (8.4–10 per cent), the academic literature (7 per cent) or commonly used by corporate managers (5–6 per cent) (Welch, 2000).[7]

Yet, the standard risk premium assumed in the academic literature, 7 per cent along with the assumption of efficient markets, implies that real dividend growth will be roughly 12 per cent going forward from the 1999 valuations. Some proponents of the EMH hold such growth to be implausible and therefore attribute the run-up in US equity values principally to a fall in the risk premium (Fama and French, 2001; Sharpe, 2000; Siegel, 1999). Fama and French (2001) write:

> Growth rates of dividends and earnings are largely unpredictable, so there is no basis for extrapolating unusually high long-term future growth. This leaves a decline in the expected stock return as the prime source of the unexpected capital gain. In other words the high 1950–99 returns seem to be the result of low expected future returns (p. 21).

This hypothesis is backed up with high-quality empirical work. Blanchard (1993) finds that the 1980s witnessed a significant decrease in the equity premium to between 2 per cent and 3 per cent. Wadhwani (1999), Pastor and Stambaugh (1998) and Claus and Thomas (1999) all arrive at estimates for the risk premium between 1.5 per cent and 3 per cent for the late 1990s. Fama and French (2001), Jagannathan et al. (2001) and Siegel (1999) report an expected risk premium in the neighborhood of zero (consistent with the standard asset-pricing model) for the recent era.

However, these works are balanced by rigorous empirical studies on the ex ante risk premium that challenge such low estimates. For example, Moyer and Patel (1997) arrive at an estimate for the equity premium of roughly 7 per cent for the 1985–95 period. Correspondingly, Hayes et al. (1998) document evidence that the risk premium has not significantly declined in the United States and several other G5 countries between 1983 and 1997. Mayfield's (1999) estimates based on market volatility, while illustrating that the risk premium has trended downwards considerably, achieves results that are inconsistent with an expected risk premium below 4.2 per cent for the late 1990s. Here, the estimated model confirms a structural break in the historical risk premium series (albeit in 1940) but the lower bound on the estimate is 4.2 per cent over the return on treasury bills. Despite this contradictory evidence, a substantial fall in the risk premium is a more plausible explanation for the 1982–99 rise in US stock market capitalization than the new economy theory.

The empirical work showing a decline in the risk premium is accompanied by supporting theories, which hold that the change in the required rate of return is permanent. In some cases the falling risk premium is attributed to rising market participation in the United States, driven primarily by the increase in indirect household ownership through mutual funds and retirement accounts (Heaton and Lucas, 1999; Mankiw and Zeldes, 1991). In 1989 32 per cent of all US households held corporate equity directly or indirectly but in 1995 the percentage was 41 per cent, and by 1999 approximately one-half of all households had invested in the stock market (Diamond, 2000; Wolff, 2000). Thus, as a result of the consequent risk spreading, it is contended that the market should support a lower equilibrium risk premium (Heaton and Lucas, 1999; Siegel, 1999).

The presumed fall of the risk premium is often linked to the rise in the importance of institutional investors, given that institutional money mangers are assumed to be more knowledgeable about corporate operations, more forward looking and, therefore, more sophisticated investors than individuals. Furthermore, it has been pointed out by several observers that institutional investors are less risk averse than are individuals and therefore their dominant presence has transformed the risk–return characteristics of the stock market (Campbell and Viceira, 1999). Thus, to the extent that these investors have come to dominate trading activity (see Chapter 5), participants should be willing to hold stocks for longer periods, resulting in a decline in market volatility. Additionally, it is maintained that institutional investors have promoted a lengthening of individual investors' time horizons by encouraging the expansion of individual retirement accounts and 401(k)s (Diamond, 2000).

However, others argue that institutional investors have a shorter horizon since money mangers are evaluated at shorter frequencies and are subject to career pressures and concern (Diamond, 2000, p. 41).[8] Mutual funds flows, in particular, are composed of a collection of finances from small, inexperienced investors (Edwards and Zhang, 1998, p. 261). Thus, mutual fund corporations can only be as 'sophisticated' as the shareholders who pressure them for high returns. As detailed in Chapter 3, several studies produce evidence that suggest institutional investors pursue short-term investment strategies, often herding into the same stocks and contributing to volatility (Dennis and Strickland, 2000; Wermers, 1999). Friedman (1996) argues that the shift of equity ownership from individuals to institutions, especially mutual funds, has contributed to market volatility and price risk. These arguments run counter to the case for a decline in the risk premium stemming from the increased institutional ownership of corporate equity.

Blanchard (1993) holds that the falling risk premium during the 1980s can be partially accounted for by the rising importance of the pension fund portion of the institutional investor sector since the latter are considered more farsighted than individuals and, implicitly, mutual fund corporations. The idea that pension funds, especially government retirement funds, have a mandate to focus on longer-term investment strategies is extremely popular. There is evidence that this particular mandate reveals itself in the willingness of public pension fund managers to take seriously their ownership rights in the corporate sector, exercising corporate control whereas others have remained passive. McCauley et al. (1999) write:

> To some extent, institutional investors are prepared to speak up in the presence of poor corporate performance ... Thus far, representatives of pension funds for public sector employees have been most active in making their views known; the divided and perhaps conflicted managers of corporate pension funds rarely speak up; whereas managers of mutual funds appear to have spoken up only in isolated instances (p. 340).

Given pension fund involvement in corporate government, an important point we are willing to concede is that this segment of the institutional investor population may be a stabilizing force in stock markets. However, this also suggests that understanding the differences across institutional and individual investors is critical in evaluating the tenability of this version of falling risk premium hypothesis.

Another plausible reason for a decline in the US equity risk premium is the decrease in the cost of obtaining a diversified equity portfolio because of the existence of mutual funds. As the argument goes, in the absence of mutual fund companies, small investors would not be able to make the purchases in different companies necessary to obtain a diversified portfolio due to financial constraints. Mutual funds, on the other hand, by pooling together resources from small investors, allow shareholders the opportunity to hold an otherwise inaccessible diversified equity portfolio at a lower cost and spread risks accordingly (Diamond, 2000; Heaton and Lucas, 1999). Therefore, it can be argued that the equity risk premium has fallen over the 1980s and 1990s due to the rise of mutual funds. The lacuna in this theory is that mutual funds have been around for a long time – the first two mutual funds were formed in 1924 (Blume et al., 1993, p. 96). Therefore, one must credibly explain why it took investors until the 1980s and 1990s to finally exploit a vehicle for diversification that had been available for 75 years.

The final theory and most popular often cited to explain why the equity premium may have trended downwards over the last two decades is the investor-learning hypothesis. It is also one of the most implausible justifications. Here the falling risk premium is attributed to the popular presentation of information (through academia and the media) that has led to greater public understanding about the return and risk characteristics essential to stock market investment (Diamond, 2000, p. 41). Principal to this expansion in the knowledge base of investors is the 'learning' that average stock market returns are more stable relative to bonds than had been previously acknowledged and that their past risk aversion to equity was inconsistent with historical statistics. For example, Siegel (1994, 1998) utilizes 200 years of US data to illustrate that stocks dominate bonds, commercial paper and treasury bills over long horizons both with respect to return and risk. Siegel (1998) summarizes his main point succinctly, writing:

> The growth of the purchasing power of a diversified equity portfolio not only dominates all other assets but is remarkable for the stability of its long-term after-inflation returns. Despite extraordinary changes in the economic, social and political environment over the past two centuries, US stocks have yielded between 6.5–7 per cent per year adjusted for inflation in all major sub-periods (1998, p. 6).

Thus, it is argued that such studies documenting the consistency of long-term equity investments have educated the investing public, resulting in a decrease of the required rate of return on stock. However, if education is possible then, all things being equal, so is miseducation. Bernstein (1998b) expresses concern over the 'logical and troublesome inconsistencies' with the idea advanced by Siegel (1994, 1998) that stocks are the dominant assets over the long run and the certainty with which it is maintained (p. 183). Employing close to 200 years of data back to 1800, Bernstein does observe that stocks outperformed bonds 57 per cent of the time. Yet, this period includes 32 years, 1950–81, in which bonds returned a meager 2.3 per cent per annum and real bond returns were negative for 18 of those years. Thus, Bernstein concludes 'stocks are the superior investments with a high degree of certainty only in environments where bonds are getting killed' (p. 184). Furthermore, it is also noted that prior to 1950, practitioners had 150 years of history to support a contention that bonds were the premier asset and nearly 30 years passed before this belief was revised. Now that 50 years of history supports the superiority of equity conviction, it should be considered just how likely is it that the United States will experience another period where bond markets perform as poorly as they did during the 1950–81 era.

Figure 4.1, which graphs the logarithmic value of the total return indices for S&P stocks, government bonds, treasury bills and AAA corporate bonds, illustrates Bernstein's points concisely. First, it is clear from the graph that equity investments significantly outperformed bills and bonds from 1951 onwards. However, it is also apparent that the performance of non-equity assets was indeed abysmal during the 1950–81 period. Figure 4.1 also shows clearly that those investing their entire savings in AAA corporate bonds in 1908 and cashing out between the 1936 and 1948 period would have done as good as or better than those with portfolios composed solely of equity. Moreover, in terms of total returns, bonds outperformed the equity market during the entire 1900–1927 era. Although not illustrated in Figure 4.1, this domination of bonds over equity extends to well before 1900 (Shiller, 2000a; Bernstein, 1998b). Thus, Shiller (2000a) argues that 'the evidence that stocks will always outperform bonds over long time intervals simply does not exist … So the "fact" of the superiority of stocks over bonds is not a fact all' (p. 195). Nonetheless, the domination of stocks over bonds from 1950 onwards is an important stretch not to be so readily dismissed.

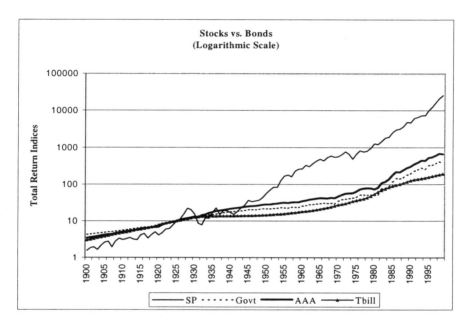

Note: SP, Govt, AAA and Tbill are the total return indices for the S&P 500, US government bonds, corporate AAA bonds and US treasury bills, respectively.

Source: Global Financial Data, www.globalfindata.com.

Figure 4.1 Stocks versus bonds

Investor survey data does not corroborate the claim that investors are expecting lower returns and yet, ironically, the investor-learning hypothesis implies expected returns will be much lower going forward. And despite the claim of lower expected returns, the certainty that stocks will dominate bonds over the long horizon is still maintained. Moreover, the superior performance of equity over bonds over the last three decades does not necessarily imply a continued denomination of one asset over the other since the economic environment is subject to change. This is especially true for the most recent era if (as we contend below) the supply and demand for equity has pushed stock prices up to unsustainable values. That is, the stock market would have undoubtedly become more risky since the probability of prices reverting to more justifiable levels is more likely. Viewed in this light, appealing to historical averages may justify high stock prices and investor euphoria but does not change the fundamental facts about the required rate of return. Diamond (2000) acknowledges this possibility:

> Popular perceptions may, however, be excessively influenced by recent events – both the high returns on equity and the low rates of inflation. Some evidence suggests that a segment of the public generally expects rates of increases in the prices of assets to continue, even when those rates seem highly implausible for a longer term (p. 41).

It should also be noted that a risk premium falling to zero (or slightly below) for the 1990s suggested by some of the empirical models discussed above is inconsistent with the fundamental differences between stocks and bonds. Such a value would imply that stock market investments (diversified or otherwise) are without risk. Yet, while US government securities are in effect risk-free and corporate bonds are relatively safe (even in the likelihood of bankruptcy), stock market investments are not guaranteed. Thus, the risk premium should always be greater than zero to compensate shareholders for the fact that they are residual claimants. Shiller (2000a) notes:

> The public has not learned a fundamental truth. Instead, their attention has shifted away from some fundamental truths. They seem not to be so attentive to at least one genuine fundamental truth about stocks: That they are residual claims on corporate cash flow, available to stockholders only after everyone else has been paid. Stocks are, therefore, by their very definition, risky. Investors have also lost sight of another truth: that no one is guaranteeing that stocks will do well. There is no welfare plan for people who lose in the stock market (p. 195).

Clearly then, without a premium, it is unlikely that anyone would choose hold equity over bonds or treasury bills. In all, the case for the investor-learning hypothesis appears weak.

RETURNING TO THE DIVIDEND DISCOUNT MODEL

The new economy theory implies a high rate of growth in stock market dividends (g), while the falling risk premium theory implies a lower required rate of return on stocks ($i + \rho$). Table 4.2 presents fundamental value estimates for the S&P Index using the Gordon growth model with varying assumptions about the risk premium and dividend growth rates. For simplicity, we use nominal values for all model parameters. The actual value of the S&P Index at the end of 1999 was 1428.68. The results of the experiment show that with a risk premium of 7 per cent, the weighted average of the estimates used by 226 financial economists

(Welch, 2000), the market was extraordinarily overvalued no matter what assumption is made about dividend growth rates.

Table 4.2 Value estimates for the S&P 500

Dividend Growth rate (g) (%)	Risk Premium (ρ) (%)						
	1	2	3	4	5	6	7
5.46	967.6*	624.5*	461.0*	365.3*	302.6*	258.2*	225.2*
6.46	2167.9*	976.7*	630.4*	465.4*	368.8*	305.4*	260.7*
7.46	–	2188.3*	985.9*	636.3*	469.7*	372.3*	308.3*
8.46	–	–	2208.6*	995.1*	642.2*	474.1*	375.7*
9.46	–	–	–	2229.0*	1004.3*	648.1*	478.5*

Notes: S&P DRI Database. (*) Denotes the value estimates arrived at by the Gordon growth model, P $= D(1 + g)/(i + \rho - g)$, where i denotes the yield on the ten–year bond (the risk-free asset) at the end of 1999, 6.28%. The Dividend value of the S&P 500 Index (D) was $16.70 at the end of 1999 while the actual value of the S&P Index was 1428.68.

The same is true for risk premia of 5 per cent and 6 per cent. Even with a risk premium of 4 per cent and a dividend growth rate of 8.46 per cent (a 3 per cent increase over the historic growth rate) the S&P 500 at the end of 1999 was significantly overvalued by roughly 30 per cent. Correspondingly, assuming dividend growth of 5.46 per cent into perpetuity (the actual historic growth rate) the market is overvalued even when assuming a risk premium of just 1 per cent (this holds for a premium of 0 per cent as well). In fact, in order to get an estimate close to the actual value of the S&P Index in 1999 we must assume a risk premium of 2.5 per cent and a dividend growth rate of 7.5 per cent (or some other equally implausible combination). These results are consistent with Ritter and Warr (2001) who, based on a more complicated residual income valuation model, find that with an equity risk premium of 0 per cent the market was still overvalued in 1997. (Note well, the July 31, 2002 close of 911.62 may still represent a level still unjustifiable by fundamentals.)

From the dividend discount model we can decompose changes in equity valuations into three sources: (1) expected changes in dividend growth rates, (2) changes in the required rate of return, or (3) 'valuation errors' (Ritter and Warr,

2001, p. 30). As we laid out explicitly in Chapter 2, the efficient markets theory rules out valuation errors by attaching the rational expectations hypothesis to the standard model. Modeling investor expectations in this manner presumes stock price changes can be linked directly to long-lasting changes in g and r (i or ρ) in equations (4.1a)–(4.1d). Yet, from our discussion immediately above and Table 4.2, it is clear that unless one is willing to make historically implausible assumptions about the growth rate of stock dividends or the equity risk premium, the conclusion of overvaluation is inescapable. Therefore, we deduce that both theories are individually and collectively unable to explain the dramatic run-up in US equity values during the 1990s.

It appears, then, that a theory of 'valuation errors', investor 'irrationality' or speculative bubbles is necessary to systematically explain US equity price dynamics over the last two decades. The overly restrictive EMH cannot explain the recent phenomenon since theoretically it denies the existence of overvaluation and speculative frenzy. On the other hand, alternative theories of equity price fluctuation are often labeled as unmethodical and categorically dismissed as if no analytical and internally consistent model has ever been developed. To the contrary, many of the speculative theories surveyed in Chapter 2 (Shiller, Keynes, Veblen) are indeed systematic and provide rich insight into equity price behavior, thus serving as the initial point of reference for our empirical investigation of US stock price dynamics. Ironically, insights from such theories are usually tacked onto conventional models in an ad hoc manner to explain the day-to-day phenomena in equity markets especially during times of obvious overvaluation.

We therefore make use of speculative theory to advance a credible case for the hypothesis that although the stock market boom was rooted in corporate profitability, it was to a larger extent driven by forces beyond fundamentals. Specifically, the increase in equity values can be linked to the shrinkage in the volume of equity outstanding, the growth of mutual funds (domestic demand in general) and the influx of foreign capital into US equity markets. In brief, it can be shown that the 1982–2000 bull market can be understood with a flow theory of speculative price behavior that is consistent with Hyman Minsky's broader conceptual framework, which emphasizes the tendency of capitalist financial structures to move endogenously from a robust to a fragile state.

A SUPPLY AND DEMAND APPROACH TO EQUITY PRICING

Beyond the Dividend Discount Model Towards Net Flows

The standard valuation model equates the fundamental value of a share with the present discounted and risk-adjusted value of all future dividend payments. Yet, the ability of the market to produce actual prices which approximate the true value of the claims on illiquid, capital assets is complicated by the fact that one of the primary functions of financial markets in general 'is to provide liquidity to asset holders' (Davidson, 1999, p. 4). Given other vehicles through which individuals can transport purchasing power over time, namely bonds, money and consumer durables, stocks are considered assets to the wealth-holding public with several competing rivals. As a store of value, the demand for equity conforms to the conventional determinants of asset demand. Here the determinants of equity demand are taken to be wealth, the expected return to holding equity relative to all alternative assets, and the risk and liquidity characteristics associated with equity vis-à-vis all other assets.

Assuming for simplicity a world with four competing assets we can more formally write the demand for equity as:

$$E^d = f(W, r_m - r_e, r_b - r_e, \pi^e - r_e, \sigma, \vartheta) \tag{4.2}$$

where W denotes wealth, σ and ϑ represents the risk and liquidity premium on equity, π^e is expected inflation, and r_m, r_e, and r_b are the returns on money, equity and bonds, respectively. E^d is negatively related to all the arguments with the exception of wealth with which it co-varies positively. The difference, $\pi^e - r_e$, represents the expected return to holding consumer durables over equity and justifies the negative relationship between inflation and equity prices often thought to be a paradox in the mainstream literature (that is Modigliani and Cohn, 1982; Fama, 1981; Balduzzi, 1995).

From equation (4.2) (the actual substitutability of assets notwithstanding) it is quite straightforward to envision cases where increases in the demand for equity could prompt asset appreciation inconsistent with the fundamentals suggested by the standard valuation model. For example, initial capital gains in the stock market increase household wealth, which in turn stimulates the demand for equity and, consequently, positive feedback loops can emerge. Likewise, underperformance in the bond market, which leads to a widening of $r_e - r_b$ spread, can increase equity demand irrespective of whether or not the economic environment augurs well for future corporate profits. The net result in both cases can be equity prices out of line with the income streams emanating from the underlying capital assets and dividend payouts to shareholders. Note well, this theory of under- and overvaluation is independent of investor irrationality.

Thus, it would appear that the supply and demand for stock as an asset, which ultimately determine market prices, does not necessarily mesh well with the notion of the stock market as an unbiased predictor of future corporate profitability. When we tack on fundamental uncertainty over the future values of the relevant economic variables from which to measure the true worth of stock, the concept of an efficient equilibrium stock price becomes even more implausible, especially in the face of bull and bear markets. Instead, equity markets may generate 'unsustainable increases in prices brought on by investors' buying behavior rather than by genuine, fundamental information about value' (Shiller, 2000a, p. 5). Thus, while the dividend discount model and its many variants yield insight into the fundamental value of stock, equation (4.2) makes it clear that equation (4.1) is not enough to explain actual market price dynamics at all times.

This portfolio theory is enhanced when we integrate supply issues into the analysis along the lines suggested by the flow theory of capital market price fluctuation (Toporowski, 1999a, 1999b) discussed in Chapter 2. A cursory glimpse of Toporowski's (1999) theory reveals a hypothesis that demystifies stock markets, describing literally how they operate in the real world. However, stating that equity prices have increased over the decade simply because the net financial inflow has increased leaves questions as to whether the resulting appreciation was justified or not. And, like its adversary, the strict version of the EMH, it is difficult to disprove such a theory in an empirical court. However, when augmented by a portfolio theory of demand-side flows the result is an informative 'voting' theory of speculative markets. The resulting theory acknowledges the collaboration of supply *and* demand forces in asset price fluctuation while the EMH considers the supply of equity to be relatively inelastic and most of the remaining Keynesian theories focus attention completely on demand-side price pressure as well.

Supply issues are critical to the formation of speculative bubbles, considering that price pressures emanating from increases in demand can be counterbalanced by an increase in the amount of corporate equity outstanding. For that reason, a necessary condition for the existence of speculative bubbles is at the very least a constant supply of equity (Binswanger, 1999, p. 189). Correspondingly, a shrinking supply of equity can expedite the bubble formation process. The variants of the standard valuation model presented above, which exclusively consider investor demand for equity, miss this important insight and, therefore, an important reason why prices might deviate significantly from fundamental value. In fusing the portfolio theory with Toporowski (1999), it becomes clear why we must go beyond the dividend discount model and the EMH to understand equity price dynamics.

However, equities are special assets in the sense that their underlying value is derived from the ability of corporations to pay out dividends to shareholders. In this light, a more systematic theory of equity price determination and fluctuation must make room for corporate profitability or 'fundamentals'. While profits and economic growth may be a poor anchor for stock values during times of financial euphoria or speculative panic, they nevertheless play an important role in both the supply and demand of equity. Consequently, any investigation into the 1982–2000 US stock market boom that ignores corporate profitability potentially misses an important portion of the equity appreciation puzzle. While the dividend discount model is not enough to understand market prices fully, it is still illuminating. As we argued in Chapter 2, the speculative theories advanced by Keynes, Veblen and Minsky place emphasis on profitability and macroeconomic performance as an initial impetus to portfolio shifts towards equity. Grounding the flow theory to Minsky's model of financial fragility provides for a general theory of equity price determination and gives us the insight to more completely explain the 1982–2000 stock market boom.

A Complete Supply-and Demand-Based Theory

The portfolio model sketched above illustrates why market prices may deviate from the value suggested by the standard valuation model. The book's supply and demand approach to equity price determination takes as its point of departure this 'voting' concept of equity markets. The theory, however, never claims that fundamentals do not matter, only that their role in the determination and fluctuation of prices is not as central at all times as is postulated by the conventional theory of equity valuation. While departing from the standard valuation equation with a Keynesian theory of expectation formation, the theory closely follows Minsky's model of endogenous financial fragility or the financial instability hypothesis (Minsky, 1975, 1982, 1986, 1995). The outcome is a theory which holds that the stock market naturally evolves from a robust to fragile state, as reflected by the excessive appreciation in asset prices, validated only by the buying behavior of euphoric investors and unjustified in terms of economic fundamentals. Hence, the flow theory finds the theoretical underpinnings necessary to explain a sustained net inflow into the stock market and systematically unpack the stock market boom of the 1980s and 1990s.

At the core of the theory is the familiar principle of fundamental uncertainty that renders difficult the assessment of the aptness of investment projects, the future state of the economy, and the growth of aggregate demand. The presence of fundamental uncertainty, which cannot be reconciled by the calculus of probability, makes accurate forecasts of stock price behavior nearly impossible. The flow theory is also premised in the reliance of wealth-holders on adaptive (extrapolative) expectations to navigate the environment of uncertainty. These precepts give rise to rules of thumb, conventions, herding, and bandwagon behavior, as individuals grope for information regarding the future value of corporations and the capital embodied within each. To these ends, agents view market prices as correctly summing up the present state of affairs and believe that the future 'will look like the relevant past extrapolated' (Keynes, 1964, chapter 12; Crotty, 1993, p. 63). As has been posited above, stock prices become more reflective of the flow of funds into the market than the discounted value of future expected profits or dividend payments, at least in the short run. Given fundamental uncertainty and adaptive expectations, the standard valuation model becomes the 'conventional expectations' valuation model, and marrying the flow theory to Minsky's model of financial fragility becomes straightforward. These results conflict with the rational expectations hypothesis, which holds that agents know the underlying model, the values of all the relevant parameters and understand that all others have such knowledge and therefore the notion of market efficiency.

As we asserted in Chapter 2, the financial instability hypothesis was developed by Minsky to explain the tendency of firms, encouraged by strong profitability, to take on unsustainable debt levels that eventually outpace incoming cash flows, leading to financial distress, fragility and collapse. As such the theory is developed without actually focusing on stock market dynamics. Yet, as is evident from the quotation opening this chapter, the readings of the late Hyman Minsky reveal a view of the asset price–money expansion nexus as 'an engine of instability' (Goodhart and Hoffman, 1999, p. 1). Minsky contended that as the economy moves from a state of robustness to speculative advance – encouraged by a period of realized profits and macroeconomic stability – expected future profitability and the ratio of debt financing rise. To the extent that wealth-holders exist in the identical 'expectational climate', the portfolio preferences of individual investors shift towards equity, leading to a rise in equity prices. As the willingness to hold money declines, the resulting asset price inflation encourages an overly optimistic or euphoric boom, and consequently credit, investment and consumption expand.

This phenomenon, which ultimately leads to the fragility of the stock market and the economy at large, is captured succinctly in Taylor and O'Connell's (1985) formal Minsky model, which takes a multi-asset approach to the monetary side of the economy. Here, the price of equity is formulated as a function of the proportion of wealth held in equity, which in turn is jointly determined by expected profits and the rate of interest. Adding the variables suggested in equation (4.2), we can write the price of equity more formally and completely as:

$$P_e = f\left[\varepsilon(\iota, \Pi, r_a - r_e, \sigma, \vartheta), W\right] \tag{4.3}$$

where ε, Π, ι and r_a are the proportion of wealth held in equity, expected profits, the discount rate and the returns on other assets, respectively. W, σ, ϑ, r_e denote wealth, the risk and liquidity premiums and the return on equity as indicated previously. P_e is positively related to W and ε, which itself co-varies negatively with ι, $r_a - r_e$, σ, and ϑ and positively with Π. Thus, Minsky's theory is captured by the fact that as euphoria spreads through the economy, via increases in Π (anticipated profits), wealth-holders shift portfolios away from money, durable goods and bonds to claims on 'real capital assets' (equity) and the resulting inflow of funds into stock markets serve to increase equity prices.

Adding our insights regarding equity as a store of value emphasizes again the potential endogeneity of flows with respect to equity prices and the possibility of feedback loops, speculative bubbles and Ponzi behavior.[9] The increase in Π by triggering growth in P_e, subsequently causes an increase in W and possibly a decline in $r_a - r_e$ spreads, both which feedback positively on P_e through ε. It should be well noted, however, that the speculative theory advanced here is not dependent on investors exhibiting return-chasing behavior. This generally distinguishes all Keynesian-inspired theories of speculative price movements from noise trading theories, which conceive of speculative bubbles as the net result of flows lagging returns, or, more explicitly, that investors pursue positive feedback strategies.

Instead, with investors exhibiting adaptive expectations, all that is necessary to initiate a stock market boom within Minsky's flow theory is a period of strong profits (fundamentals) that might increase the long-term earnings expectation of equity investors (Parenteau and Veneroso, 1999, p. 1). From here, information cascading transforms the boom to euphoria and investors into portfolio plungers.[10] It should also be emphasized that the fragility of the stock market results both from an over-exaggeration of the economy's profit potential and the underestimation of the uncertainty and riskiness inherent in equity and relative to alternative investments. Several studies have shown that the implicit equity risk premium does exhibit cyclically and, moreover, there is evidence that high periods of economic growth correspond to the undervaluing of the stock market risk (Barsky and De Long, 1983; Shiller, 1989, 2000a; IMF, 2000).

Implicitly, Minsky departed from the dividend discount model, which underscores the fact that long-term profit expectations are held to be relevant for equity market pricing. Likewise, this book's supply and demand approach to equity price determination includes fundamentals but not in the standard manner advocated by EMH proponents. Instead, information regarding fundamentals must be placed in its proper environmental and behavioral context (Glickman, 1994). One cannot assume away complexity by modeling an environment of probabilistic uncertainty and modeling agents as automatons with perfect foresight. Instead, the proper environment is that of fundamental uncertainty and the behavioral context is individuals with emotion, affected by various psychological propensities such as decision regret, fads, fashions and the acquiescence to popular opinion. The prices emerging from the market mechanism then:

> reflect not only the expectations about the influences of changes in the economic fundamentals on future expected earnings, but also the expectations about how investors will tend to behave in response to perceived changes in expectation ... If all investors start to think that all other agents will think that a variable not included in the original information set reveals relevant information, their conjecture becomes validated as each 'rationally' acts on the basis of that expectation (Raines and Leathers, 1996, p. 143).

And as Glickman (1994) notes, any 'financial event may qualify as information either because it is indicative of underlying real conditions or simply because it is suggestive of possible reactions by market participants' (p. 327). Keynes' notion of stock exchanges as a 'beauty contest', where popular opinion reigns, is implicit here.

Clearly equation (4.3), which includes fundamentals and extrinsic factors, provides a more general model of equity price determination than equation (4.1). This having been said and despite departing from the dividend discount model, we maintain that robust profits and low discount rates encourage a boom but do not necessarily constrain it or rule the market in a systemic fashion. Thus, the rupturing of prices from their fundamental values can persist for long periods of time so that even a long-run equilibrium relationship will be weak. With agents grossly overestimating the future profit potential of the economy and underestimating the inherent risk of equity vis-à-vis other investment vehicles, equity prices respond to the increased demand and the consequent inflow of funds into the market. These flows being the outcome of an uncomfortable mix of ingredients – conventionally determined expectations, sentiment and investor psychology – implies that stock prices are, as Keynes (1964) states in *The General Theory*, moved more by purchase orders which reflect 'spontaneous optimism than mathematical expectations'.

Thus, the core of the theory of capital market price fluctuation is captured in the Minskian flow approach to equity price determination in that both smart and 'not-so-smart' flows, which overestimate profit potential and underestimate risk, influence equity prices. Yet, the euphoria theorized here must be placed in a global context. Minsky, noting the movement towards financial market integration, held that 'the significance of financial disturbances and instability is, if anything, greater than if each of these economies were treated in isolation' (Minsky, 1982, pp. x–xi). The elimination of barriers to international capital flow results in a growth in the ownership of US assets and liabilities by foreigners. Thus, foreigners can participate in the domestic euphoric boom and act in ways to reinforce the upward movement in domestic equity prices. Moreover, the term $r_a - r_e$ in equation (4.3) underscores the fact that the portfolio demand for US equity is contingent on the performance of foreign assets. Consequently, financial crisis in a particular region, as well as general underperformance, shifts the demand toward those countries with relatively stronger market performance. These dynamics uncover a potential linkage between relative currency movements, interest rate spreads, and differing risk characteristics across countries and stock market valuations.

As the prices advance during a euphoric boom, and agents (domestic and foreign) become portfolio plungers, some 'blindly following the herd like sheep', the market renders itself fragile and more vulnerable to negative shocks to investor confidence about expected profits or other relevant variables. Corporations follow suit expanding investment and accumulating debt, transforming themselves from hedge to speculative and finally Ponzi units as they struggle to meet Wall Street's expectations. Nevertheless, once investors become skeptical about the value past trading has imparted to the stock market, outflows can detonate bearish expectations and lead to an informational avalanche, ultimately culminating in market collapse (Lee, 1998). Furthermore, the demand for equity, which is ultimately constrained by domestic savings and the willingness of both the banks to supply credit and foreigners to extend savings, cannot continue uninterrupted.

In summary, the supply and demand theory of equity price fluctuation traces the speculative dynamics in stock markets through four phases: (1) the recovery phase, (2) robust expansion, (3) euphoric boom and (4) the deflation or crisis phase (Minsky, 1995, p. 205). In the recovery phase, economic fundamentals are strengthening as the market rebounds from a bearish climate. Cautiously, wealth-holders begin to regain confidence and the inflow of funds into the equity market responds to the expansion in corporate profitability and economic growth. During the robust expansion phase, both profits and equity prices increase significantly, and any under- or overvaluation is due to random errors associated with fundamental uncertainty.

In the euphoric boom phase, profit growth slows and even turns negative as equity price appreciation accelerates. Some corporations during this stage of the boom in the United States found creative ways to mask the decline in profitability but were forced to reconcile eventually via earnings restatements and/or bankruptcy. Here, overvaluation is due mainly to overly optimistic investors who have dropped the possibility of a stock market collapse completely from their personal calculus (Gray and Gray, 1994, p. 145). This phase is, of course, contingent on the ability of net inflows to determine the course of stock price movements irrespective of the fundamentals.

Finally, in the deflation phase, both profits and equity prices fall as bearish sentiments dominate the market. The decrease in equity prices will be greater than that in profits given the past overvaluation and indeed, may even descend further than that justified by the economic fundamentals due to informational avalanches. Moreover, just prior to the deflation phase, an immediate crash can occur if the market is unable to encourage the excess inflow of funds necessary to negotiate the existing desired net sales of stock. Often, as was the case in the 1930s and recently in 2001 and 2002, corporate fraud and malfeasance is uncovered. Not surprisingly then, 'the decade of the 1920s has been called the greatest era of crooked high finance the world has ever known' (Kindleberger, 1996, p. 77). When all is said and done, the question of corporate behavior and financial felony revealed during 1996–2002 may challenge this claim.

This, of course, is only the demand side of the story. When we add supply-side considerations, it is clear that declining equity issuance (supply changes) can encourage the euphoric boom phase of the Minsky cycle, and hasten the recovery stage. In fact, this is exactly how McCauley et al. (1999) interpret the junk bond leveraged buyouts of the 1980s (see below). Moreover, while a relatively constant supply is necessary for the formation of speculative bubbles, the net flow theory implies that a shrinking supply of equity in the wake of growing demand can generate upward pressure on market prices as well. Because investors can act in ways to counteract supply-side price pressure, and changes in the supply of equity can attenuate demand-side price pressure, it is more appropriate to consider both forces jointly (that is net flows). The flow theory, therefore, implicates both investor demand and changes in the volume of corporate equity outstanding in the 1982–2000 bull market in the United States.

EXPLAINING THE 1982–2000 STOCK MARKET BOOM

The supply and demand theory of price determination, which maintains elements of many of the speculative the theories recounted above, namely Keynes, Veblen and Minsky, underpins our main hypotheses regarding the bull market of 1982–2000. Accordingly, the run-up in US equity values can be attributed to four inter-related developments. The first necessary development is the increase in corporate profits during the 1980s and early 1990s. The second key development is the growth in the domestic demand for corporate equity, facilitated by institutional investors. The third crucial factor is the influx of foreign capital into US financial markets, especially foreign portfolio equity investment. Finally, these demand-side elements have been aided and abetted by equity retirements stemming from merger and takeover activity as well as stock buybacks on behalf of US corporations.

Collectively, the hypotheses imply that the stock market boom, while it might find its origins in increased corporate profitability, has to a larger extent been driven by the enormous flows of funds into the stock market unrelated to fundamentals. Consequently, the rise in corporate profits and therefore future expected dividend growth, while fundamentally important, is not adequate in itself to explain equity price increases. In fact, as the boom advanced, profits may have explained less of the variation in equity price movements in typical Minskian fashion. This explains the overvaluation or 'valuation error' uncovered earlier using the Gordon growth model and even when making strong assumptions about dividend growth rates and equity risk premia.

The Growth in Demand and Equity Price Appreciation

As is stressed by the Minsky-inspired supply and demand theory, an important factor behind the increase in demand for corporate equity and, therefore, the run-up in US equity prices is corporate profitability. The smooth functioning of the capitalist economy ultimately rests upon profits as they indicate the adeptness of past investment decisions and establish the existing conditions with respect to investment, employment and financing (Minsky, 1982, p. xvii). Thus, expected profitability *should* be a major determinant of the level of equity prices, since the latter reflect future profitability and aid in assessing the true value of enterprising firms. As noted above, a period of strong profit growth serves as the catalyst behind the euphoric expectations about the future corporate performance and stock market returns. In acknowledging the importance of profitability to equity price determination and fluctuation in the 1990s, it is first imperative to place the recent behavior of equity prices in the proper context, acknowledging the economic environment in which the developments occurred.

A noteworthy consideration for the performance of US corporations is the pro-profit climate initiated by the Reagan administration in the 1980s and continued by the monetary and government authorities during the 1990s. Of principal importance here was the large pro-investment tax cut implemented in 1981 that served as a positive shock to the growth rate of corporate profits. Indeed, the 1980s and early to mid- 1990s, minus a few setbacks, were a time of persistently strong earnings growth. Real, before-tax, corporate profits grew from roughly $346.5 billion to approximately $858.3 billion from 1982 to 1998 or from 7.7 per cent to 11.5 per cent of national income, respectively. Between 1992 and 1997 real earnings doubled and 1994 saw a 36 per cent increase in real S&P 500 earnings from the previous year (Shiller, 2000a, p. 20).

Simultaneously, declining unionization and increasing globalization placed a check on wage and inflation growth. The unionization rate in the United States fell from 20 per cent of the labor force to just 16 per cent in 1993 (Browne, 1999, p. 7). Greenspan pledged his allegiance to a continuance of this environment, suggesting that the United States relax the existing immigration laws to ease potential wage pressure from tight labor markets.[11] In turn, the employment cost index, which measures total labor compensation costs (wages and salaries, total benefits costs), declined during the late 1990s (Browne, 1999, p. 5). These developments helped to sustain the growth in corporate profits without which foreign and domestic investors would not have undertaken the activity that engendered the further explosion in equity prices. That is, stock prices would not have mushroomed to the extent that they had by 1999 if the economy in which they burgeoned fostered an environment that was at least beneficial to prospective corporate profits. Inasmuch as wages had stagnated, inflation remained tame, the push towards deregulation continued successfully, and globalization permitted access to new markets and placed downward pressure on prices, an environment amicable to profits had been established.

The performance of the United States was indeed novel, if not remarkable, given the profit growth of the 1980s coupled with the length of economic expansion during the 1990s. Subsequent to the brief recession that ended during the first quarter of 1991, the US entered into an economic growth phase that, by the first quarter of 2000, had spanned 35 quarters. By 1999, unemployment and inflation rates reached their lowest levels in 30 years, while average labor productivity continued to increase (ibid., p. 3). Between 1993 and 2000, 23 million new jobs were created, albeit much of it low-wage employment such that some have pointed out the deterioration in job quality (Paulre, 2000, p. 16). Nevertheless, a stable macroeconomic environment coupled with this type of job creation favors corporate profits and results in a higher share of income accruing to corporations and, therefore, shareholders.

We argue that the US economic boom along with pro-profit climate was collectively processed as information to investors who revised upwards their forecasts of the expected profitability of firms. In accordance with the supply and demand theory of equity price determination, this resulted in a shift of domestic and foreign portfolios towards claims on real capital (equity) and away from alternative assets. More importantly, investors began to accept the historically long economic boom and stable profit growth as an augur of unprecedented, long-lasting future earnings and dividend growth. With the possibility of a downturn disregarded, future US economic growth and extraordinary stock market performance is taken as a certainty.

It should be noted that financial analysts, academicians and journalists alike put forth ideas that reinforced investors' appetite for stock and bolstered this increase in the demand. As discussed above, studies that championed stock as the premier assets over the long run (Siegel, 1994; Elias, 1999) and suggested a new economy seemed to validate the longest economic boom and greatest bull market in US history. The view of equity as less risky was also enhanced by the growth of derivative instruments, which led to a growing number of passive investors who believed that options, futures, swaps, and options on indexes could permit the lock-in of high returns and completely eliminate risk. These developments fueled the growth in the demand for corporate equity already existing from the euphoria endogenously generated by the open economy Minsky cycle, leading to overconfidence about future dividend growth rate and an underpricing of the equity risk premium.

However, outside of the longevity of the economic boom, it has been well documented that the economic performance of the United States is not too remarkable in historical terms (Paulre, 2000; Shiller, 2000a; Browne, 1999; Krugman, 1997; Carlson and Sargent, 1997). While the average annual growth rate of GDP over the 1991–99 and 1982–90 periods was 3.6 per cent and approximately 4 per cent respectively, the growth rate was 4.5 per cent over the 1959–73 period (Paulre, 2000, p. 14). Neither was the profit growth experienced over the 1980s and 1990s unprecedented. Shiller (2000a) points out that during the 1921–26 period real earnings quadrupled and during the five years subsequent to the depressions of the 1890s and 1930s real earnings doubled as well (p. 7). Thus, the GNP and profit growth was not as extraordinary by US historical standards as popularly held, especially if we consider the fact that as profits may have been somewhat exaggerated towards the end of the cycle. However, the strong economic performance of the 1980s and 1990s was enough to spawn Minskian-type euphoria, as investors believed the future would look much like the past extrapolated and therefore plowed money into US corporate equity. This ensured that the consequent stock price appreciation over the 1982–2000:1 period, unlike the underlying economic performance, was indeed unparalleled by historical standards.

The poor performance of foreign markets during the same time frame, by altering the relative return on US corporate equity, also helped to further increase domestic demand and attracted foreign capital flows into the stock market. In the 1990s, the Asian countries experienced financial crises, currency runs and deep recessions while Japan's economy remained stagnant over most of the entire decade and the Nikkei Index performed poorly, with an annualized mean return of just 0.2 per cent over 1990–97. While the markets of many emerging economies and Japan deteriorated, other developed countries saw significant increases in stock prices. However, even those stock markets grew at a less vigorous pace relative to the United States. Germany, France and the United Kingdom saw a doubling of their major indices from 1994 to 1999, while over the same period the S&P 500 tripled (Shiller, 2000a, p. 4). We argue that this geographical relativity caused a further shift in domestic portfolios towards US corporate equity and away from foreign assets, as well as an increase in portfolio equity flows into the US stock market.

Institutional Money

Institutional investors played a significant role in the shift of household savings towards equity and away from alternative assets since they have come to dominate equity markets and now possess a larger proportion of household savings than banks. In 1950, 80 per cent of all trading on organized exchanges involved individual investors, but by 1975, individuals accounted for just 25 per cent of all trade (Blume et al., 1993, p. 105). The initial result of this shift was a more conservative domestic portfolio. Recall that prior to 1974, institutional money was constrained by the 'prudent man' rule of 1830. The rule effectively mandated investment managers to 'preserve the capital value of each investment and avoid risk' (Blume et al., 1993, p. 96). While some maverick mutual fund managers pursued more aggressive asset management strategies, the bulk of the profession remained cautious for fear of violating the prudent man rule. However, academic research significantly changed the defensive nature of institutional money management with the theory of portfolio diversification.

Harry Markowitz, in his 1952 doctoral dissertation, showed that investors should not necessarily concern themselves with the riskiness and return of each individual asset but instead focus on the suitability of the entire portfolio. By focusing on the entire portfolio and minimizing its overall riskiness even assets, which by themselves may have been unacceptably risky investments, were given a role in a well-diversified portfolio. This finding would eventually lead to an increase in the demand for stock and 'also made investing in foreign countries respectable as the breakdown of international capital controls made foreign investing more feasible' (Blume et al., 1993, p. 99). More importantly, the theory of portfolio diversification, after further refinement, provided the basis the passage of the Federal Employee Retirement Income Act (ERISA) of 1974. ERISA, among other things, effectively replaced the prudent man rule with the rule of diversification, allowing pension fund mangers to focus on the return and risk of the entire portfolio and implement more aggressive and profitable strategies. As Blume et al. (1993) appropriately note, while ERISA applied specifically to pension funds, 'in effect it psychologically liberated all institutional money to be invested more creatively and aggressively' (p. 107).

Institutional money managers got an additional boost in May 1975 (May Day) when fixed commissions were jettisoned in favor of a standardized fee system for brokerage services. Prior to 1975 a party to a transaction involving 1,000 shares was charged ten times more in commissions than a 100-share transaction even though the cost difference in transferring both orders was negligible. May Day dismantled this system, allowing institutional investors to trade on more competitive and cheaper terms. Thus, by 1975 the stage was set for these flows to move into the stock market and place unprecedented upward pressure on market prices. Of course an environment of strong profit growth was necessary to trigger flows into the stock market, whose power to impact prices was magnified by the fact that institutional investors had come to dominant trading activity. This increased corporate profitability was indeed forthcoming along with the euphoric expectations it encouraged, resulting in a substantial shift in the domestic portfolio composition. With our conception of the stock market as a voting machine, the argument that the rise of institutional investors has abetted equity inflation can be fully appreciated.

Supply Issues

With the demand for equity growing and the euphoria extending across national borders, encouraging foreign portfolio equity investment, the significant reduction in the supply of equity from merger, takeover and restructuring activity as well as stock repurchases during the 1984–90 and 1995–99 intervals accelerated the run-up in US equity values. More than just a sideshow, McCauley et al. (1999) interpret 1984–90 as an example of financial market mania that can be understood formally within Minsky's model of financial fragility. The authors note that leveraged buyouts (LBOs), especially those financed through the use of junk bonds, became a new source of profit during the 1980s. This process was ignited by William Simon's 'stand out deal' in which the financier procured $66 million from a LBO deal involving Gibson Greetings with only $1 million of his own money (ibid., p. 15). During the entire period over 18,000 US corporations 'underwent leveraged buyouts, and the total dollar value of these deals exceeded $250 billion' (ibid., p. 167). These highly speculative LBOs, hostile or otherwise, quickly became the way to make profits and even the largest firms on the New York Stock Exchange became targets. It is estimated that nearly one-half of all major US companies received 'hostile' takeover bids in the 1980s, 'where hostility is defined as bids pursued without the acquiescence of target management' (Holmstrom and Kaplan, 2001, p. 124).

One of the most important effects of this financial innovation is that it dramatically altered investors' perception of debt and the relationship between risk and return. Institutional investors and stockholders attracted to the large profits and consequent surges in stock prices joined the trend, implicitly viewing debt as shareholder value. Thus, demand changes that could have counteracted the supply-side price pressure were instead accommodating and increased leverage enhanced firms' market value instead of decreasing it. The positive response of investors to this financial innovation generated directly from the strong profit growth of the early 1980s and the expectations it encouraged. In this environment it is not surprising that 'only the most conservative corporations refrained from increasing leverage after 1984', some repurchasing their stock at a premium using borrowed funds ('greenmail') to thwart hostile takeover bids (McCauley et al., 1999, p. 158). The fact that the result of these developments was increases in the market value of firms refutes the Modigliani–Miller (1958) theorem, which maintains the value of the firm to be independent of its financing policy.

McCauley et al. (1999) suggest that the Minsky cycle came to the distress stage in 1989–90 as junk bond defaults soared and a record number of firms filed for bankruptcy. However, the authors suggest that a booming stock market provided the remedy for debt-ridden, cash-strapped US corporations. With the collapse of the junk bond market, the 1991–94 period witnessed an unprecedented increase in equity issuance and reverse LBO initial public offerings. The authors document evidence that indicates that those corporations issuing equity were those who were less profitable and burdened with debt and, furthermore, that very few were actually seeking financing to expand business operations (p. 158). If this analysis is correct, the ability of corporations to float equity, and thereby avert the transformation from speculative to Ponzi units, was fostered by the growth in domestic and foreign demand for corporate equity. In this manner, it was robust stock market valuations that allowed a booming economy to refuel itself. Nevertheless, aggregate corporate profitability remained strong and the stock market boom after stagnating slightly was extended into the 1990s.

While leveraged buyout deals declined significantly, stock repurchases persisted throughout the 1990s as they continued to be interpreted as a way of creating value for shareholders. In the early 1990s it was primarily more profitable firms that undertook stock buybacks, but by the 1995–2000 period even firms with more modest profits were engaging in stock repurchase programs. With the bond market collapse a distant memory, debt-financed buybacks began to resurface in the late 1990s (albeit not to the extent seen in the 1980s). Moreover, individuals became preoccupied with the stock market and the gains to be had from stock ownership, making stock options more attractive and thereby encouraging more stock repurchase programs. This served to make the mergers and takeovers in the 1990s less hostile, as loyalty shifted from corporation to the shareholder. Holmstrom and Kaplan (2001) note:

> Managers and, boards and institutional shareholders had seen what leveraged buyouts and other market-driven restructurings could do. Thanks to lucrative stock options plans, managers could share in the market returns from restructured companies. Shareholder value became an ally rather than an enemy. This explains why restructurings continued at a high rate in the 1990s, but for the most part on amicable terms. There was less of a need for high leverage, since deals could be paid for with stock with less worry that managers would abuse privilege (p. 122).

It is crucial to understand that institutional investors factor prominently into these developments. Donaldson (1994) and D'Arista (1994) point out that the rise of institutional investors has resulted in a shift in the balance of power from corporate managers to shareholders. Moreover, Holmstrom and Kaplan (2001) argue that fund managers are more likely to be interested in shareholder value and less loyal to management given the mandate to provide high returns for their constituents. The authors note that institutional investors were important sellers of large blocks of corporate stock during takeovers (p. 132). D'Arista (1994) notes that the shift in stockholdings from individual to institutional investors was strongly positively correlated with the number of cash-related merger and takeovers in the 1980s (p. 268). Furthermore, institutional investors facilitated the leveraged buyouts of the 1980s by readily purchasing the junk bonds that financed them (Holmstrom and Kaplan, 2001, p. 132).

While the leveraged merger and takeover activity was the spontaneous result of financial innovation, the dramatic rise in share repurchases would have never happened if not for a critical Securities Exchange Commission (SEC) policy change in the early 1980s. Prior to 1982, the SEC discouraged share repurchases in order to eliminate the potential for price manipulation. However, in 1982, in order to improve liquidity in market downturns, the SEC reversed its previous policy stance and approved Rule 10b-13 which effectively established a 'safe harbor' for corporations that repurchased their own shares. Accordingly, corporations could now engage in repurchase programs without the threat of an SEC inquiry or being held liable for price manipulation (Greenspan, 2002). Also, corporations were no longer prohibited from repurchasing shares in the first or last half-hour of trading and were permitted to repurchase an amount of stock equal to up to 100 per cent of the average daily trading volume up from 25 per cent before the policy change. As a direct result of Rule 10b-18 share the policy change. As a direct result of Rule 10b-18 share repurchases exploded, with the number of firms initiating programs rising steadily to 84.2 per cent by 2000 (Grullon and Michaely, 2002). (We fully discuss the implications of Rule 10b-18 in the next chapter.)

Whatever the theory for the dramatic rise in merger and takeover activity and the stock repurchases, the outcome was a significant reduction in the volume of equity outstanding on secondary markets and intense upward pressure on stock prices. Not surprisingly, many have passed over the supply issue when attempting to unravel the equity appreciation puzzle of 1982–2000. Notable exceptions are Jane D'Arista (1994), who noted the phenomenon extremely early in its development, Binswanger (1999) and, of course, Jan Toporowski (1999a, 1999b) in his theory of 'capital market inflation'. Hence, one of the major differences between the bull markets of the 1920 and 1960 and the 1982–2000 run-up is that net issues of corporate equity were significantly negative over the latter period.

Summary

The supply and demand, speculative price theory rooted in Minsky's model of financial fragility provides an entry point into the investigation of US equity price dynamics during the 1982–2000 period. However, we do not propose to query whether the Minsky model is consistent with the stylized facts as that would go well beyond the scope of this book. Instead we utilized the model to give a contextual framework to our flow theory of equity price determination that is, in turn, used to identify three main forces behind the stock market boom outside of corporate fundamentals. Here it is maintained that the run-up in equity values can be attributed to the shift in domestic portfolio towards equity facilitated by institutional investors (especially mutual funds), the influx of foreign savings in the US stock market and the reduction in the volume of equity outstanding. Moreover, we argue that by the first quarter of 2000, these forces moved US stock returns above that level that could be reasonably justified by economic fundamentals.

The stock market boom had its roots in corporate profitability and therefore the ability of the firm to pay out dividends to shareholders can explain a portion of the escalation in stock values. However, this environment of strong profit growth led to an increased demand for equity that pushed stock prices to unsustainable levels. The growth in the demand for stock was further encouraged by research, which extolled equity as the superior investment with respect to both risk and return, and the belief that technology in the United States had birthed a 'new economy'. The new economy concept appears to have surfaced in the 1990s as an ex post justification for the longevity of the economic boom, exorbitant stock prices and historically unparalleled price–earnings ratios and dividend yields. Nevertheless, it helped to subdue suspicion about overvalued stock prices and encouraged the steady inflow of funds until the second quarter of 2000. Institutional investors played a crucial role as instruments executing individual investors' insatiable demand for stock. Their ability to aggressively pursue stock market investments had been sanctioned a decade earlier by ERISA and the theory of portfolio diversification which surfaced out of academia in the 1950s. To the extent that institutional investors held a major share of household assets by the 1980s and dominated the stock market by 1975, flows were more able to move prices without reference to corporate profits and changes in discount rates.

The euphoria could not be contained within the borders of the United States given the significant reduction in the barriers to capital flow. Consequently, domestic demand was intensified by the purchases of corporate equity over the 1990s (as we detail at greater length in the following chapter). Financial crisis induced excess volatility and poor returns in the financial markets of other countries, making US assets relatively more attractive and reinforcing the demand for US corporate equity on behalf of both domestic and foreign investors. This demand might have been dampened had corporations satisfied foreign and domestic demand for equity by floating new equity issues. Instead, the merger and takeover movement (often financed by debt instruments, particularly junk bonds) coupled with stock repurchases, initiated by SEC Rule 10b-18, led to a decrease in the supply of corporate equity during the period and resulted in further price appreciation. Moreover, it encouraged even greater demand for stock as investors reinterpreted debt in a positive light in the 1980s, and stock buybacks as creating shareholder value in the 1990s independent corporate profitability.

This nexus between supply and demand precipitated an explosion in equity values during the 1982–87 and 1995–2000:1 periods. Rising equity prices also served to make the stock market a safe haven for many of the corporations who surfaced from the 1980s with poor balance sheets and unduly burdened with debt. Having escaped crisis by raising capital on equity markets, the corporate sector was able to rebound from the 1990 recession with a positive indication of future profitability and little sign of financial trouble. Therefore, foreign savings and domestic funds continued to pour into the stock market. Again the belief in a new era and stock as the dominant asset, bolstered by strong corporate performance in the recent past, provided the justification for the explosion in all the measures of stock market performance. Even high-tech firms with no clear market or products and no profits were given high valuations by the indiscriminate market mechanism (Perkins and Perkins, 1999).

CONCLUSION

Both the falling risk premium theory and the new economy justification for the extraordinary performance that surfaced in academia and the business press have roots in the theory of efficient capital markets. The new economy hypothesis conceives the market valuations as an extension of the longest economic boom in US history and, therefore, an indicator of future prosperity. The falling risk premium theory attributes the run-up in equity values to the willingness of investors to accept a lower rate of return on equity going forward. Although there may be some truth in both theories, it is not probable that either one, or a combination of them, explains the bulk of the rise in equity prices given the values of dividend growth rates and risk premia that must prevail in order to validate them. Consequently, the EMH is ill equipped for an assessment of the 1982–2000 stock market boom.

On the other hand, we have established theoretically the possibility that the flow theory of equity price determination and, therefore, the hypotheses that shrinking supply, the growth of domestic demand and international capital inflow all contributed to the stock market boom is plausible. The supply and demand approach to the stock market permits us to tell a logical story of how the stock market evolved to such an overvalued state by the first quarter of 2000. However, systematic empirical work is necessary to separate these hypotheses from pure conjecture. In Chapter 5, we show empirically that the theories advanced here are at the very least consistent with the stylized facts. Having established a prima facie case for our position, Chapter 6 assesses US equity price dynamics, by way of more formal econometric analysis.

5. Empirical Analysis I: The Stylized Facts

> How do we know when irrational exuberance has unduly escalated asset values, which then become subject to unexpected and prolonged contractions...? (Alan Greenspan, February 1997).

INTRODUCTION

In the preceding chapter we utilized a simple supply and demand-based theory of speculative asset price movements to systematically advance three main hypotheses regarding the US stock market boom. Accordingly, the run-up in equity values was attributed to the domestic portfolio shift towards equity, foreign capital inflow (both stemming in part from euphoric expectations) and the reduction in the volume of equity outstanding on secondary markets. The hypotheses are in harmony with the broad conceptual frameworks advanced by proponents of several speculative market theories outlined in Chapter 2 and suggest that forces outside of corporate profitability must be jointly considered to comprehensively unpack the unparalleled phenomenon. In this chapter we examine the stylized facts and juxtapose these events to the interpretations offered by both speculative and efficient market approaches to asset pricing.

According to the efficient market hypothesis (EMH), stock prices reflect all available, relevant information and, thus, random fluctuations in security markets derive from new information becoming accessible. This again does not imply that supply and demand forces are absent in equity markets, only that the demand for stock originates with rational investors trading solely on fundamentals and, given the high substitutability of stocks, market prices are largely independent of supply. That is, the excess demand curve is perfectly elastic at the full information price, ensuring that the market equilibrium process maintains the fundamental value of stock. Thus, the term 'efficient capital market' generally means that asset prices are determined in perfect competitive financial markets dominated by rational traders (Cuthbertson, 1996, p. 93). In such markets, flows – domestic or foreign in origin – do not impact equity returns unless they contain valuable information about the future discounted and risk-adjusted value of dividend payments enabled by corporate profits.

However, the supply and demand-centered model, which inspires our investigation, implies that fundamentals, while imposing a constraint on speculative price movements, are not always the main constituents of stock prices. Instead, this Keynesian view of financial markets holds that equity price dynamics are strongly influenced by investor demand, which can create a premium or discount on stock unjustified by the underlying fundamentals. Furthermore, in integrating the insights of the flow theory of capital market price fluctuation, the approach acknowledges the collaboration of supply *and* demand forces in asset price fluctuation, thus maintaining that the excess demand curve for equity is not perfectly (or nearly) elastic. As is noted by Binswanger (1999) 'an unchanging or shrinking supply of an asset is a perquisite for the existence of bubbles' (p. 189). Share repurchases and equity retirements, by this reasoning, can augment the increase in equity values and in some cases can be the prime movers themselves.

Consequently, we hold that any theory regarding the 1982–2000:1 stock market boom which focuses exclusively on the demand side may neglect a significant portion of the story. While Shiller's (2000a) irrational exuberance theory makes a significant contribution to the understanding of US equity prices over the 1982–2000:1 period it is incomplete in that it focuses only on investor demand. Furthermore, it omits foreign considerations from the framework therefore missing the connection between foreign capital inflows and stock market returns. Given this conjecture it is appropriate to analyze both the recent developments pertaining to both the changes in the supply and demand of equity in the United States over the respective period. The evidence provided below demonstrates that at the very least the explanations for the boom advanced in the previous chapter are consistent with the trends in the data and provide justification for a more formal and rigorous investigation.

CHANGES IN PORTFOLIO COMPOSITION AND INCREASED DEMAND

Aggregate Changes in Portfolios

The most important prerequisite for the formation of a speculative bubble is a growth in the demand for equity unwarranted by fundamentals. The evidence presented below clearly illustrates that the principal equity-holding sectors of the US economy exhibited an increased demand for corporate equity as reflected in the growth of equity as a proportion of total financial assets. Table 5.1 records both the aggregated portfolio of US corporate equity-holders as well as the portfolios of the separate wealth-holding sectors, namely, depository and non-depository institutions, households, government (state and local), foreign entities and security dealers and brokers. Collectively these sectors account for 100 per cent of the US corporate equity outstanding, with households (3), non-depository institutions (2) and foreign entities (5) consistently holding 90–96 per cent of the total during the 1980-99 period.

The depository institutions (a large segment of which were constrained by the Glass–Steagall Act prior to its repeal in 1999) have traditionally maintained a small percentage of equity in their financial portfolios.[1] Table 5.1 (line 1) shows that corporate equity made up just 4.79 per cent of the total financial assets of depository institutions in 1982 and by 1999 that amount fell to approximately 4 per cent. However, this small decline in the demand for corporate equity was more than balanced by the growth in demand by non-depository institutions, that is, insurance companies, mutual funds, closed-end funds and pension funds. In 1982 these institutions held 27.84 per cent of their financial portfolio in the form of corporate equity. This amount increased to just 28.32 per cent by the end of 1989. However, by 1996 corporate equity made up 43.5 per cent of the financial portfolios of the non-depository institution sector and by the end of 1999, over one-half of financial assets were held in the form of US corporate equity.

The household sector also (more thoroughly discussed below) increased the amount of equity held as a percentage of their total financial assets. As Table 5.1 (line 3) illustrates, between 1982 and 1999 corporate equity increased from 10.9 per cent to 24.72 per cent as a proportion of the total financial portfolio. Correspondingly, the US corporate equity increased as a percentage of the total US financial assets held by foreign entities from roughly 15.2 per cent to approximately 24 per cent during the same period. Likewise, Table 5.1 shows that even state and local governments (line 4) found corporate equity attractive during the 1980s and 1990s. In 1982 and as late as 1985 state and local government held no corporate equity, but by 1999, the latter made up approximately 9 per cent of the total financial assets held by this sector.

Looking at the sectors in aggregate (all equity-holding sectors including security dealers and brokers), the growth in the demand for corporate equity during the period corresponding to the stock market boom is made unambiguously clear. Line 8 in Table 5.1 indicates that the proportion of equity in the total financial portfolio of the equity-holding public grew from 11.73 per cent to 28.56 per cent during the 1982–99 interval. If we consider just the principal equity-holders, households, foreign entities and non-depository institutions, which hold the lion's share of the amount of corporate equity outstanding, the increase in demand is more dramatic. Line 7 shows that the collective portfolio of these principal sectors shifted significantly towards equity over the previous two decades. In 1982 corporate equity comprised just 13.77 per cent of the aggregate portfolio of these wealth-holding sectors of the US economy (less than one-seventh). In 1992 corporate equity made up one-fifth of the total financial assets held by these sectors and by 1999, approximately one-third of the aggregate portfolio of households, foreigners and non-depository institutions consisted of corporate equity.

Table 5.1 Equity as a percentage of total financial assets (by sector)

	1980	1981	1982	1983	1984	1985	1986
(1) DI	5.53	4.76	4.79	4.91	4.15	4.40	3.88
(2) NDI	28.21	25.84	27.84	30.53	28.51	29.75	28.31
(3) Households	13.25	11.10	10.90	11.11	9.60	10.41	11.82
(4) Government	0.00	0.00	0.00	0.00	0.00	0.00	0.03
(5) Foreign Entities	15.16	14.43	15.19	15.92	13.29	14.14	15.57
(6) Brokers	7.27	5.85	5.88	11.05	7.52	9.04	9.59
(7) 2+3+5	15.86	13.77	14.18	15.05	13.46	14.75	15.69
(8) Total (1+2...+6)	13.12	11.36	11.73	12.45	10.97	12.01	12.65

	1987	1988	1989	1990	1991	1992	1993
(1) DI	3.48	3.54	4.24	3.88	4.77	4.33	3.55
(2) NDI	27.48	26.23	28.32	25.43	30.43	31.55	34.07
(3) Households	10.94	12.11	13.52	11.98	15.53	16.52	17.43
(4) Government	0.09	0.20	0.36	0.50	0.62	0.75	0.86
(5) Foreign Entities	13.95	13.52	14.57	12.20	14.01	14.39	14.10
(6) Brokers	7.76	8.98	5.96	3.66	4.30	3.88	5.05
(7) 2+3+5	14.85	15.33	16.94	15.09	18.90	20.01	21.40
(8) Total (1+2...+6)	11.93	12.38	13.87	12.45	15.76	16.64	17.75

	1994	1995	1996	1997	1998	1999	
(1) DI	3.09	3.88	3.88	4.19	3.63	3.97	
(2) NDI	34.40	39.14	43.51	47.68	50.16	54.00	
(3) Households	15.92	18.68	19.39	21.42	21.80	24.72	
(4) Government	1.03	2.64	4.64	7.65	8.64	9.07	
(5) Foreign Entities	13.67	15.11	15.64	18.71	20.83	23.98	
(6) Brokers	4.42	6.02	5.96	6.66	5.91	6.68	
(7) 2+3+5	20.52	23.77	25.50	28.40	29.69	32.85	
(8) Total (1+2...+6)	17.05	20.08	21.77	24.49	25.59	28.56	

Notes: Depository Institutions (DI) include commercial banks, saving institutions and bank personal trusts and estates. Non-depository Institutions (NDI) include mutual and closed-end funds, pension funds and insurance companies. Total includes all US corporate equity holding entities.

Source: Flow of Funds Accounts of the United States, Federal Reserve Board.

These aggregate changes in portfolios (line 7 and 8) as well as the variation in portfolios across sectors establishes the growth in the demand for, and the willingness to hold, appreciating US stock by the wealth-holding public necessary for the tenability of the book's main hypothesis. It remains to be shown that this collective increase in demand placed pressure on stock prices unjustified by economic and corporate fundamentals. Of course this trend could also reflect a passive phenomenon on behalf of some of the principal equity-holding sectors. For example, some institutions, just by holding corporate equity during the stock market boom, would necessarily experience an increase in equity as a percentage of total financial assets. Yet, the trends documented in Table 5.1 are suggestive since they at the very least illustrate that households, non-depository institutions and foreign entities were willing to tolerate a growing share of equity in their financial portfolios. Moreover, the demand on the part of local and state governments cannot be considered passive since this sector held no equity in 1985.

This notwithstanding, these stylized facts provide an incomplete story without an analysis of the net flows (or net purchases) into the stock market. In this manner we will be more able to represent the active demand on the part of the various wealth-holding sectors of the domestic and international economy. Therefore, it is appropriate at this juncture to further scrutinize and decompose the principal equity-holding sectors, looking at their portfolio composition as well as their net purchases of financial assets to further identify the main entities driving the increase in the demand for US stock. In turn, we will use these sector cash flows from these sectors to proxy for the economy-wide increase in demand for corporate equity.

Households

At first glance, an unexpected observation regarding the household sector is that the latter has been the net seller of corporate equity for the period corresponding to the greatest bull market in US history. In fact, during the years of the most tremendous run-up in equity values, 1995 through the end of 1999, households sold roughly $1.9 trillion worth of corporate shares ($2 trillion in real terms), $507.1 and $455 billion in 1997 and 1998 alone ($530.4 and $468.6 in real terms). Figure 5.1 records the real net purchases of the chief financial assets historically held in household portfolios, revealing the negative net purchases of corporate equity. This seemingly makes the equity price appreciation puzzle somewhat of an enigma, especially when we add the fact that households purchased more deposits than any other asset in 1998.[2] Moreover, we have the question of why, instead of withdrawing funds, did the household sector not plow more savings back into stocks to take full advantage of the explosive rates of return?

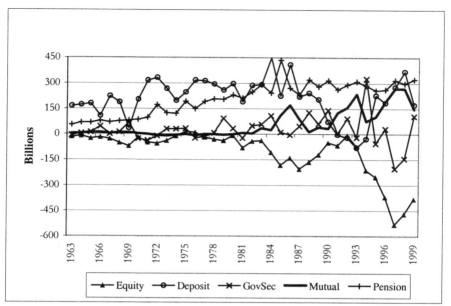

Notes: Net purchases in real terms (inflation corrected).

Source: *Flow of Funds Accounts of the United States*, Federal Reserve Board, Table F.100.

Figure 5.1   Household net purchases

The answer to the latter question may be quite simple since the phenomenon is perfectly consistent with the notion of portfolio rebalancing. That is, the appreciation of assets creates new wealth, which is then redistributed among other assets to maintain some desired or ideal asset allocation strategy. This process should manifest itself in the selling of a portion of the assets whose value has increased, thus justifying negative net purchases of corporate equity by the household sector. Figure 5.1 illustrates that households did indeed increase the amounts of other financial assets in their portfolios, namely deposits, pension fund reserves, and mutual fund shares from 1982 through 1999. In addition to agents rebalancing portfolios, equity price appreciation initiates a wealth effect, which implies that a portion of the new-found wealth is transferred from equity to cash or deposits and spent on consumer goods. Therefore, it is not surprising at all to observe the household sector vigorously selling corporate equity in the wake of the US stock market boom.

Figure 5.1 not only documents households' rapid selling of corporate equity but also demonstrates that the 1982–99 period is not anomalous. Referencing the entire 1963–99 interval, it is clear that households were net purchasers of corporate equity only in 1975 and 1976. This period includes the last four years of the 1953–67 bull market during which households sold $67.9 billion worth of corporate equity in real terms. This, then, points towards a trend that is to be expected in light of the fact that households held the bulk of corporate shares in 1963 (approximately 85 per cent) and mutual and pensions funds have aggressively sought to increase their equity holdings since the 1970s. Thus, the household sector's shedding of corporate equity indicated by negative net purchases is also a necessary and expected consequence of the rise of institutional investors. With the supply of equity shrinking institutional investors were ultimately forced to satisfy their demand for equity by purchasing them from the household sector.

Figure 5.1 also illustrates that mutual fund shares and pension fund reserves made up of the bulk of household positive net purchases, suggesting that a significant portion of the decline in direct ownership of corporate shares was balanced by an increase in indirect ownership of equity through pension and mutual funds (see below). Table 5.2a, which presents a partial balance sheet of households and non-profit organizations from 1973 through 1999, details this historical trend – households shifting their portfolios away from direct equity holdings towards indirect ownership of corporate shares. As late as 1981, only 20 per cent of all equity held by the household sector was held indirectly through a financial intermediary. During the 1982–99 interval the portion of equity held directly fell substantially from 80 per cent to roughly 59.3 per cent. Again, this important transition manifests itself in household negative net purchases during the entire 1977–99 interval. The net selling of corporate equity and net purchasing of mutual funds shares during the 1990s also reflects risk spreading by households as they sought diversification through the ownership of mutual fund shares. Thus, households' net selling of corporate equity does not reflect an aversion for corporate equity but a change in the manner in which sector chooses to hold it.

The evidence suggests that institutional investors were the major catalyst behind the phenomenal growth in US equity prices. Yet, because both sell and buy orders are ultimately responsible for changes in equity prices, households can still be viewed as a having a direct role in the stock market boom if they demanded a premium unjustified by fundamentals in satisfying institutional investors' demand for equity. In fact, households, while shifting the manner in which they held corporate shares, have also exhibited a penchant for both indirect and direct equity holdings. As was illustrated in Table 5.1 and discussed above, one of the most important developments as it pertains to the stock market boom has been the significant increase in equity as a percentage of total financial assets in domestic portfolios, reflecting the growth in the demand for corporate equity.

Figure 5.2 shows that there has been an increase in equity and pension fund reserves and a decline in deposits as a proportion of total assets held for household and non-profit organizations during the 1982–99 period. In 1982 households held just about 11 per cent of their wealth directly in corporate equities, approximately

17 per cent in pension fund reserves and 24.6 per cent in bank deposits. By the end of 1999 the corresponding proportions were 25 per cent, 30 per cent and 12 per cent, respectively.[3] While the growth of pension fund reserves may be partially reflective of a passive phenomenon (an appreciating stock market), it also reflects the growth of defined contribution pension plans. Nevertheless, it is clear that the sizeable net selling of corporate equity on behalf of the household sector was not significant enough to prevent corporate equity from expanding significantly as a percentage of total financial assets. Direct equity holdings of corporate equity and mutual fund shares make up approximately one-third of the portfolio. Therefore, the stylized facts point to a clear shift in desired portfolio composition in favor of equity despite the household sector's negative net purchases of direct corporate shares during the 1982–99 period.

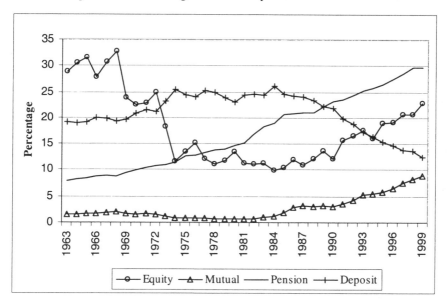

Source: Flow of Funds Accounts of the United States, Federal Reserve Board, Table L.100.

Figure 5.2   Household portfolio composition

The 1982–99 period saw the percentage of mutual fund shares in aggregate household financial portfolios increase from a mere 1 per cent to 9 per cent. Figure 5.2 also shows that prior to 1982 households held an insignificant proportion of mutual fund shares – an amount that fluctuated around 1 per cent for the entire period surveyed (1953–81). It should be noted, however, that mutual fund share purchases are not as dramatic as is popularly held; in fact, in 1995 households acquired more time and savings deposits and money market fund shares than mutual fund shares. However, as Figure 5.2 shows, mutual fund shares are growing rapidly as a proportion of total household financial assets while deposits are shrinking. Mutual fund shares as a percentage of households' total financial assets grew by 526 per cent between 1983 and 1999. Moreover, from Figure 5.1 it is clear that the net selling of corporate equity by the household sector has been matched for the most part by net purchases of mutual fund shares. To the extent that mutual funds and pension funds have experienced substantial increases in corporate equity as a proportion of their financial holdings (as we consider below), households have, then, also increased their indirect holdings of corporate shares.

In summation, two issues are made apparent by our analysis of the household sector's balance sheet and net purchases of financial assets. First, one should not mistake negative net purchases as an indication of household aversion to corporate equity ownership since the proportion of direct equity holdings as a percentage of total financial assets continued to grow tremendously. Instead, there has been an important change in the manner in which households choose to hold corporate shares. Specifically, households have increased their indirect holdings by way of mutual and pension funds to the extent that only 59 per cent of all equity in household portfolios is held directly. Second, the growth of mutual fund shares and direct holdings of equity in household portfolios represents a noteworthy trend that signifies an increase in demand for corporate equity. When coupled with the growing demand stemming from institutional investors, this may partially account for the unprecedented growth in US equity values.

Institutional Investors

During the 1980s and 1990s institutional investors progressed and eclipsed banks as the dominant custodian of household financial assets. In 1980 commercial banks held 50 per cent of all household financial assets, while institutional investors held approximately 20 per cent. By late 1998 this situation had changed considerably, with institutional investors increasing their holdings to 40 per cent of all household financial assets, leaving banks the eventual guardian of an amount just shy of 20 per cent – a complete reversal of the scenario observed two decades earlier.[4] More importantly, as it pertains to the run-up in US equity values, mutual funds and pension funds have demonstrated a marked preference for corporate equity over recent years. This is illustrated by the fact that the proportion of the typical pension funds portfolio held in stocks was consistently above 60 per cent during the late 1990s (Robertson and Wright, 1998).

Figures 5.3a, b, c, d and e presents the main assets held by private and public pension funds, mutual funds, life insurance companies and foreign entities as a percentage of their total financial holdings, providing insight into important portfolio composition changes. All five diagrams are indicative of an increased demand for equity during the 1980s and 1990s similar to that of the household sector illustrated in Figure 5.2. Having reduced their equity holdings from 60.5 per cent to 36.6 per cent between 1971 and 1974, private pension funds show a less impressive increase in equity as a percentage of total financial assets. As Figure 5.3a illustrates, from 1975 to 1989, private funds maintained a portfolio composed of approximately 40 per cent equity before shifting back towards corporate shares in the 1990s. By the end of 1999 private funds held roughly half of their assets in the form of corporate equity, an amount not seen for almost two decades. Furthermore, Figure 5.3a verifies that private funds have historically held an insignificant portion of their assets in the form of mutual fund shares and by 1990 the latter made up just 1.8 per cent of the total. However, that amount increased to 15 per cent by the end of 1999, illustrating a substantial increase in the indirect ownership of corporate shares as well.

The trend towards equity for public pension funds, illustrated in Figure 5.3b, is more conspicuous and dates back to 1975. In 1974, the year ERISA came into effect, public funds stored 62 per cent of their financial wealth in the form of bonds and just 18.72 per cent in corporate stocks. From 1975 to 1999, however, equity grew tremendously as a proportion of all financial assets while the percentage of bonds dwindled to roughly 10 per cent. The most dramatic shift in portfolio composition occurred during the 1982–99 period, demonstrating an increased appetite for stock both on the part of public pension fund managers and individuals. Figure 5.3b documents that corporate stock comprised nearly 70 per cent of the aggregate public pension fund portfolio in 1999, up from approximately 37.7 per cent in 1987 and 23 per cent in 1982. During the 1987–99 interval when the portfolio shift was the most significant, government securities were reduced from about 35 per cent to a little over 12 per cent of the total portfolio.

Figure 5.3c makes it apparent that the mutual fund sector adheres to a phenomenon in the literature known as 'portfolio plunging' – the rapid pursuit of a particular type of financial asset which comes to dominate the portfolio. During the bull market of the late 1960s, for example, mutual funds maintained a portfolio consisting of roughly 90 per cent equity. During the 20-year period following the stock market peak of 1968 the proportion of equity held declined dramatically to 37.4 per cent while government securities and municipal bonds as a percentage of total financial assets grew from 2.15 per cent and 0 per cent to 28.6 per cent and 16.6 per cent, respectively. This relatively balanced portfolio was short lived as the 1989–99 period saw corporate equity swell to 74 per cent of total mutual fund financial assets.

(a) Private fund portfolio composition

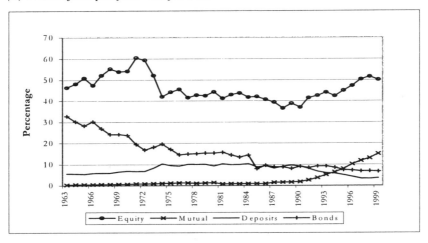

Source: *Flow of Funds Accounts of the United States*, Federal Reserve Board, Table L.119.

(b) Public fund portfolio composition

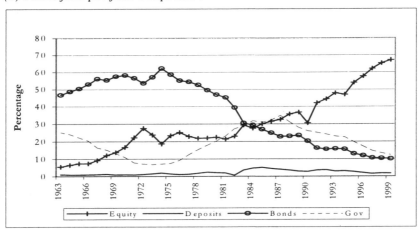

Source: *Flow of Funds Accounts of the United States*, Federal Reserve Board, Table L.120.

Figure 5.3   Institutional investor portfolios

(c) Mutual fund portfolio composition

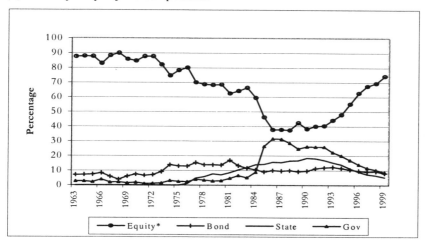

Source: *Flow of Funds Accounts of the United States*, Federal Reserve Board, Table L.121.

(d) Life insurance portfolio composition

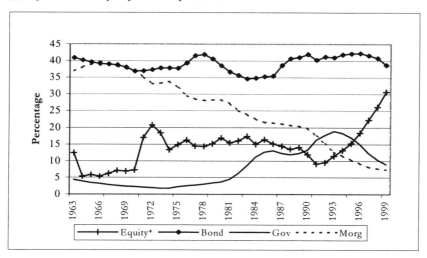

Source: *Flow of Funds Accounts of the United States*, Federal Reserve Board, Table L.117.

(e) Equity as a proportion of all US financial assets held by ROW

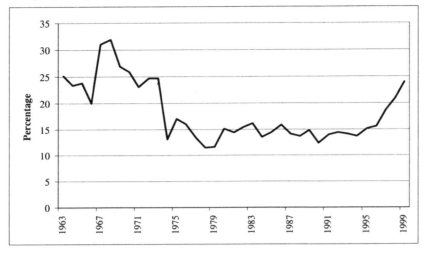

Source: *Flow of Funds Accounts of the United States,* Federal Reserve Board, Table L.107.

The pattern of skewed portfolios during bull markets is characteristic of one of three realities; either mutual funds are return chasers, their activity partially causes equity price increases, or both. Nevertheless, Figure 5.3c makes it quite clear that the demand for equity on behalf of mutual fund managers has grown remarkably over the last decade. The identical trend exists when analyzing life insurance companies, whose change in portfolio composition over the 1963–99 period is represented in Figure 5.3d. In 1991 life insurance held only 9.18 per cent of their financial assets in the form of corporate equity. By 1999 this amount ballooned to over 30 per cent of total financial assets.

Clearly, institutional investors have developed a penchant for corporate equity during the last two decades, and boasted portfolios biased towards equity especially in the 1990s. Institutional investors, then, have utilized the funds acquired from the household sector to secure corporate equity. Between the years 1960 and 1985 institutional investors increased their stockholdings from 10.7 per cent to 30 per cent of all US corporate equity outstanding. This amount improved to 39.6 per cent in 1990 and to 48 per cent by 1998. These developments are shown explicitly in Table 5.2b, in which the percentages of equity held for each of the major sectors are recorded from 1965 through 1999. As the table indicates, households' share of corporate equity has been significantly reduced from nearly 84 per cent to less than 45 per cent over the period in question. Table 5.2b suggests that individually mutual funds have made the biggest gains with respect to equity accumulation during 1982–99 and as such, the intensity of bull market of the 1990s is often attributed to their activity.

Table 5.2a   Household direct and indirect ownership of corporate equity

	1973	1974	1975	1976	1977	1978	1979	1980
Holdings	761.3	491.2	644.3	808.1	697.6	711.0	850.7	1093.1
Direct	597.5	373.4	499.0	637.4	542.5	550.3	674.9	884.0
Indirect	163.8	117.8	145.3	170.7	155.1	160.7	175.8	209.1
%Direct	78.5	76.0	77.5	78.9	77.8	77.4	79.3	80.9
%Indirect	21.5	24.0	22.6	21.1	22.2	22.6	20.7	19.1

	1981	1982	1983	1984	1985	1986	1987	1988
Holdings	985.1	1064.6	1220.0	1144.4	1561.9	1870.8	1895.5	2207.4
Direct	789.1	843.9	950.8	878.7	1058.1	1330.3	1306.2	1587.0
Indirect	196.0	220.7	269.2	265.7	503.8	540.5	589.3	620.4
%Direct	80.1	79.3	77.9	76.8	67.7	71.1	68.9	71.9
%Indirect	19.9	20.7	22.1	23.2	32.3	28.9	31.1	28.1

	1989	1990	1991	1992	1993	1994	1995	1996
Equity Holdings	2754.5	2551.5	3557.6	3989.6	4629.1	4581.5	6148.7	7293.0
Direct	1963.6	1806.5	2570.9	2873.2	3242.1	3070.9	4121.6	4642.1
Indirect	790.9	745.0	986.7	1116.4	1387.0	1510.6	2027.1	2650.9
%Direct	71.3	70.8	72.3	72.0	70.0	67.0	67.0	63.6
%Indirect	28.7	29.2	27.7	28.0	30.0	33.0	33.0	36.4

	1997	1998	1999
Equity Holdings	9207.6	10573.6	13196.2
Direct	5689.6	6328.7	7829.4
Indirect	3518.0	4244.9	5366.8
%Direct	61.8	59.8	59.3
%Indirect	38.2	40.2	40.7

Notes: Equity holdings are the market value of the equity held by the household sector.

Source: *Flow of Funds Accounts of the United States*, Federal Reserve Board, Table B.100e: Balance Sheet of Households and Nonprofit Organizations with Equity Detail.

Why the Bubble Burst

Table 5.2b   Percentages of equity outstanding held by sector 1965–99

	1965	1969	1975	1977	1978	1979	1980	1981
HH	83.83	69.11	59.00	58.41	56.30	58.17	58.56	56.48
Mfunds	4.20	4.81	3.98	3.43	3.24	3.05	2.84	2.71
Insurance	2.86	3.12	4.93	5.32	5.58	5.49	5.26	5.69
ROW	1.99	3.15	3.95	4.29	4.31	4.16	5.00	5.41
Privpen	5.55	7.22	12.77	13.31	15.38	15.12	15.52	16.46
Pubpen	0.34	0.86	2.87	3.23	3.41	3.20	2.96	3.46
Other	1.22	11.72	12.49	12.01	11.80	10.81	9.86	9.83
Total	100.00	100.00	100.00	100.00	100.00	100.00	100.00	100.00

	1982	1983	1984	1985	1986	1987	1988	1990
HH	53.28	50.44	48.24	46.60	49.60	48.19	51.61	50.68
Mfunds	3.16	4.01	4.50	5.01	6.01	6.70	6.10	6.58
Insurance	5.85	5.94	5.87	5.77	5.13	5.37	4.97	4.57
ROW	5.65	5.91	5.98	6.03	6.83	6.97	6.95	6.88
Privpen	18.84	19.66	20.94	22.72	19.52	19.65	16.75	17.11
Pubpen	3.85	4.83	5.39	5.29	5.60	6.28	6.91	7.64
Other	9.36	9.22	9.08	8.58	7.31	6.83	6.71	6.54
Total	100.00	100.00	100.00	100.00	100.00	100.00	100.00	100.00

	1992	1993	1994	1995	1996	1997	1998	1999
HH	52.51	51.00	48.12	47.92	45.70	44.77	43.25	44.70
Mfunds	7.39	9.63	11.20	12.06	14.33	15.29	16.26	17.16
Insurance	4.58	4.83	5.66	5.29	5.49	5.64	6.06	6.00
ROW	6.06	5.92	6.28	6.21	6.40	6.97	7.62	7.78
Privpen	16.13	16.15	16.10	15.17	14.27	12.85	12.33	11.02
Pubpen	8.21	8.38	8.80	9.31	10.06	10.85	11.40	10.43
Other	5.12	4.09	3.84	4.03	3.74	3.64	3.09	2.92
Total	100.00	100.00	100.00	100.00	100.00	100.00	100.00	100.00

Notes: HH, Mfunds, Insurance, ROW, Privpen and Pubpen denote households, mutual funds, insurance companies, private pension funds and public pension funds, respectively. Other includes depository institutions, closed-end funds and security brokers and dealers.

Source: *Flow of Funds Accounts of the United States*, Federal Reserve Board, Table L.213: Corporate Equities.

There is a good reason to place special emphasis on mutual funds. First, if we separate public and pension funds it becomes apparent that mutual fund investment companies now hold more corporate equity than any other institutional investor (17.2 per cent in 1999). Second, the stock market boom closely corresponds to the rapid growth of equity mutual funds in the United States. In 1982 there were just 340 equity mutual funds and 6.2 million mutual fund accounts, but by 2000 there were 4,395 equity mutual funds and 162.5 million mutual fund shareholder accounts. The number of households owning mutual funds reached 51.7 million in May 2000, implying that more than half of the households in the United States now hold the asset.[5] While some attribute this growth to long-term demographic forces, others point towards the societal preoccupation with the stock market and irrational exuberance.

Finally, mutual funds investors are popularly held to be small, 'unsophisticated' and 'uninformed' relative to the average stock market investor. We surveyed the empirical literature in Chapter 3 that indicated mutual fund shareholders exert external pressure on fund managers moving money into those funds with higher returns and the propensity of mutual funds towards herding behavior and their consequent contribution to market volatility was also documented (Wermers, 1999; Gompers and Metrick, 1998; Warther, 1995). Thus, mutual funds can only be considered as 'sophisticated' as the clients they serve. These points allude to a crucial difference among institutional investors, suggestive of the fact that mutual funds may differ significantly from other institutional investors.

Looking specifically at differences between the clientele of mutual and pension funds is enlightening. While the typical pension fund sponsor has $21 million invested with the median manager, the medium mutual fund account is below $15,000 and the minimum investment requirement for 51.4 per cent of all mutual fund companies is $1000 or less.[6] Moreover, pension fund clients are typically finance specialists with years of experience in investment management. On the other hand, mutual fund shareholders are relatively inexperienced investors with little expertise in finance. Pension fund sponsors also have the power to meet with managers, monitor investments and examine asset holdings. Survey evidence suggests pension fund sponsors value personal contact, with 78 per cent of all clients meeting at least once a year with high-level management (Del Guerico and Tkac, 2000). Correspondingly, pension fund managers rely on reputation, investment style and specialty when making hire and retention decisions. An important empirical finding documented by Guerico and Tkac (2000) is that sponsors punish managers who deviate from stated investment objectives even if it results in outperformance.

To the contrary, the probability that the average mutual fund shareholder will have contact with portfolio managers is extremely small. Instead, these investors must rely on performance track records to assess fund manger competency. This underlines the propensity of mutual fund shareholders to herd towards funds with higher returns. Therefore, in an attempt to attract inflows mutual fund managers are pressured into more unsophisticated investment strategies than their pension fund counterparts. Del Guerico and Tkac's (2000) empirical work assessing the relationship between Jensen's Alpha and equity flows support the contention that pension funds are more financially sophisticated than mutual funds.

Survey evidence also suggests that mutual fund investors are not well informed about their mutual fund investments. Capon et al. (1996) note that 75 per cent of all mutual fund investors were unfamiliar with fund investment style and an amazing 40 per cent did not even know if they were invested in load or no-load funds! Furthermore, 50 per cent of all investors with mutual fund accounts in 2000 held no mutual fund shares in 1990.[7] Thus, a large segment of the mutual fund investor population had only experienced bull market stock valuations up until 2000, partially explaining the over-exuberant expectations about the market going forward at the end of 1999.

Given the disparities in clientele across institutional investors, fund managers differ in terms of their activity in stock markets. Dennis and Strickland (2000), in their investigation of institutional investor herding, find that mutual fund owner-ship, as a percentage of total ownership of corporate shares, is more closely correlated with abnormal turnover and returns than is the proportion of equity held by other institutional investors. In fact, the authors maintain that the difference can be explained by the fact that mutual fund mangers 'are evaluated more frequently than other types of managers, and the focus is on short-term performance' (p. 22). Not surprisingly then, many of the initial public offerings (IPOs) of the 1990s, especially those in the high-growth sectors, were purchased by mutual funds. Moreover, a good portion of the equity mutual fund sector focuses exclusively and aggressively on capital appreciation rather than income (Investment Company Institute, 1999). This makes mutual fund flows one of the most logical sources to tap as a proxy for domestic sentiment and therefore crucial to the investigation into whether changes in domestic flows move market returns independent of economic fundamentals.

Nevertheless, the US stock market has become increasingly dominated by the collective activities of institutional investors, accounting for over 75 per cent of all trading on the market. Gompers and Metrick (1998) report that by 1996, large institutional investors (that is, those that manage at least $100 million) 'held dis-cretionary control over more than half of the US equity market'. Furthermore the 'one hundred largest institutions increased their share of the market from 19 per cent in 1980 to 37.1 per cent in 1996' (p. 1). It is important to note that the bulk of the rise of institutional investors shown in Table 5.2b had occurred prior to the most recent bull market. This underscores the fact that to pin the stock market boom merely on the rise of institutional investors is far too simple. Such a theory would not be able to explain the poor performance of the stock market during the years in which the largest shift of equity from individuals to institutions took place – 1967–77.

Based on this simple analysis alone, serious questions are raised about the consistency of at least one version of the falling risk premium theory with the stylized facts. If the most dramatic shift in equity ownership occurred between 1965 and 1975 why did it take another decade to materialize into higher stock prices and a lower required rate of return? Moreover, collectively the proportion of direct equity holdings by pension funds has remained relatively constant during 1982–99 (private pension funds decreased holdings while public pension funds increased holdings) and actually held slightly less of the market value of equity outstanding in 1999 than they did in 1982. While pension funds increased their share of US corporate equity by approximately 4.4 per cent between 1982 and 1985, it was mutual funds that dramatically increased the percentage of total value of equity outstanding (from 3.16 per cent to 17.2 per cent) during the entire 1982–99 interval.

Blanchard (1993) partially attributes the fall in the risk premium exclusively to the rise of pension funds, understanding the monumental difference between pension and mutual funds. Yet, Table 5.2b demonstrates that if the falling risk premium theory related to the rise of institutional investors is to be tenable, mutual funds must be a large portion of the story. Thus, the theory that attributes a decline in the risk premium to mutual funds lowering the cost of equity portfolio diversification is consistent with the data. However, given the caveats raised above about the mutual fund sector's susceptibility to the pursuit of short-horizon investment strategies and herding behavior, it is questionable that a falling risk premium stemming from the mutual fund-driven rise of institutional investors can account for the escalation stock prices over the last decade. This remains true even though the largest institutional investors increased their holding significantly during the 1982–99 period. Instead, consistent with the model of financial fragility, we argue that the under-pricing of risk (that is a faulty belief in a declining risk premium) rises out of the strong profit growth and euphoria that it stimulates, leading to stock market inflows that move prices away from their more realistic values.

The Impact of Accelerating Domestic Demand on Equity Prices

The household sector and institutional investors have operated in an identical fashion for most of the 1982–2000 stock market boom, shifting their portfolios towards equity and away from alternative assets. The only exception is life insurance companies which only began to seriously expand their holdings of equity in 1991. These stylized facts are consistent with the model of endogenous financial fragility, which suggest that the proportion of wealth stored in corporate equity increases as the economy moves from a state of recovery to robust expansion and ultimately euphoric boom. While we have established clearly the growth in demand for corporate shares, it is quite another matter entirely to illustrate that the shift in demand has impacted equity values above and beyond economic fundamentals.

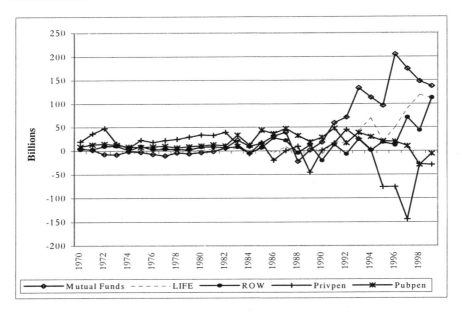

Notes: Net purchases in real terms (inflation corrected).

Source: *Flow of Funds Accounts of the United States*, Federal Reserve Board, Table F.213.

Figure 5.4   Net purchases of corporate equity by sector (I)

One rudimentary way to determine whether the flow theory of equity price fluctuation is consistent with the data is to examine the relationship between the S&P Index and net purchases of corporate equity during the period leading up to and including the time under investigation. Figure 5.4 graphs the net purchases of corporate stock for public and private pension funds, life insurance companies, the foreign sector and mutual funds from 1970 to 1999. From 1970 to 1983 private pension funds were, on balance, net purchasers of corporate equity but fluctuated between seller and buyer status during the 1984–95 period. However, like the household sector (represented previously in Figure 5.1), private pension funds were strong net sellers of corporate equity during the height of the run-up in US stock prices (1995–99), unloading $144 billion in 1997 alone. Likewise, public pension funds were consistent net purchasers for the 1970–97 period before selling a total of $35.2 billion at the height of the boom (1998–99). Evidence then, suggests some portfolio rebalancing on the behalf of pension funds, as collectively the sector was a net seller of corporate equity over the 1990s.

In comparison, mutual funds purchased on net $1.5 trillion worth of corporate stock during the 1990s. Moreover, mutual fund net purchases appear to track stock market performance reasonably well. During the 1970–81 period when the market performed poorly, mutual funds were net sellers of corporate equity with the exception of 1970 and 1971 during which time they purchased a relatively small $6.7 billion. However, during the 1982–99 interval, which corresponds to the great bull market, mutual funds were positive net purchasers of corporate equity – the exception being 1988 when they were net sellers of roughly $16 billion. Life insurance companies and foreign portfolio investors, on the other hand, did not purchase significant amounts of equity until 1991, but for the subsequent years up to 1999 the real value of their purchases were $538.4 and $288 billion, respectively.

Table 5.3 reports descriptive statistics for the real net purchases of each sector for the 1970–99 period and the sub-periods, 1970–81, 1982–99, 1989–99 and 1995–99. The table reiterates that on average households were net sellers of stock for the entire period including the relevant sub-periods, while private pension funds were net sellers on average with the exception of the 1970–81 interval. However, private and public pension funds behaved in a slightly asymmetric fashion for the 1982–99 period, as the latter were positive net purchasers for all sub-periods in question. The foreign sector (labeled ROW) and life insurance companies were also significant net buyers of corporate equity. Additionally, the table confirms that mutual funds sold shares on average during the 1970–81 period but purchased them in large amounts from 1982 onwards. The 1982–99, 1989–99 and 1995–99 sub-periods make the aggressive accumulation of stock on behalf of mutual funds abundantly clear.

Consequently, Table 5.3 confirms that during the 1982–2000 stock market boom, and in the wake of the shrinking supply of corporate shares, mutual funds, life insurance companies, public pension funds and the foreign sector were purchasing stock principally from households and private pension funds. According to the EMH, households and private funds should have readily sold without demanding a premium unless they held private information, or believed the remaining institutional investors possessed genuine information, that suggested favorable movements in corporate profits or discount rates. The flow theory contends that regardless of the future path of profits or other economic fundamentals, the inflow of funds into stock markets engenders equity price increases. Thus, distinguishing which of these theories is more accurate in the context of the 1982–2000 boom requires careful empirical analysis that shows that the price appreciation emanating from the transfer of stock from households and private funds to other sectors was unjustified by economic fundamentals. Analysis of these flows will shed light on whether the growth of equity as a proportion of total financial assets reported in Table 5.1 was unrelated to underlying performance of the corporate sector.

Table 5.3 Means and standard deviation of net purchases of corporate equity

	HH	Mutual Funds	Life Insurance	ROW	Private Funds	Public Funds
1970–99						
Mean	− 124.22	40.52	20.65	13.01	1.76	17.71
StDev	144.69	63.52	31.30	22.64	41.83	16.23
1970–81						
Mean	− 26.84	− 3.69	6.72	5.37	25.39	10.21
StDev	27.45	4.34	5.52	3.49	11.17	2.52
1982–99						
Mean	− 189.14	69.98	29.93	18.10	− 14.19	22.71
StDev	155.14	67.62	37.72	28.24	47.23	19.47
1989–99						
Mean	− 229.80	105.25	47.34	24.05	− 28.13	17.57
StDev	183.35	63.37	39.32	34.15	55.03	21.03
1995–99						
Mean	− 400.15	152.10	73.55	48.29	− 70.72	2.79
StDev	106.15	40.96	37.35	35.45	47.46	20.70

Notes: Descriptive statistics by sector in inflation-adjusted billions of dollars. ROW denotes rest of world. HH denotes households.

Source: *Flow of Funds Accounts of the United States*, Federal Reserve Board, Table F.213: Corporate Equities.

Table 5.4 reports the correlation coefficients for changes in net purchases, interest rates (Yield), and stock prices (Sp) and profits (Prof) in first differences, and one-step ahead first differences ($t + 1$). The coefficients indicate a strong, positive pair-wise relationship between the net corporate equity purchases of mutual funds (Mf) and changes in the S&P Index at time t for the 1970–99 period. The relationship is weaker for 1970–81 and stronger for the period corresponding to the stock market boom, 1982–2000. However the net purchases for both public pension funds (Fund) and life insurance companies (Life) exhibit extremely weak correlation with the changes in the stock market index for 1970–99. The 1982–99 sub-period – the period most germane to our investigation – once again confirms a smaller positive relationship between these institutional investor flows and stock market performance.

For both the 1970–99 and 1982–99 intervals, the coefficients confirm a relatively strong positive correlation between the equity purchases of public pension funds (and to a smaller extent life insurance companies) and contemporaneous changes in corporate profits. However, the correlation coefficients are significantly smaller for the relationship between mutual fund net purchases and contemporaneous changes in corporate profits, indicative of a weak relationship at best. This suggests that the relationship between mutual fund net purchases and profits is weaker than that between mutual fund net purchases and stock prices. On these grounds it would appear that if these institutional investor flows moved prices they might have done so in a manner unrelated to fundamentals. However, mutual fund net purchases are positively and more strongly related to $\Delta Prof_{t+1}$, thus establishing some relationship to corporate performance. Yet, the correlation coefficients between $\Delta Prof_{t+1}$ and changes in the S&P Index at time t is remarkably small across all time periods given that the stock market is held to be forward looking with respect to developments on the real side of the economy.

Descriptive evidence, then, indicates that mutual fund flows are closely correlated with US stock market performance and weakly correlated with contemporaneous changes in corporate profits. On the other hand, pension fund and life insurance funds are weakly correlated with the S&P Index but more strongly correlated with corporate profits. Thus, the preliminary evidence suggests that the growth of defined contribution plans and pension fund activity in the stock market cannot be implicated in the explosion in US stock prices over the last decade. Instead, it would appear that the run-up in US equity values could be linked to the growth of mutual funds. This correlation, and the fundamental differences between mutual funds and pension funds expressed above, suggests that the run-up in equity values was not the result of a declining risk premium related to stabilizing institutional investor flows.

However, citing strong positive correlation alone is not sufficient to conclude that mutual fund flows cause equity prices since we cannot rule out a bi-causal relationship, or that causality runs unidirectionally from equity prices to flows. Furthermore, both equity prices and flows, or its proxy, positive net purchases, could exhibit correlation simply because they respond analogously to other variables more relevant to stock market valuations. That is, funds may flow into the stock market for purely fundamental reasons. After all, this line of justification would be consistent with the contentions put forward by proponents of the efficient markets paradigm. Thus, not only is correlation between prices and flows not sufficient to conclude causality but it is also inadequate for differentiating between the rival theories.

Table 5.4 Correlation coefficients net purchases

1970–99	Fund	Life	Mf	Row	ΔProf_{t+1}	ΔProf_t	ΔSP_{t+1}	ΔSP_t	Yield
Fund	1.00								
Life	0.24	1.00							
Mf	0.19	0.05	1.00						
Row	0.08	0.10	0.39	1.00					
ΔProf_{t+1}	− 0.05	− 0.21	0.16	0.12	1.00				
ΔProf_t	0.23	0.15	0.03	0.02	0.10	1.00			
ΔSP_{t+1}	0.03	− 0.03	− 0.18	− 0.09	0.10	− 0.01	1.00		
ΔSP_t	0.05	0.08	0.50	0.62	0.20	0.04	0.15	1.00	
Yield	− 0.01	− 0.06	− 0.03	− 0.02	− 0.32	− 0.21	− 0.19	− 0.21	1.00

1970–81	Fund	Life	Mf	Row	ΔProf_{t+1}	ΔProf_t	ΔSP_{t+1}	ΔSP_t	Yield
Fund	1.00								
Life	0.10	1.00							
Mf	− 0.13	0.12	1.00						
Row	− 0.00	− 0.14	− 0.08	1.00					
ΔProf_{t+1}	0.25	− 0.20	0.12	− 0.12	1.00				
ΔProf_t	0.03	0.34	− 0.12	0.14	0.09	1.00			
ΔSP_{t+1}	0.15	0.05	0.03	− 0.07	− 0.08	− 0.08	1.00		
ΔSP_t	− 0.00	0.18	0.26	0.21	0.20	− 0.20	0.10	1.00	
Yield	0.06	0.12	0.02	0.13	− 0.49	− 0.15	− 0.11	− 0.17	1.00

1982–99	Fund	Life	Mf	Row	ΔProf_{t+1}	ΔProf_t	ΔSP_{t+1}	ΔSP_t	Yield
Fund	1.00								
Life	0.24	1.00							
Mf	0.19	0.05	1.00						
Row	0.08	0.10	0.39	1.00					
ΔProf_{t+1}	− 0.07	− 0.23	0.17	0.14	1.00				
ΔProf_t	0.25	0.15	0.03	0.02	0.07	1.00			
ΔSP_{t+1}	0.02	− 0.04	− 0.21	− 0.10	0.06	− 0.05	1.00		
ΔSP_t	0.05	0.07	0.51	0.65	0.16	0.02	0.07	1.00	
Yield	− 0.01	− 0.09	− 0.04	− 0.04	− 0.25	− 0.24	− 0.19	− 0.22	1.00

Notes: Fund, Life, Mf and Row are the changes in the net purchases of corporate equity by pension funds, life insurance companies, mutual funds and foreign portfolio investors. ΔProf and ΔSp are changes in after-tax profits and the S&P 500 Price Index. Yield is the three-month treasury bill rate. All data are quarterly.

Source: Federal Reserve Board and Standard and Poor's (S&P) DRI Database.

Foreign Demand and Equity Values

Unrestricted capital movements have had important consequences for the US stock market since, being one of the largest and most vibrant, it attracts more foreign capital than any other stock market in the world. The relative superiority of its stock markets with respect to risk and return, the size and liquidity of its secondary government bond market, and the central role of the dollar in the international monetary system have all served to make the United States an attractive haven for foreign capital. The internationalization of US equity markets has resulted in one-fourth of all equity transactions in the United States either involving foreign equity or involving a foreign party on either side of the transaction (Tesar, 1999, p. 236). Moreover, international capital flows and the attractiveness of its domestic financial markets along with a steady trade deficit have all helped to transform the United States into a net debtor nation, whose net debt to the rest of the world stood at $2.19 trillion in 1999, roughly 22 per cent of gross domestic product (GDP) (D'Arista, 2001). Much of this capital inflow has come courtesy of the foreign purchases of US corporate equity.

Foreign portfolio activity, while making up only 5.2 per cent of market capitalization in 1980, reached a peak of 18.6 per cent in 1987 before declining to 11 per cent in the early 1990s and remaining steady at approximately 8 per cent throughout the decade (Aggarwal and Schirm, 1995, p. 258; D'Arista, 1999). It should be noted that this decline stems from an increase in US stock market capitalization and not a decline in international equity portfolio flows. Certainly, US equity market capitalization increased from $2.2 trillion in 1985 to $5.5 trillion in 1994 and to $17.2 trillion by 1999. As for bilateral relations between the United States and the European Union (EU), equity flows are typically larger than trade flows and have increased dramatically between the two areas since 1992, with the relaxation of capital controls in the EU15 (Portes and Rey, 1999, p. 10).

This evidence suggests that any investigation into US equity price dynamics during the current era that considers domestic factors exclusively may also be overlooking an important driving force behind the 1982–2000 bull market. The finding that foreign savings have buoyed the US stock market would be consistent with the increased integration and internationalization of financial markets and the consequent interdependencies between national economies that result. According to the flow theory of equity price determination, which incorporates the openness of global financial markets, US equity prices and foreign capital flows growing together may be far from a coincidence. Indeed, foreigners may fuel a speculative boom, providing the domestic economy with the liquidity it needs to encourage further credit expansion and keep speculative and Ponzi units afloat.

Figure 5.4 and Table 5.3 shows that foreign portfolio investors have been significant net purchasers of corporate equity in the 1990s, purchasing on average

$48.3 billion per year during the 1995–99 period and $112.3 billion in real terms in 1999 alone. Their activity closely approximates that of life insurance companies and, in fact, Table 5.2b confirms that the rest of the world holds a slightly larger proportion of US corporate equity outstanding than the life insurance sector, approximately 7.8 per cent. Moreover, Figure 5.3e illustrates (reiterating the evidence presented in Table 5.1) that after remaining relatively constant around 15 per cent from 1980 to 1986, the proportion of corporate equity in the financial portfolios of foreigners actually fell to 12.2 per cent in 1990 before increasing to 13.7 per cent in 1994. However, the percentage of equity holdings as a percentage of the total portfolio of US financial assets increased significantly to roughly 24 per cent during the last half of the decade.

Foreigners may possess a smaller share of US corporate equity (7.8 per cent) relative to domestic individual investors (44.7 per cent) and pension funds (21 per cent), yet may effectively move prices along with mutual funds and other smaller institutional investors. However, these stylized facts make one important issue clear. Attributing the potential influence of foreign flows on stock prices to a shift in the risk–return characteristics of the market is inconsistent with trends in foreign ownership. Since the proportion of US corporate equity outstanding held by foreigners has only increased from approximately 5.7 per cent to 7.8 per cent, foreign activity in the stock market cannot account for the large alleged fall in the risk premium during the 1982–2000 period. Nor can it be said that a sector which holds less than 8 per cent of total value of US equity outstanding has altered the risk–return characteristics of the market such that the remaining 92 per cent of the participants are willing to accept a lower expected rate of return going forward. Thus, if foreign equity flows moved US stock prices it has done so either in a manner related to 'rational' assessments of expected dividend payments or in a manner unjustified by economic and business fundamentals.

Table 5.4 illustrates that, like mutual funds, portfolio equity flows are highly correlated with changes in stock prices but nearly uncorrelated with changes in corporate profits. In fact, the correlation coefficients for foreign purchases and the S&P Index are larger than those between mutual fund flows and the measure of stock market performance for both the 1970–99 and 1982–99 periods. This militates in favor of the hypothesis that foreign savings have buoyed US equity prices and in a manner unjustified by corporate fundamentals. Moreover, the statistics reported above on net purchases and portfolio composition may still seriously understate the role of the foreign sector. This is because the information contained in Table F.213 and L.213 in the Federal Reserve Board's *Flow of Funds Accounts* used as a source for Figures 5.3e and 5.4, includes only 'portfolio' equity flows. That is, only purchases by single foreign investors that 'result in ownership of less than 10 per cent of the outstanding equity of the issuing US firm'. Alternatively, 'purchases by a single foreign investor that result in ownership of 10 per cent or more of the firm's outstanding equity are considered foreign direct investment' (FDI) and therefore excluded from the source tables, F.213 and L.213 (*Guide to the Flow of Funds*, p. 850).[8]

Yet, the issues of ownership or the source, while important, are inconsequential as far as price appreciation generated through an impersonal market mechanism is concerned. Unquestionably, flows impact price regardless of whether they are concentrated from a single investor or aggregated from several smaller investors. Consequently, unpacking the equity portion of FDI, using Table F.230: 'Identified Miscellaneous Financial Claims' from the *Flow of Funds Accounts*, would appear imperative in determining whether foreign equity flows are important to US stock market performance during the 1982–2000 period. When we decompose FDI we find that equity accounted for over 85 per cent of the flows from 1982 to 1999. From 1987 to 1997, equity accounted for 94 per cent to 100 per cent of all FDI. The remaining portion of FDI is made up of reinvested earnings and inter-company loans.[9] Unfortunately, there is no related levels table that might have been used to clear up the equity ownership issue, but suffice it to say that foreigners are most likely to hold more than 8 per cent of the value of US equity outstanding.

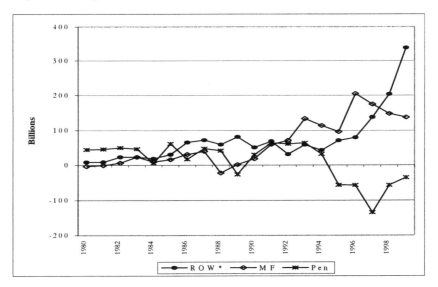

Notes: Net purchases in real terms (inflation corrected). ROW* denotes foreign portfolio equity flows plus FDI equity flows. Pen denotes total Pension fund flows (public and private).

Source: *Flow of Funds Accounts of the United States*, Federal Reserve Board, Tables F.213 and F.230.

Figure 5.5 Net purchases of corporate equity by sector (II)

Nonetheless, augmenting portfolio investment with the equity portion of FDI reveals a different picture when returning our attention to the net purchases of corporate equity. Figure 5.5 updates Figure 5.4 with the adjustments to net purchases of the foreign sector. The graph illustrates clearly that the foreigners have played a much more prominent role in US equity markets than was previously indicated, accumulating $806 billion worth of shares during the 1995–99 period alone. The amount increases to $894.7 billion if we include 1993 and 1994 making the foreign sector the largest net injectors of funds into the stock market outside of mutual funds during 1993–99 (primarily due to the abnormally large net purchases of 1998 and 1999). Referencing the entire 1982–99 period it is clear that foreign purchases have indeed rivaled domestic flows, including those of mutual funds. We have included the net purchases of mutual and pension funds (public and private) in Figure 5.5 along with foreign purchases of US corporate equity to place the role of the latter in a different perspective. Seen in this light, unclouded by the ownership issue that disconnects portfolio flows from foreign direct flow, the contention that foreigners have contributed significantly to equity price inflation appears even more convincing.

Furthermore, capital inflow can be transmitted to the US stock market through several mechanisms with FDI equity and direct portfolio equity flows being only the most obvious channels. However, portfolio bond and treasury inflows place downward pressure on interest rates, lowering yields on alternative assets and the discount at which expected profits are capitalized. The transmission of the effect of foreign flows on stock prices via an interest rate channel can aid explaining the low rates that prevailed in the United States despite the booming economy of the 1990s. Additionally, foreign flow of funds to domestic banks increases reserves, allowing for the extension of marginal credit and other loans that may ultimately bid up share prices.[10] Accordingly, these loans may take the form of consumer credit, which ultimately bolsters corporate profits and consequently, the ability to pay out dividends to shareholders.[11]

Figure 5.6 highlights the net debtor status of the United States. It shows that foreigners have been accumulating corporate equity, corporate bonds and US government treasuries over the last two decades. In real terms, foreigners purchased roughly $88, $126 and $158 billion worth of corporate bonds in 1997, 1998 and 1999, respectively, topping off an upward trend set in motion since 1989. The growing accumulation of government securities dates back to 1982 and culminated in an injection of $925.6 billion into US financial markets during the 1995–99 period. A further impetus to international purchases of government securities were the large and persistent budget deficits run by the Republican government which served to make Reagan the largest seller of government bonds to foreign parties. Figure 5.6 also illustrates that FDI (heavily equity flows) made a large portion of the capital flow into the United States during the late 1990s.

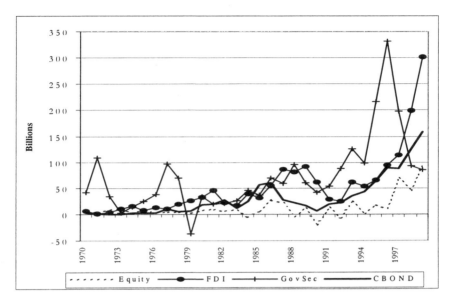

Notes: Net purchases in real terms (inflation corrected).

Source: *Flow of Funds Accounts of the United States,* Federal Reserve Board, Table F.107.

Figure 5.6   Net capital inflow (by instrument)

The collapse of the Bretton Woods agreement saw an immediate increase in foreigners' share of treasuries outstanding from just 3.72 per cent in 1969 to 16.89 per cent in 1973 and to 21.61 per cent in 1978.   Although their share dropped to 14.72 per cent in 1984, the foreign sector accumulated treasuries at a tremendous pace for the remainder of the decade.   Throughout the 1990s the for-eigners dominated US treasury markets and held 35.78 per cent of all securities outstanding by the end of 1999.   Likewise, the foreign sector increased their cor-porate bond holdings from a meager 1.47 per cent to 17.95 per cent of all bonds outstanding, making them a significant player here as well.   The net result is that the activity of the foreign sector ultimately codetermines the path of US interest rates, which are of immediate consequence to the stock market.   Thus, it is quite plausible that the recent bull market was critically linked to the fact that by 1999 estimates the US was utilizing 72 per cent of the world's net savings (*Business Week*, November 1, 1999).

Again, analysis of correlation coefficients establishes the a priori plausibility of international flows impacting on US equity prices both directly and through indi-rect channels.   Table 5.5 presents the correlation between corporate bonds

(CBOND), treasury security purchases (GOV), foreign direct equity (FDI) and portfolio flows (EQUITY) and interest rates and the stock market variables discussed in the previous sections of this chapter. The coefficients suggest a strong positive relationship between the equity component of FDI and changes in the S&P Index, ΔSP_t, for both the 1970–99 and 1982–99 periods. The 1970–81 period, as we have seen in our analysis of domestic institutional investors, is distinct from the others reporting a significantly weaker pair-wise relationship between portfolio equity flows (also illustrated earlier in Table 5.4), FDI and ΔSP_t.

Table 5.5 ROW impact on US financial markets (correlation coefficients)

1970–99	CBOND	EQUITY	FDI	GOV	ΔSP_t	YIELD
CBOND	1.0000					
EQUITY	0.1410	1.0000				
FDI	− 0.1675	0.2857	1.0000			
GOV	0.3176	0.1479	0.2497	1.0000		
ΔSP_t	0.2893	0.6379	0.1535	0.1488	1.0000	
YIELD	− 0.1268	− 0.0328	− 0.0243	− 0.1192	− 0.2121	1.0000
1970–81	CBOND	EQUITY	FDI	GOV	ΔSP_t	YIELD
CBOND	1.0000					
EQUITY	− 0.1120	1.0000				
FDI	− 0.3054	− 0.1386	1.0000			
GOV	− 0.0490	− 0.0211	− 0.0746	1.0000		
ΔSP_t	− 0.0859	0.2098	0.0779	0.0513	1.0000	
YIELD	0.1734	0.1282	0.1103	− 0.0286	− 0.1711	1.0000
1982–99	CBOND	EQUITY	FDI	GOV	ΔSP_t	YIELD
CBOND	1.0000					
EQUITY	0.1403	1.0000				
FDI	− 0.1681	0.2874	1.0000			
GOV	0.3282	0.1528	0.2568	1.0000		
ΔSP_t	0.2889	0.6620	0.1598	0.1599	1.0000	
YIELD	− 0.1496	− 0.0513	− 0.0418	− 0.1245	− 0.2184	1.0000

Notes: CBOND and GOV are the changes in net purchases of corporate bonds and government securities by ROW (rest of the world). EQUITY denotes portfolio equity flows and FDI represents foreign direct equity flows.

Source: S&P/DRI Database, *Flow of Funds Accounts of the United States*, Federal Reserve Board, Table F.107: 'Rest of the World' and F.230: 'Identified Miscellaneous Financial Claims'.

For 1970–99 and 1982–99, the table also reports a negative, albeit weak, relationship between CBOND and GOV and the three-month treasury constant maturity rate (YIELD), consistent with the hypothesis that net purchases of bonds and treasuries placed downward pressure on interest rates. In turn, both periods suggest a relatively strong negative correlation between YIELD and the S&P Index. Additionally, both net purchases of corporate bonds and government treasuries are positively correlated with ΔSP_t, in fact, the coefficients suggest an even stronger relationship than those between foreign direct equity flows and stock market performance. Collectively, these data weakly support the contention that flows into bond markets indirectly impact the stock market through an interest rate or other indirect channels.

The usual caveats apply here – correlation does not necessarily imply causation nor does causation mean international flows move equity prices irrespective of economic fundamentals. This is important to note since international flows into domestic markets could reflect a spreading of risk across more investors and thus justify price changes based on reduction in the risk premium. Moreover, international investors may engage in positive feedback trading or exhibit return-chasing behavior, in which case equity prices may cause capital flows into the stock market instead of the other way around. Neither of these eventualities can be completely ruled out based on our empirical work utilizing correlation coefficients and analyzing the trends in the data. Furthermore, high interest rates have historically encouraged global capital flows. To the extent that international flows may have influenced equity prices, the traditional relationship between discount rates and the latter will be compromised. Therefore, Granger causality tests, the multivariate VAR technique and instrumental variable analysis will more properly permit us to query deeper into these issues and investigate the role of international forces in the bull market of 1982–2000.

THE DECLINE IN THE SUPPLY OF EQUITY

Since 1980 domestic corporations trading publicly in the United States have significantly reduced the amount of equity on the secondary market by way of mergers, leveraged buyouts and stock buybacks (Figure 5.7). During the stock market boom years, 1982–99, the decline in the volume of domestic shares outstanding averaged nearly $61 billion per year ($73.5 billion in real terms), despite the IPO boom of the late 1990s. This period can be divided into four separate phases, two shorter phases with positive net issuance, 1982–83 and 1991–94 and two where net issuance was negative, 1984–90 and 1995–99. While, the 1984–90 phase is associated with intense merger and leveraged buyout activity, firms also began to repurchase their own shares in record amounts as a defensive strategy to prevent hostile takeovers (McCauley, et al., 1999, p. 170; D'Arista, 1994,

p. 226). SEC Rule 10b-18, which established a safe harbor for firms to carry out
share repurchases, was instrumental in the dramatic rise in repurchase programs
for a variety of purposes since 1982. In 1989 alone, $120 billion in equity was
removed from the market – an amount that was, in absolute value, roughly 51 per
cent of net corporate profits. It should be noted that this followed a year in which
the volume of domestic equity was reduced by $108 billion, or 44 per cent of net
corporate profits. In stark contrast, net issues increased by an amount equivalent
to 7.4 per cent of net corporate profits per annum during the 1953–81 period.
This is an important stylized fact to keep in mind when we turn to the econometric investigation in Chapter 6.

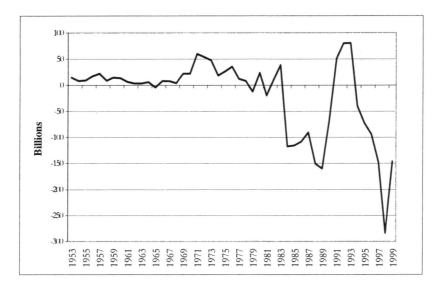

Notes: Net issues in real terms (inflation corrected).

Source: *Flow of Funds Accounts of the United States*, Federal Reserve Board, Table F.213.

Figure 5.7   Net issues of domestic corporate equity

After the 1991–94 phase of intense equity issuance, 1995–99 saw a return to the
negative issuance phenomena prevalent in the 1980s. In 1998, an extraordinary
$267 billion in domestic corporate equity was extracted from public markets by
non-financial corporate businesses. The consequent influx of funds amounted to
54 per cent of 1998 after-tax corporate profits. This made publicly listed financial and non-financial corporations themselves the largest net purchasers of corporate equity (bigger than both mutual and pension funds) and, thus, the ultimate

providers of liquidity to the market. Including the positive net issues of the foreign sector, the total reduction in corporate shares of publicly listed companies was $165.8 billion. In fact the foreign sector took full advantage of the stock market boom, issuing $421.5 over the 1995–99 period. However, the net issues of foreign firms listed on US exchanges were swamped by the retirement in shares undertaken by domestic corporations (– $707 billion).

With mergers undoubtedly still an important part of the story, stock buybacks, to provide stock options to employees or otherwise, made up a considerable portion of the reduction in the volume of corporate equities outstanding. The 1995–99 phase witnessed approximately 3.6 per cent of GDP going into stock buybacks.[12] The largest 150 non-financial firms in the S&P 500 repurchased on average 2 per cent of their stock per annum between 1994 and 1998 (1 per cent of which made up stock options to employees) (Liang and Sharpe, 1999). Share repurchases by all S&P 500 companies alone more than tripled between 1995 and 1998 and actually exceeded dividend payments to common shareholders in 1997 and 1998 (ibid., p. 1).

Table 5.6 Net issues, and stock price, profit and earnings growth

Interval	Net Issues	Per Annum S&P Growth (%)	Per Annum Profit Growth (%)	Per Annum S&P Earnings Growth (%)
1982–83	29.2	18.9	8.2	– 3.8
1984–90	– 562.1	14.3	8.6	6.8
1991–94	143.6	9.6	12.3	11.1
1995–99	– 706.5	41.4	6.0	8.0

Source: Federal Reserve Board and S&P/DRI Database

Using data on the S&P 500 Composite Index, we have calculated the nominal price appreciation for the various sub-periods along with the figures for net issuance and profit growth. The results, illustrated in Table 5.6, are highly suggestive. The years 1984–90 and 1995–99 when the volume of equities outstanding declined by $562.1 and $707 billion the market appreciated remarkably, 14 per cent and 36.7 per cent per annum, respectively. In contrast, the years when the volume of equities increased significantly, 1991–94, the S&P Index appreciated at a slower rate, approximately 10 per cent per year. It should also be noted that in the 1982–99 sample, periods of positive issuance correspond not only to poorer stock market performance but generally to *higher* profit growth as well. This remains the case whether we look at aggregate corporate profits or S&P earnings. The two-year period, 1982–83, however, is characterized by strong stock market performance, poor S&P earnings growth but aggregate net issues of corporate equity were positive.

The 1995–99 segment of the bull market, with stock prices appreciating well over 180 per cent, has no equal. Although profit growth was significantly lower than that for both 1982–83 and 1991–94, the average yearly growth in equity values was two to over three times greater. Figure 5.8 underscores the difference between the aforementioned intervals. The upward slope of the S&P Index curve is clearly steeper when net issues of corporate equity are negative. In fact, visually there appears to be a remarkable structural break in the data on the S&P Index at precisely the same time corporations began to reduce again the volume of equity outstanding, 1995, the origin of the most dramatic portion of the US stock market boom.

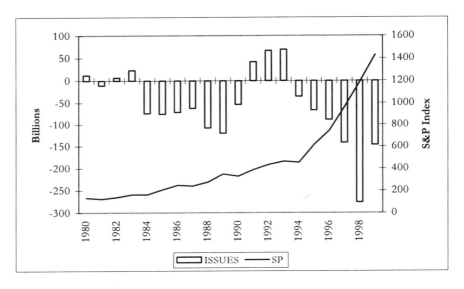

Notes: SP is the S&P 500 Stock Market Index.

Source: *Flow of Funds Accounts of the United States*, Federal Reserve Board, Table F.213 and S&P /DRI Database.

Figure 5.8 Net issues of domestic corporate equity and stock market performance

Table 5.7 reports the correlation coefficients for net issues (issue), stock price changes (ΔSP), profits (Profit) and dividends (Divid) one period ahead, and interest rates (Tbill). The results indicate a negative pair-wise relationship between net issues at time t and time $t - 1$ and changes in the S&P index for 1953–99. The correlation coefficients are particularly sizeable (– 0.425 and – 0.536) and they are larger than those between ΔSP and $Divid_{t+1}$, $Profit_{t+1}$ and the three-month T-bill rate. The relationship between ΔSP and net issues appears slightly weaker (– 0.330 and – 0.463) for 1982–99 and significantly weaker for lagged issuance and changes in the index (– 0.095) for the 1953–81 period. The correlation coefficients between contemporaneous net issues and changes in the stock price index tell an entirely different story, suggesting a weak positive relationship (0.100). However, concentrating on the 1990–99 period, both lagged and contemporaneous net issues exhibit strong negative correlation with changes in the S&P Index.

Table 5.7 Correlation coefficients for stock performance and potential factors

1953–99	ΔSP	Divid(t+1)	Profit(t+1)	Issue	Issue(t–1)	Tbill
ΔSP	1					
Divid(t+1)	0.53143	1				
Profit(t+1)	0.52127	0.98686	1			
Issue	– 0.42496	– 0.59287	– 0.55164	1		
Issue(t–1)	– 0.53639	– 0.59420	– 0.55379	0.68966	1	
Tbill	– 0.04734	0.10097	0.15877	– 0.10342	– 0.10047	1
1953–81						
ΔSP	1					
Divid(t+1)	– 0.00388	1				
Profit(t+1)	0.00336	0.95431	1			
Issue	0.10077	– 0.03694	0.04212	1		
Issue(t–1)	– 0.09474	0.07640	0.12405	0.68905	1	
Tbill	– 0.15422	0.89246	0.80749	0.00104	0.09111	1
1982–99						
ΔSP	1					
Divid(t+1)	0.47767	1				
Profit(t+1)	0.47250	0.98547	1			
Issue	– 0.32962	– 0.43602	– 0.38205	1		
Issue(t–1)	– 0.46327	– 0.44437	– 0.39227	0.60721	1	
Tbill	– 0.21841	– 0.61535	– 0.61463	– 0.02378	– 0.03115	1

Notes: ΔSP, Divid, Profit denote the change in the S&P 500 Index, S&P dividends and after-tax corporate profits, respectively. Issue denotes net issues of domestic corporate equity and Tbill is the three-month Treasury bill rate. All data are quarterly.

Source: Federal Reserve Board and S&P/DRI database.

Negative correlation between net issues and stock prices substantiates an association between the variables but is insufficient to conclude a causal relationship running from supply changes to market valuations. First, the opposite line of causation could also be true. Such a negative causal relationship could emerge in the recent era owing to institutional factors such as the compensation of employees and corporate managers in the form of stock options. To the extent that an appreciating stock market makes stock options more attractive, employees are more likely to accept packages heavy on shares and lower on traditional forms of remuneration, thus also enhancing corporate profitability since stock options were not expensed. These dynamics would justify a negative relationship running from stock prices to net issues and corporate profits. In turn, this creates an incentive for managers to embrace a policy of share repurchases in lieu of dividend payments to further boost stock prices (Shiller, 2000a, p. 24). Mutual causality between the variables in question is then likely. The data suggests that stock options were prevalent when the market boomed in the 1960s but waned during the bear market of the 1970s only to rise again in the recent era (Holmstrom and Kaplan, 2001).

Second, other economic forces may cause stock prices and issues of corporate equity to move in a manner that induces negative correlation between the variables. Specifically, increases in corporate profitability permit the repurchase of shares, justifying a negative relationship between net issues of equity and profits. At the same time, the forward-looking (leading indicator) nature of stock prices engenders a positive correlation between equity prices and profits. Therefore, the predictability of stock valuations for profits and the negative relationship between the latter and share retirements implies a negative correlation between net issuance and stock prices.

Moreover, if one considers profits as the enabler of share buybacks, it should be emphasized that in the 1990s companies benefited substantially from their own stock market investments. For example, Microsoft, Compuserve Computer Corporation and Intel boasted stock portfolios of $19.8, $8.3 and $8 billion, respectively in 1999.[13] Also, corporations booked considerable profits from their pension funds, whose proceeds greatly appreciated with the stock market boom. Furthermore, the stellar stock market performance made stock options more attractive vis-à-vis more traditional forms of compensation and to the extent that options were not expensed profits may have been artificially inflated as a result. These developments suggest endogeneity between stock prices and profits. Therefore, equity price appreciation may have given rise to the excess profits that might have facilitated the aggressive share repurchases of the late 1990s. Thus, the case for mutual causality and a supply-side bubble becomes even more convincing. We examine this more systematically below.

Share Repurchases and Fundamental Value

Although we established a prima facie case for our position, it not clear from such an analysis that supply issues move prices independent of profit growth and real developments that impact stock prices. Thus, the complicated question of whether supply issues move prices beyond business and economic fundamentals requires more systematic empirical work. Certainly, the fact that correlation exists and is theoretically indicative of a causal relationship still does not imply that a reduction in the supply of equity initiates unwarranted stock price increases. The reasoning is quite simple. First mergers and takeovers may send positive signals to investors about increased profitability and thus the decline in equity supply conveys new information about future dividend prospects.[14] More importantly, there are two ways corporations can transfer income from their operations to shareholders, the most popular manner historically being the distribution of periodic dividend payments. However, corporate profits can just as easily be distributed to a segment of the existing shareholders through share repurchase programs.

There has indeed been serious deviation from the historic norm in the last two decades since dividend payout rates have fallen and share repurchases have risen sharply (Fama and French, 2000). Liang and Sharpe (1999) point out that from 1994 to 1998 stock repurchases of S&P 500 corporations have increased by over 200 per cent while dividend payments rose by only 35 per cent. They conclude that the dividend discount model, the standard framework for evaluating stock prices, 'has lost some appeal as an equity valuation tool' (p. 1). However, it should be noted that although share repurchases are not explicitly accounted for within the dividend discount model, it is not an oversight that affects the validity of the model. Campbell et al. (1997) aptly note that equity repurchases merely affect the time pattern of expected future dividend payments with the respective totals remaining the same (p. 256).

Fama and French (2001), Jagannathan et al. (2001) and Wadhwani (1999) all show that prices remain properly valued within the present-value framework when corporations pay dividends and repurchase shares. For example, a corporation with N shares outstanding at market price P, by repurchasing shares valued at S, would initiate an increase in per share earnings growth of $s = S/NP$ (Liang and Sharpe, 1999, p. 3; Campbell, et al., 1997, p. 287). Consequently, the widely accepted Gordon growth model would simply reflect the higher growth rate of dividends: $P_t = D_t(1 + g + s)/i + \rho - (g + s)$[15], where P, D, i, ρ and g denote the price of stock, dividends paid, risk-free interest rate, risk premium and growth rate of dividends, respectively.[16] The earnings growth model (focusing on earnings instead of dividends) allows one to sidestep the issues of share repurchases altogether (Fama and French, 2001, pp. 16–17). On the other hand, earnings growth has a much larger standard deviation than dividends, resulting in a loss in precision when estimating expected stock returns (ibid., p. 17).

Consistent with standard valuation analysis, dividend payouts to shareholders alter the preexisting stock prices by forcing investors to consider the future, long-term stream of such payments. Likewise, it would appear on the surface that share repurchases function analogously, by rewarding some shareholders immediately, buying back their stake in the firm, while others who were not inclined to sell are compensated by the consequent price appreciation. This price appreciation is directly linked to growth in future dividend payments, thus, the conclusion that share repurchases fit neatly within a standard valuation model, justifying fundamental changes in equity prices alongside dividends and discount rates. The implicit assumption here is that the funds used to repurchase shares would have been used to pay dividends. However, if dividend payments are maintained and the share repurchase funds would have been otherwise used for investment purposes, shareholders should view the policy in an entirely different light. For this reason the dynamic Gordon growth model (dividend–ratio model) advanced by Campbell and Shiller (1988) is more appropriate for equity valuation since it holds price changes to be a function not only of expected dividend growth but also whether the growth will be temporary or permanent.[17]

To some, repurchases should simply be incorporated into the analysis of stock valuations by treating outflow of funds analogous to dividend payouts. In this manner, Cole et al. (1996) utilizing data on net share repurchases, which from 1986 to 1995 were 48 per cent of dividends, calculate a 'share repurchases yield'. Correspondingly, Lamdin (2000) augments the Gordon growth equation with a 40 per cent increase in actual dividends paid at the beginning of 1999. With justifiable assumptions about future growth rates and the risk premium, Lamdin deduces that in 1999 the S&P 500 was not significantly overvalued. Unfortunately, share repurchases and dividend payouts are only superficially equivalent and thus simply adding a 'share repurchase yield' to dividend growth rate is an inadequate way to measure the fundamental value of the stock market.

First, if the EMH is correct, the market should react differently to increases in dividend payments than to share buybacks. Increases in dividends are derived from current profits, which signal to investors' higher future corporate profitability. The increase in stock prices is, therefore, premised on the expectation that the new increase in payouts will be maintained. As a result, corporations generally do not increase dividends temporarily since wary investors penalize those that do so. On the other hand, share repurchases, which are typically financed by excess profits or temporary surpluses and transitory, are much more flexible, imposing no such requirement on corporations to buy back shares in the future (Liang and Sharpe, 1999, p. 4).

Jagannathan et al. (2000) show that dividend-paying companies have more stable earnings than those that rely on share repurchases. Three studies, John and

Williams (1985), Bernheim (1991) and Allen et al. (2000) argue that corporations use dividends to signal quality and are therefore not interchangeable with share repurchases. Thus, increases in dividends and share repurchases may place asymmetric demands on companies and profits transmitted via share repurchases create more uncertainty for shareholders. Therefore, it is not immediately evident that investors should react to both in the same manner if we take the standard approach to asset prices. Yet, despite the earnings stability and 'firm quality' attributes of dividend-paying corporations, the 1990s rewarded share repurchasing companies disproportionately. While a portfolio indexed to the S&P 500 returned 579 per cent a similar portfolio indexed exclusively to share repurchasing companies would have returned 1203 per cent.[18]

Since dividends in all future periods enter the present value formula underpinning equity valuations, an increase in payouts in one period is but a small component of price. What looms larger in the valuation of current stock prices is the expected growth rate of dividends. Thus, it is only when increases are held to be permanent that one should expect large effects on the market price (Campbell et al., 1997, p. 253). Since share repurchases do not necessarily imply future repurchases, their immediate effect on current prices should be related to future increases in dividend payments that come from a reduction in the amount of shareholders sharing profits in the future. Liang and Sharpe (1999) argue that for S&P 500 companies to maintain the current pace of share repurchases while maintaining current dividend payout rates, 90 per cent of their earnings would be exhausted (52 per cent and 38 per cent, respectively). Therefore, share repurchases can be considered a permanent source of income to shareholders only if investing 10 per cent of profits in the 'new economy' is sufficient to secure the future earnings that will enable the current payout rates to persist. On the other hand, if the growth rate of future profits necessary to validate current prices is not sustainable with a 90 per cent payout rate, the dynamic dividend discount model should value equity prices understanding the transitory nature of recent repurchases.

Finally, it is clear that shareholders, trading solely on fundamentals, should not regard the two methods as indistinguishable if debt instruments or loans finance share repurchases. While there are several reasons why firms might borrow funds to repurchase equity, none of them justify an increase in share valuations if the purchase is unrelated to the future profitability of the firm. Moreover, there is a limit to the amount of debt a corporation can take on, and therefore *if* the market is a precise discounting machine it should not impute additional value to the shares of corporations who decrease the amount of their equity outstanding continually through increased leverage. After all, if it were uncovered that firms were borrowing to make dividend payments to shareholders, it would be accused of Ponzi financing, warranting a decline in its stock prices. Thus, the claim that share repurchases can be incorporated into the standard valuation model is in need of serious qualification.

If, indeed, it is increased corporate profits that have permitted corporations to buy back shares over the last two decades then share repurchases (and perhaps negative net issuance) can be deemed an intrinsic part of the rise in market valuations. That is, the portion of the stock market boom that is explained by the shrinking supply of equity is justified by fundamentals. Yet, evidence presented in Chapter 4 suggests that debt-financed takeovers, mergers and stock buybacks became increasingly prevalent in the 1980s and 1990s. The late 1990s alone is replete with examples such as the EDS Corporation, which borrowed $1.5 billion on the bond market to finance an aggressive share buyback program, or Dupont, which raised an additional $2 billion on debt markets to acquire Pioneer High-Bred International.[19] One of the most infamous examples is WorldCom that grew at an unsustainable pace in the 1980s and 1990s primarily through more than 65 mergers partially financed by debt. This behavior is quite reminiscent of the leveraged buyout behavior that came to an abrupt end with the collapse of the junk bond market in the late 1980s discussed in the previous chapter. If it is the case that such debt-financed ventures have contributed to the stock market boom in a manner unrelated to the future profitability, the efficiency of financial markets is immediately called into question.

Nevertheless, properly valued, high stock prices generally imply high dividends for shareholders in the future. Conversely, improperly valued, high stock price augur in favor of lower future returns. Recall Table 4.1, which reports the real and nominal growth of dividends on S&P 500 stock. The table illustrates that share repurchases and merger activity has translated into an increase in real dividend growth rates. Over the entire 1952–99 sample the average yearly real growth in S&P dividends is approximately 1.42 per cent. The growth rate for the 1990s was roughly 1 per cent, with the greatest increase occurring between 1995 and 1996 when dividends grew 4.57 per cent. However, dividends grew 2.42 per cent (1 per cent over the historical average) during the 1995–99 period, although real dividend growth was just 0.33 per cent for 1999. The evidence therefore suggests that the recent share retirements have boosted earnings per share but not by as much as necessary to justify the explosive stock prices witnessed over the last decade. This conclusion is consistent with recent research which finds that share repurchases due to stock options did not translate into increases in long-run dividend payments.

Perhaps we need to know future dividends growth rates to unravel the story completely but we can say that hitherto the aggressive share repurchases and merger activity of the 1980s and early 1990s have not produced the dividend growth expected.[20] On the other hand, we have experienced unprecedented growth in stock prices. As we demonstrated in Table 4.2 of the previous chapter, fundamental value estimates for the S&P Index suggested that even when assuming an additional 2 per cent to 3 per cent increase over the historic growth rate of nominal dividends and a modest risk premium of 4 per cent to 5 per cent the S&P

500 at the end of 1999 was significantly overvalued. The scenario is worse if we assume that dividend growth will be boosted by just 1 per cent more per year (a growth rate of 6.46 per cent). Here, even taking a risk premium of 2 per cent over the market is, by our estimates, overvalued by roughly 31 per cent.

There is also the possibility that share repurchases are viewed as corporations 'paying themselves first', sending positive signals about future earning prospects. Thus, when announcements about repurchases are made, investors may buy the stock in expectation of future price increases. In this manner positive information is conveyed by flows into the market from stock buybacks. Several mutual funds now offer equity portfolios made up exclusively of firms that buy back shares, reinforcing the idea that share repurchases symbolize firm quality.[21] Again, this information may send false buy signals to investors if share repurchases are decapitalizing or do not actually translate into higher growth in dividends per share. In this case shrinking supply calls forth demand increases that pushes prices up further than that which can be justified by reasonable assessments of fundamentals.

The speculative market theory inspired by the model of financial fragility emphasizes this nexus between supply and demand with the exception that investors are understood within the context of intractable uncertainty and mass psychology. Here too, the effects of declining supply, by altering investor perceptions about future profitability, can be intensified by demand changes that encourage further net inflows and price appreciation. However, once we move beyond the theory of efficient markets, investors may indeed have short-term horizons and are therefore unconcerned about what happens to the market valuations over the long run. That is, investors may purchase stock simply to reap gains by unloading it at a higher price. This is the essence of J.M. Keynes' comments about the stock market approximating a game of 'Old Maid', 'Snap' or 'Musical Chairs' (Keynes, 1964, p. 156). To use the WorldCom example, euphoric investors were not concerned that many of the mergers and acquisitions were not adequately synthesized into the enterprise to increase profitability, only that the stock price would continue to rise.

This situation is enhanced by the rise of mutual fund investors who are evaluated at a shorter frequency, both by their managers and the public, thus leading to a bias towards the securing of short-term gains over the type of trading that would be deemed 'rational' by the EMH theorist. As such, the market may favor firms with high payout ratios since institutional and individual investors do not plan to be around when the verdict is handed down as to whether or not the ratios were sustainable and/or translate into future cash flow in the long run. Worse still, financial euphoria causes investors to overlook the rising debt burdens of corporations and, in fact, interpret the developments as an augur of future increases in dividends per share.

At the very least, from the preliminary evidence, it would appear that the decline in the amount of US corporate equity outstanding on secondary markets intensified the growing demand for stock market instruments. As was noted above, a relatively fixed supply of equity is necessary for the formation of a speculative bubble. Otherwise price pressure effects from the increased demand can be attenuated by a steady increase in the supply of equity. (This remains the case whether the asset prone to speculative bubbling is real estate, bonds or tulips.) To the extent that the supply of equity was actually shrinking during the 1982–99 period, the increase in prices was unprecedented and the empirical evidence thus far suggests that supply not only intensified the growing demand but impacted market valuations independent of demand-side effects. This implies that unpacking the run-up in US equity values requires more than a theory of 'irrational exuberance' or a falling risk premium.

SUMMARY

In the previous chapter we argued theoretically that the flow theory of equity price determination is well equipped to understand US stock market dynamics over the last two decades. Therefore, the hypothesis that shrinking supply and the growth of domestic and foreign demand has contributed to the run-up in equity values was held as a plausible explanation for the unprecedented boom. In this chapter we have shown empirically that the theory is at the very least consistent with the stylized facts, thus more clearly establishing a prima facie case for the hypothesis advanced in this study. The trends in the data, correlation coefficients and other pragmatic empirical evidence tend to favor the flow theory over the theories emanating from the theory of efficient capital markets. While the hypotheses that mutual fund and foreign capital flows as well as the reduction in the volume of equity outstanding appear legitimate, more sophisticated empirical work is necessary to resolve the qualifications we have discussed above. The next chapter of this book analyzes the growing demand and shrinking supply hypotheses in terms of more formal econometric analysis.

6. Empirical Analysis II: Formal Econometrics

INTRODUCTION

This chapter focuses on both the supply and demand sides of the excess demand curve for stock, investigating the role foreign capital flows, institutional investor net purchases and the decline in volume of corporate shares outstanding played in the recent run-up in US equity values. Specifically, we analyze the causal relationship between net purchases and issuance of corporate equity and stock returns, employing the vector autoregression (VAR) technique and auxiliary procedures as well as the structural model approach to control for fundamental economic forces. The supply and demand approach employed here is not novel and, in fact, is similar to Friedman's (1977, 1982) flow of funds methodology used to study the impact of changes in net purchases and net issues of corporate bonds by corporations and finance companies on long-term bond yields.

The econometric studies closely related to ours exploring the demand-side determinants of equity valuations are Edwards and Zhang (1998) and Warther (1995) – both surveyed in detail in Chapter 3. To the best of our knowledge this is one of the first studies to inquire into the supply side of the horizontal excess demand corollary. The other empirical study is Baker and Wurgler (1999) who find that the proportion of equity in total new issues (equity issue plus debt issue) has stronger predictive power for market index returns than the dividend yield. The authors document that stock returns tend to be high following years where the equity share of new issues is low. We go further to identify causality and assess whether the causal relationship is robust in the presence of variables that proxy for fundamental value of aggregate stock market indices looking at actual net issues of corporate equity.

The chapter proceeds as follows. Immediately below we describe the data and define the variables employed in the study. Second, we outline the Granger causality and VAR approach and present the empirical results. We find evidence of causality between net issues of corporate equity, demand-side flows and stock returns for the 1982–99 period on the basis of both bivariate and multivariate tests of Granger causality. Further, we uncover evidence from variance decompositions and impulse response functions that strongly support the hypothesis that supply changes are important for understanding US equity price dynamics during the 1982–99 period. Innovation accounting techniques also favor the contention that mutual fund flows and foreign portfolio flows explain market returns but the results are extremely sensitive to restrictions placed on the VAR model, although we hold them to be appropriate.

The fourth section presents the structural model technique and corroborates the results documented above. With the unrestricted reduced form (VAR) approach we cannot ascertain whether contemporaneous flows impact prices. Nor can we address whether the causal relationship between contemporaneous net issues, demand-side flows and market valuations is robust in the presence of proxies for fundamental value. Therefore, using a standard set of macroeconomic and financial variables popularized by Fama (1981, 1990) and Chen et al. (1986) to capture the fundamental value of the Standard and Poor's (S&P) Index, we re-examine the structural relationship between stock market returns and net purchases and issues of corporate equity. We find that, even when controlling for fundamentals, lagged net issues remain a significant explainer of equity returns and improves the R^2 obtained from regressions of stock returns on the variables assumed to determine the equilibrium level of broad stock market indices. Likewise, the ordinary least squares (OLS) and instrumental variables (IV) techniques indicate that contemporaneous mutual fund and foreign portfolio flows were important determinants driving US equity values during the 1982–99 boom. It must be noted that regardless of the econometric methodology employed we find no evidence that public pension fund or life insurance flows were instrumental in the run-up in stock price during the 1990s. Finally, we provide a summary and implications of our findings linking the latter to speculative market theory.

VARIABLES AND DATA DESCRIPTION

The financial and economic data used in this investigation are obtained from S&P/DRI database, Datastream and the Federal Reserve Board. All the variables and derived series employed in this chapter are defined in Table 6.1. We examine the causal relations between aggregate net issuance, foreign and institutional investor flows and broad stock market performance using quarterly data from 1953:1 to 1999:4. To these ends the S&P 500 Index is employed as a proxy for the stock market portfolio. Currently, the market value of S&P 500 stocks comprise roughly 75 per cent of the market value of all stock traded publicly on the major US exchanges and is therefore considered the broadest proxy for US stock market performance. In turn, stock returns are calculated as the quarterly change in the S&P Index plus the quarterly dividend yield. Mutual fund, public pension fund, life insurance and foreign portfolio and foreign direct investment (FDI) flows serve as our proxy for the increased demand for US corporate equity given that these sectors make up the bulk of the net purchases during the period under investigation.

Table 6.1 Glossary of primary variables

Symbol	Variable	Definition
	Basic series	
SP	Stock price index	S&P 500 Quarterly Index
DY	Dividend yield	S&P 500 Quarterly Dividend Yield
Issues	Net issues of domestic corporate equity	Dollar value of net new issues of domestic corporate equity. Quarterly Flow (QF)
Mutual	Mutual fund purchases of corporate equity	Dollar value of net purchases of domestic corporate equity. QF
Pubpen	Net purchases of corporate equities by state and local government retirement funds	Dollar value of net purchases of domestic corporate equity. QF
Life	Life insurance companies' purchases of corporate equity	Dollar value of net purchases of domestic corporate equity. QF
Portfolio	Foreign portfolio equity investment	Dollar value of net purchases of domestic corporate equity by ROW. QF
FDI	Foreign direct equity flows	Net purchases of equity by foreign agents holding more than 10% of the firm's equity. QF
IP	Industrial production	Monthly industrial production index
Profit	Corporate profits	Quarterly corporate profits after tax at book value
Tbill1m	1-month treasury bill rate	Monthly rates (annualized)
Tbill3m	3-month treasury bill rate	Monthly rates (annualized)
10yrB	10-year government bond yield	Monthly rates (annualized)
Fyaaac	High-grade bond yield	Moody's AAA bond yield (annualized)
Fybaac	Low-grade bond yield	Moody's BAA bond yield (annualized)

Table 6.1 (Continued)

Symbol	Variable	Definition
	Derived series	
Returns	Equity returns	$[SP(t) - SP(t-1)] + DY$
Uissues	Unexpected net issues of corporate equity	Generated as residuals from an AR(3) model fit to series Issues
Umutual	Unexpected mutual fund flows	Residuals from AR(5) model fit to Mutual
Upubpen	Unexpected public pension fund flows	Residuals from AR(7) model fit to Pubpen
Ulife	Unexpected life insurance flows	Residuals from AR(6) model fit to Life
Uportfolio	Unexpected foreign portfolio flows	Residuals from AR(7) model fit to Portfolio
Ufdi	Unexpected foreign direct equity flows	Residuals from AR(8) model fit to FDI
Totpen	Net purchases of corporate equities by all public and private pension funds	$Pubpen(t) + Privpen(t)$
Instinvest	Net purchases of corporate equities by all institutional investors	$Pubpen(t) + Privpen(t) + Mutual(t) + Life(t)$
QIP	Quarterly change in industrial production	First difference of IP
Qprofit	Quarterly change in after tax profits	First difference of Profit
Term	Term structure or term premium	$10yrb(t) - Tbill1m(t-1)$
Risk	Default spread or risk spread	Fybaac - fyaaac

Notes: *Includes other insurance companies and closed-end funds.

Source: Federal Reserve Board, Datastream and S&P/DRI Database.

The question of whether supply and demand changes impact prices when controlling for fundamentals is made difficult by the fact that the true worth of a company's shares are unknowable. The macro-oriented approach permits us to focus on the issue of broad market valuation, thereby avoiding complex micro-details such as industry risk, investment strategies across firms, and relative management efficiencies and technical expertise. This study closely follows Chen et al. (1986), Keim and Stambaugh (1986), Fama (1990) and Edwards and Zhang (1998) in our choice of variables to proxy for ex post, unobservable fundamentals. These variables, which include the term structure, default or risk spread, industrial production, and short-term interest rates were laid out in great detail in Chapter 3. Our extensive survey of variables was conducted in part so that readers themselves could judge how adequately they proxy for fundamental economic information.

There are two long-term aggregate corporate equity issues series reported by the Federal Reserve Board that serve as possible candidates for observing changes in supply. One is the monthly gross total of equity issues reported in the Federal Reserve Bulletin. Although the use of monthly data is appealing, this series does not net out share repurchases. Consequently, it is useless for our study since it obscures the fact that net issues were negative during the 1980s and 1990s. Therefore, we utilize the net issues of domestic corporate equity series reported in the Federal Reserves' Flow of Funds Accounts (Table F.213). Net issues are the dollar value of the quarterly increase in the amount of equity outstanding. As Baker and Wurgler (1999) point out, retirements due to merger activity comprise a significant portion of the flow of funds series. However, this is not a disadvantage for our purposes since we are concerned with the broad question of the effect of supply changes on stock prices, that is, supply changes due to mergers and takeovers as well as repurchases.

Tables F.107, F.117, F.120 and F.122 of the *Flow of Funds Accounts* provide information on the dollar value of the net purchases of corporate equity on behalf of domestic institutional investors and foreign investors. The Federal Reserve Board seasonally adjusts mutual fund net purchases using the X-11-ARIMA procedure. Net purchases of corporate equities by life insurance companies, public pension funds and the rest of the world exhibit no significant seasonality and are, therefore left unadjusted. We utilize Table F. 230, which decomposes FDI, to extract the equity component of FDI for our investigation. The net purchases of these sectors represent a significant amount of the inflow of funds into the stock market over the 1982–99 period. It should be emphasized that net issues of corporate equity represent flows in and out of the stock market as well. Thus, negative net issuance, or share retirements, is equivalent to net purchases as far as the impersonal pricing mechanism is concerned – both eventuate in an inflow of funds which may place upward pressure on equity prices. Our primary purpose is to investigate whether it is true that these flows help explain the bull market of the 1980s and 1990s.

These supply and demand flow series are significantly serially correlated and, thus, predictable. Therefore, autocorrelated flows in one period may generate expectations of future inflows into the market. To the extent that stock prices are forward looking, it could be argued that market prices may very well predict future inflows. Also recall that Keim and Stambaugh (1986) and Fama and French (1988, 1989) document evidence that expected returns vary over time (see Chapter 2). Therefore, it could also be the case that the trending component of net issues and demand flows and stock returns move together in a manner that induces correlation. It is then seemingly appropriate to strip away the correlation between these trending variables and time-varying returns to address the relationship cleanly in our investigation using OLS and the instrumental variables methodology.

Chen et al. (1986) set the standard by using the residuals from an autoregressive model on a particular explanatory variable to represent unanticipated movements in that series. The authors hold, 'the general impact of a failure to adequately filter out the expected movement in an independent variable is to introduce an errors-in-the-variables problem' (p. 386). Similarly, the predictable component is extracted from all the flow series to generate unexpected net issues and purchases for our investigation utilizing the OLS and IV approaches. Both Warther (1995) and Edwards and Zhang (1998) proceed similarly with this 'two-step procedure' in their investigations of the impact of mutual fund flows on asset returns.

The data-generating process for the supply series was identified as an AR (3) model using the standard Box–Jenkins modeling procedure, over-fitting a univariate autoregressive model and paring down to the appropriate lag length using tau-statistics, Akaike's Information Criterion and ensuring the residuals from the resulting regressions were white noise. Portmanteau tests on residuals from the AR (3) process suggested white noise and over-fitting to an AR (4) model resulted in deterioration in Akaike's Information Criterion. Consequently, unexpected net issues, Uissue, are estimated as the residuals from a regression of net issues on three lags of itself. Likewise, utilizing Akaike's information criterion and tests for white noise, we identified life insurance, mutual fund and public pension fund flows as AR (5), AR (6) and AR (7) processes, respectively. The resultant series of unexpected flows are labeled Umutual, Ulife and Upubpen accordingly. The data-generating process for foreign portfolio flows and foreign direct equity flows were best captured by AR (7) and AR (6) models, respectively and the outputted residuals were used to make up unexpected portfolio flows, Uportfolio, and unexpected foreign direct equity flows, Ufdi.

GRANGER CAUSALITY AND VAR ANALYSIS

Bivariate Tests of Causality

Granger causality analysis investigates causal relationships specifically by examining the forecasting power between variables (Granger, 1969). The test involves determining whether lagged values of variable x improve the prediction of y that is obtained from using lagged values of variable y itself. Thus, series x_t is said to 'Granger-cause' series y_t, if lagged variables of x_t enter significantly into a regression of y_t on lagged values of y_t and x_t or following Hsiao (1979), if the inclusion of x_t improves the final prediction error. In turn, the question of whether institutional investor equity purchases, foreign equity flows and net issues of corporate equity Granger-cause stock returns (or vice versa) can be determined by evaluating the null hypotheses, $B(L)x_{t-1} = 0$ and $B(L)y_{t-1} = 0$, in the following system of equations:

$$y_t = \beta_0 + A(L)y_{t-1} + B(L)x_{t-1} = 0 + \varepsilon_t \qquad \text{(a)}$$

$$x_t = \beta_0 + A(L)x_{t-1} + B(L)y_{t-1} = 0 + \varepsilon_t \qquad \text{(b)}$$

where $A(L)$ and $B(L)$ are lag operators, y_t denotes stock returns and x_t represents net issues (Issue) or either of the demand-side flow variables (Mutual, Life, Pubpen, Portfolio, FDI) consecutively. (See Table 6.1 for a description of the variables.) Following this methodology the causal relations between the fundamental variables and stock returns can be studied as well. Evaluated on the basis of a standard F test, $B(L)x_{t-1} \neq 0$ implies a variable x is at the very least a proxy for other unobservable (or uninvestigated) Granger causal forces. In turn, if the null hypothesis is rejected for equation (a) and stock returns do not Granger-cause net issues (or institutional investor and foreign flows) the latter are said to be exogenous with respect to the former.

Granger's (1969) method of examining causality tests involves little more than ensuring the stationarity of the variables under consideration and selecting the appropriate lag length, $A(L)$ and $B(L)$. To properly conduct unit root tests for stationarity we first attempted to uncover the true data-generating process of the individual time series in question (discussed above). We then performed tests for the presence of unit roots for each of the series following Dickey and Fuller (1979) and Phillips and Perron (1988). Table 6.2 presents the results of Augmented Dickey–Fuller (ADF) and Phillips–Perron (PP) tests for stationarity for 1953–99 and 1982–99. By both standards the stock returns are found to be stationary across all time periods.[1] Contrarily, the US industrial production index, profits and the three–month treasury bill are found to contain a unit root in all periods by both criteria. Thus for the remainder of this book we utilize the first differences of these variables.

The ADF procedure suggests that for the periods 1953–99 and 1953–81 (not reported), the null hypothesis of a unit root can be rejected at 5 per cent for net issues and all flow series in levels with the exception of public pension and mutual fund flows. While we could reject the hypothesis that the mutual fund series contained a unit root at the 10 per cent level of significance, we could not do so for the public pension fund series. Tau-statistics from PP tests confirm these findings with the exception that mutual fund flows are found to contain a unit root while pension fund flows are found to be a stationary process.

Table 6.2: Augmented Dickey–Fuller and Phillips–Perron tests for stationarity

Variable	ADF-Statistic	Lags	Phillips–Perron
1953–99			
Issues	− 3.48**	3	− 7.37***
Mutual	1.87*	5	− 1.06
Pubpen	− 1.99	7	− 5.06***
Life	− 2.56**	6	− 1.66*
Portfolio	2.32**	7	− 3.75***
ΔMutual	− 7.46***	5	− 23.24***
ΔPubpen	− 6.58***	7	− 28.87***
ΔLife	− 4.39***	6	− 18.70***
ΔPortfolio	− 9.54***	7	− 18.42***
Returns	3.57**	4	− 11.65***
IP	− 1.52	4	1.11
QIP	− 5.61***	3	− 9.13***
Profit	1.86*	8	3.65***
Qprofit	− 4.68***	8	− 11.61***
Term	− 4.27***	6	− 5.57***
Risk	3.78**	1	− 6.56***
Tbill3m	− 2.23	4	− 2.56
1982–99			
Issues	− 2.02	3	− 4.19***
Mutual	1.15	5	− 1.86*
PubPen	− 2.43	7	− 6.77***
Life	1.21	6	− 0.51
Portfolio	1.42	7	− 2.31**
FDI	1.41	6	5.53***
ΔMutual	− 4.56***	4	− 14.11***
ΔPubpen	− 3.97***	7	− 18.42***
ΔLife	− 2.67***	6	− 11.64***
ΔPortfolio	− 5.78***	7	− 9.09***
ΔFDI	− 1.80*	8	− 26.78***
Returns	1.34	4	− 5.96***
IP	1.28	4	2.12
QIP	− 3.34**	3	− 6.25***
Profit	− 2.14	4	− 2.10
Qprofit	− 4.65***	4	− 7.80***
Term	− 2.71*	6	− 2.74*
Risk	− 3.19**	1	− 2.98**
Tbill3m	− 2.34	4	− 2.33

Notes: Tests for stationarity of the individual time series. See Table 6.1 for a full description of the variables. Δ denotes the first difference of the series. (***) Significant at the 1% level, (**) 5% level, (*) 10% level.

However, for the 1982–99 period we cannot reject non-stationarity at the 10 per cent level for any of the series on the basis of the ADF testing procedure, suggesting that these variables be treated as difference stationary processes. PP tests, on the other hand, lead to a rejection of the null hypothesis at the 1 per cent level of significance for net issues and all demand-side flow series with the exception of life insurance company net purchases. Given that the PP procedure corrects t-statistics for autocorrelation and heteroskedasticity in the residuals it has some immediate appeal. However, it is difficult to reconcile the PP test results with those from the ADF procedure and the fact that the autocorrelation functions for the variables in question die down relatively slowly. We therefore follow the directives of the ADF tests, treating net issues, mutual fund, life insurance, public pension fund and foreign equity flows as non-stationary (Enders, 1995, pp. 260–61). The first differences (Δ) of these variables, which are found to be stationary across all time periods, are consequently utilized in our inquiry. Because the net issues are negative over most of the 1982–99 period, first differences of this series are uninformative. For completeness then, we utilize the unexpected net issues. With the trend component removed this series becomes stationary across all time periods by PP and ADF criterion.

Tables 6.3a–6.3c presents the results of the Granger causality tests characterized by equations (a) through (b), treating stock returns and unexpected net issues and flows symmetrically. Tables 6.3a and 6.3b document the F-statistics and significance levels from tests of the joint hypothesis $B(L)x_{t-1}$, $B(L)y_{t-1}$ for 1953–99, 1953–81 and 1982–99. Table 6.3a includes the results of Granger causality tests between returns and interest rates, the risk and term spreads, profits and industrial production (fundamentals). Table 6.3c summarizes the results of the causality tests in a succinct fashion for the relevant flow variables and market returns. Several different lag specifications were investigated (one through eight). For the entire sample and each of the sub-periods we report only one specification unless the results were sensitive to the choice of lag length. In general, since the test of Granger causality is an investigation of all relevant, prior information, longer lag specifications are preferable. We would expect that equity issuance responds to market valuations with a lag since the issuing of new shares is subject to the corporate decision-making process. Correspondingly, changes in net issuance of equity can have substantial effects on market valuations in subsequent periods as the demand for equity reconciles with changes in supply.

Do Unexpected Net Issues Granger-cause Returns?

For the entire sample, 1953–99, evidence of mutual Granger causality between stock returns and unexpected net equity issuance is found. In dissecting the 1953–99 period we find that the relationship is primarily driven by the 1982–99 sub-period. As Table 6.3b reports, there is no evidence of Granger causality in either direction for 1953–81 at 2 and 4–8 lags. However, at 3 lags the null hypothesis that returns do not cause equity issues is rejected. Regardless of the lag length selected net issues exhibit no predictability for stock returns. In contrast, the null hypothesis that issues do not cause returns is decisively rejected for the 1982–99 period. Causality tests also indicate a highly significant F-statistic for the null hypothesis: returns do not cause unexpected net issues. This would appear to suggest that the predictive power of issues for stock returns (and vice-versa) is driven to a large extent by the strength of the relationship during the 1982–99 interval.

Table 6.3 Bivariate Granger causality tests

(a) Test I

Null hypothesis	F-statistics and significance levels	
1953–99		
	4 lags	6 lags
Uissues does not cause Returns	8.71***	
Returns does not cause Uissues	26.42***	
ΔMutual does not cause Returns	14.37***	
Returns does not cause ΔMutual	2.37**	
ΔPubpen does not cause Returns[+]	1.34	
Returns does not cause ΔPubpen	1.33	
ΔLife does not cause Returns	4.45***	3.74***
Returns does not cause ΔLife	1.36	2.39**
ΔPortfolio does not cause Returns	5.60***	
Returns does not cause ΔPortfolio	2.49**	
ΔIP does not cause Returns	0.20	
Returns does not cause ΔIP	4.60***	
ΔProfit does not cause Returns	0.93	
Returns does not cause ΔProfit	4.64***	
ΔTbill3m does not cause Returns	0.52	
Returns does not cause ΔTbill3m	0.10	
ΔRisk does not cause Returns	2.59**	
Returns does not cause ΔRisk	1.54	
ΔTerm does cause not Returns	0.040	
Returns does not cause ΔTerm	0.23	

Table 6.3 (Continued)

(b) Test II

Null hypothesis	F-statistics and significance levels	
1953–81		
	3 lags	4 lags
Uissues does not cause Returns	0.14	
Returns does not cause Uissues	2.49*	1.90
	4 lags	6 lags
ΔMutual does not cause Returns	1.77	
Returns does not cause ΔMutual	2.26*	1.66
ΔPubpen does not cause Returns	1.47	2.43**
Returns does not cause ΔPubpen	3.52***	3.61***
ΔLife does not cause Returns	0.67	1.88*
Returns does not cause ΔLife	0.37	0.48
ΔPortfolio does not cause Returns	0.50	2.31**
Returns does not cause ΔPortfolio	2.19*	3.14***
1982–99		
	3 lags	
Uissues does not cause Returns	8.26***	
Returns does not cause Uissues	10.67***	
	4 lags	7 lags
ΔMutual does not cause Returns	5.87***	
Returns does not cause ΔMutual	0.99	
ΔPubpen does not cause Returns[+]	0.68	
Returns does not cause ΔPubpen	0.57	
ΔLife does not cause Returns	1.74	
Returns does not cause ΔLife	0.42	
ΔPortfolio does not cause Returns	1.92	3.25***
Returns does not cause ΔPortfolio	0.88	1.22
ΔFDI does not cause Returns	4.09***	
Returns does not cause ΔFDI	4.58***	

Notes: Δ denotes the first difference of the variable in question. See Table 6.1 for a full description of the variables. ***Significant at the 1% level, **Significant at the 5% level, *Significant at 10% level. [+]Results hold for total pension fund flows (Totpen) as well.

Table 6.3c Summary table for bivariate Granger causality tests

	Issues and flows cause returns?	Returns cause issues and flows?
1953–99	Yes Net issues→	Yes →Net issues
	Yes Mutual fund flows→	Yes →Mutual fund flows
	Yes Life insurance flows→	Yes* →Life insurance flows
	No Pension fund flows→	No →Pension fund flows
	Yes Portfolio flows→	Yes →Portfolio flows
1953–81	No Net issues→	Yes* →Net issues
	No Mutual fund flows→	Yes* →Mutual fund flows
	Yes* Life insurance flows→	No →Life insurance flows
	Yes* Pension fund flows→	Yes →Pension fund flows
	Yes* Portfolio flows→	Yes →Portfolio flows
1982–99	Yes Net issues→	Yes →Net issues
	Yes Mutual fund flows→	No →Mutual fund flows
	No Life insurance flows→	No →Life insurance flows
	No Pension fund flows→	No →Pension fund flows
	Yes* Portfolio flows→	No →Portfolio flows
	Yes FDI equity flows→	Yes→FDI equity flows

Notes: → denotes Granger causality, No implies no causal relationship while Yes implies a causal relationship exists. Asterisk (*) implies the relationship exists but is dependent on the lag specification.

There could be several reasons for these findings. One plausible explanation is that there is mutual causality but the lack of fluctuation in the net issues series during the 1953–81 period leads to a lack of information with which to assess the predictive power of supply changes for market returns. However, merger and takeover activity stepped up significantly during the 1980s and SEC Rule 10b-18 liberated stock repurchasing corporations from the threat of investigation for price manipulation causing significant variability in the supply of equity. It is quite conceivable, moreover, that the effect of stock market performance on equity issuance has changed significantly. As noted in Chapter 4, important institutional changes such as investors' perceptions of equity retirements enabled by debt and the payment of stock options resulted in a dramatic shift in the relationship between stock returns and net issuance.

It is also quite plausible that the impact of equity issuances on market returns cannot be properly gauged by investigations on quarterly data since net inflows are quickly impounded in prices. Thus, it could be argued that higher frequency data (monthly or weekly) might allow us to examine more properly Granger causality. However, such reasoning suggests that the impact of shrinking supply on stock market valuations during 1982–99 is so strong that it overcomes the possible bias inherent in using lower frequency data, thus strengthening the contention that net inflows effectively set prices. Nevertheless, the evidence from Granger causality analysis is consistent with the notion that net issuance has not historically been important for asset pricing but has had a significant impact on returns during the 1982–99 stock market boom.

Do Institutional Investor and Foreign Equity Flows Granger-cause Returns?

Table 6.3a indicates that for the entire sample, 1953–99, a mutual Granger-causal relationship between stock returns and life insurance and mutual funds flows exists. However, the null hypothesis that changes in public pension fund purchases do not Granger-cause returns cannot be rejected. In contradistinction, as Table 6.3b illustrates, evidence of mutual causality is found between pension fund flows and S&P returns during the 1953–81 sub-period. The weak causal relationship is one way from life insurance net purchases to market returns while the joint null hypothesis cannot be rejected for mutual funds and returns regardless of the lag length selected. When referencing the 1982–99 period we find evidence that *only* mutual fund flows have predictive power for stock returns. Again these results are summarized in Table 6.3c. The implication here is that while mutual fund flows are not a significant explainer of market returns for the 1953–81 period, the results are consistent with the hypothesis that the recent stock market boom was driven in part by this sector of the economy. These results conflict with the findings of Edwards and Zhang (1998) who upon finding no evidence of Granger causality running mutual fund flow to returns for the 1990–96 interval conclude that 'recent run-up in stock prices cannot be attributed to the rapid growth of equity mutual funds' (p. 97).

On the other hand it would appear that life insurance and pension fund flows, though demonstrating predictability for market returns in earlier periods, do not bear a relationship with the bull market of the 1980s and 1990s. These results are not surprising, given the small size of the correlation coefficients between these variables and changes in the S&P Index presented in the previous chapter. These findings, although suggesting that pension fund flows do not explain the 1982–99 bubble, do support the general contention that portfolio shifts matter. However, the conclusions regarding the 1982–99 period may be premature given that the Granger causality analysis does not permit an inquiry into whether contemporaneous institutional investor flows increase the predictability of market returns.

The results would then imply that the relationship between mutual fund net purchases and S&P returns is especially strong during the 1982–99 period. It should be well noted that no evidence of a Granger causal relationship running from returns to any of these domestic flows is found for the boom period.

Although the results are not reported, we did run Granger causality tests for total pension fund flows, total institutional investor fund flows and returns. Recall from Chapter 5 that private pension fund flows into the stock market were generally negative from 1982 to 1999. Thus, when combined with the positive net purchases of public pension funds the result is a net series that suggests a small flow of funds into the stock market on behalf of these institutional investors up until 1994 and outflow thereafter. It is not surprising, then, that we found no evidence of a Granger causal relationship between total pension fund flows and returns for the period corresponding to the recent bull market. However, we were able to reject the null hypothesis that total institutional flows (insurance company, pension and mutual funds) do not Granger-cause market returns for 1953–99 and the 1982–99 sub-period. As was expected the F-statistics were significantly smaller than those for the null hypothesis that mutual funds do not cause returns since total institutional flows includes a component (pension funds and life insurance companies) that are found to have no predictability for stock market returns.

The results for foreign equity flows into the US economy are consistent across all the relevant periods. For 1953–99, 1982–99 and 1953–81 the null hypothesis that foreign portfolio flows do not Granger-cause S&P stock returns is rejected. Alternatively, no evidence that stock returns cause portfolio flows is uncovered for the 1982–99 period. Thus, Tables 6.3a and 6.3b lends credence to the claim that foreign savings influence US equity prices. Here we also find evidence of a mutual Granger causality between the equity component of FDI and US stock market performance. Recall that prior to 1982 the Federal Reserve Board's flow of funds accounts records the equity component of FDI as zero, such that only Table 6.3b, which reports the results of causality test for the 1982–99 interval, is relevant here. It appears, then, that one needs to look beyond foreign portfolio flows to adequately assess the hypothesis that foreigners have aided in the run-up in US equity values.

Multivariate Tests of Causality and Innovation Accounting

The supposition that net issuance, mutual fund net purchases and foreign equity flows are proxies for the effect of other more important variables or that they move together with stock returns in response to an outside variable is also consistent with the results of the Granger causality analysis. On this note, Sims (1980) and others have argued that bivariate causality tests may not be reliable since other potentially important explanatory variables are not explicitly considered within the framework. In contrast, the multivariate approach provides unbiased tests of Granger causality and is part of the larger VAR procedure and innovation accounting that serves as an alternative to the structural modeling approach. It therefore makes senses to investigate these variables concurrently with other variables that may influence them and the equilibrium value of stock prices.

The VAR methodology advanced by Sims (1980) works with unrestricted reduced forms, treating all variables as potentially endogenous. It imposes no a priori structure on the data, instead allowing the existing causal relations between the variables to emerge from the statistical procedure itself. In short, each of the variables is written as a linear function of its own lagged values and lagged values of the other variables included in the system. More formally, the generalized VAR process can be written:

$$\Phi(B)Y_t = \varepsilon_t$$

where Y_t is a k × 1 vector of constants, $\Phi(B)$ is a k × k matrix of coefficients and ε_t is a vector of normally distributed, random shocks assumed to be white noise. Granger causality is said to exist within this framework if the corresponding elements off the diagonal of matrix $\Phi(B)$ (which characterize the relationship between a variable and lagged values of another) are non-zero.

It is important to note that the VAR process has the following moving average representation:

$$Y_t = \mu_t + C(s)\varepsilon_{t-i}$$

where μ_t is a k × 1 vector of the means of the constants in vector Y, $C(s)$ is an orthogonalized k × k matrix of errors and ε_{t-i} is a vector of orthogonalized residuals (Enders, 1995, p. 306). The vector moving average (VMA) process, then, expresses current values of the variables in terms of current and lagged values of the error vector. Effectively, vector ε_{t-i} is a vector of innovations and $C(s)$ is a matrix of impact multipliers. Thus, upon restricting the error matrix, we can trace the effects of shocks or innovations to one variable through the system and examine its impact on each of the other included variables. More succinctly, impulse response functions can be obtained to examine the dynamic reaction of each of the endogenous variables to shocks to the system.

Similarly, the identified VAR system, Y_t, can be exploited to produce a forecast error variance decomposition of each variable. Variance decompositions involve the calculation of the proportion of variation in one variable that is attributed to its own innovations and that which is initiated by the other variables in the system. More formally we write:

$$\Sigma_{s=0...t-1}\, c_{ij}(s)^2 / \Sigma_{j=1...k}\Sigma_{s=0...t-1}\, c_{ij}(s)^2$$

where $c_{ij}(s)$ is the (i,j) component of the k × k orthogonalized matrix $\mathbf{C}(s)$ and thus, the dynamic response of variable i to innovations in j. For the VAR with k variables, the equation above gives the variance of t step-ahead forecasting errors of i explained by shocks to variable j. Collectively impulse response functions and variance decompositions are labeled innovation accounting given their exclusive assessment of the dynamic interactions initiated by innovations to the variables within the VAR system.

We employ the VAR modeling procedure and innovation accounting techniques in our investigation of the impact of shrinking supply and growing demand on stock market performance. The sample period for the study is the same as above, 1953:1–1999:4, and sub-periods 1953:1–1981:4 and 1982:1–1999:4.[2] There is a great deal of contention as to whether or not the variables under consideration need to be made stationary to obtain reliable results from the VAR methodology (see Enders, 1995, p. 301). Sims (1980) argues that the purpose of the technique is not to estimate parameters but to uncover relationships between variables by examining their co-movements. Consequently, each variable included in the system 'should mimic the true data generating process'. This means that differencing for stationarity purposes is akin to discarding useful information. For this reason we first work with all variables in levels (before moving on), estimating a truly unrestricted VAR without consideration as to the possibility of unit roots in all three periods.

We initiated the examination with three variables – the S&P Index in levels, the nominal three-month t-bill rate, and corporate profits after taxes. Profits and interest rates are included as the fundamental factors that influence equity price changes. Traditionally, econometric studies of stock price changes using the VAR methodology utilize industrial production as a proxy for general macroeconomic activity (Lee, 1992; Gjerde and Saettem, 1999). We estimated the model with industrial production in lieu of after-tax profits, and the differences in the results were insignificant. As to be expected from our Granger causality tests, lagged values of profits, industrial production and the interest rate variable exhibit no explanatory power for stock prices. The results are unchanged when we estimate the system in first differences. This emphasizes the forward-looking nature of stock prices with respect to future developments on the real side of the economy and that it is impossible to control for fundamentals utilizing the unrestricted VAR methodology. Additionally, the S&P Index is found to be an $I(0)$ process while both profits and industrial production are $I(1)$ processes prohibiting the exploitation of a co-integrating relationship between these variables.

However, we can inquire into whether the predictability of net issuance of corporate equity and the flow variables are robust when considered concomitantly. To these ends we estimated a four-variable VAR model to examine the dynamic interaction between mutual fund net purchases of corporate equity (Mutual), foreign portfolio flows (Portfolio), equity retirements (Issue) and the measure of stock market performance. Again we initially ran the VAR in levels (Model 1a not shown). However, for consistency with the bivariate Granger causality tests conducted earlier, we also estimate the VAR model in first differences with stock returns in lieu of the market index to conduct multivariate tests for predictability (Model 2a). Because the data for FDI equity flows are not available prior to 1982, we re-estimate a five-variable model for the 1982–99 period (Model 2b). We temporarily omit life insurance and public pension fund purchases of corporate equity from our consideration since both variables failed bivariate tests of Granger causality and, like profits and interest rates, simply consume degrees of freedom, offering no additional explanatory power for market returns.

Empirical Results

The appropriate models were determined by initially estimating a VAR (10) model and then varying the lag structure to investigate the superiority of the different specifications. To these purposes we used Akaike's Information Criterion and likelihood ratio tests to judge the suitability of the various models. In general, the results for Models 1a and 1b suggested that VAR (3) and VAR (4) models were the best specifications. While Akaike's Information Criterion favored the former, we could not reject the null hypothesis that the restricted model characterized the interrelationship best. However, the residuals from the estimated model with 3 lags were not white noise, which lends support for the VAR (4) model. By the same criteria the data suggested a VAR (3) specification for Models 2a and 2b, although the selection of this lag length over a slightly longer one was rather arbitrary.

The results for the multivariate Granger causality tests from Models 2a and 2b are documented in Table 6.4.[3] The results from Model 2a confirm our earlier findings that net equity issues, mutual fund flows and foreign portfolio flows Granger-cause market returns during both the 1953:1–1999:4 and 1982:1–1999:4 periods but no evidence of a Granger causal relationship in either direction is found for 1953:1–1981:4. Employing the VAR (3) model on the latter sub-period yields results that indicate net issuance and the demand-side flow variables have little explanatory power for S&P returns. This once more emphasizes that the relationships are driven primarily by the strength of the association in the most recent time period. However, when we introduce foreign direct equity flows into the system (Model 2b) the null hypothesis that mutual fund flows do not cause stock returns cannot be rejected for 1982:1–1999:4. Instead, FDI equity flows are found to Granger-cause returns along with foreign portfolio flows and net issues.

Why the Bubble Burst

Table 6.4 Multivariate Granger causality tests

Null hypothesis	F-statistics and significance levels	
1953–99		
	Model 2a	Model 2b
Issues does not cause Returns	7.37***	
Mutual does not cause Returns	2.88*	
Portfolio does not cause Returns	3.33***	
1953–81		
Issues does not cause Returns	0.40	
Mutual does not cause Returns	0.29	
Portfolio does not cause Returns	1.38	
1982–99		
Issues does not cause Returns	2.94**	2.74**
Mutual does not cause Returns	2.28*	1.63
Portfolio does not cause Returns	2.32*	3.48**
FDI does not cause Returns[+]		5.00***

Notes: Results of the four-variable VAR (3) and [+]five-variable VAR (3) models in first differences. See table 6.1 for a full description of the variables. ***Significant at the 1% level, **Significant at the 5% level, *Significant at 10% level.

The impulse response functions and variance decompositions illustrated in Figures 6.1a and 6.1b and Tables 6.5a and 6.5b shed more light on these issues. Here, the dynamic responses of returns to innovations in the other variables included in the system are traced over a two and a half-year interval. In order to execute innovation accounting we must identify the primitive (structural) form of the VAR (3) model. This is impossible unless we are willing to impose six restrictions on the model ($n^2 - n/2$). Therefore, for identification purposes we ordered the variables in the models as follows: mutual fund flows, foreign portfolio flows, stock returns and net issues. Note well, this Choleski decomposition gives causal priority to stock returns over net issues but demand-side flows over stock returns as mandated by the large F-statistics in prior Granger causality tests. Changing the manner in which the errors are orthogonalized, giving priority to net issues, yielded results that suggested that the response of stock returns to innovations in net issues was slightly stronger. However, the results for foreign portfolio and mutual fund flows are not robust to all other alternative rankings of the variables. Giving causal priority to stock returns over portfolio and mutual flows significantly reduces the predictive power of these variables on stock returns.

As Panels A through C of Figure 6.1a illustrate, shocks to net issues have a strong negative impact on the time path of stock returns for both 1953:1–1999:9 and 1982:1–1999:9, albeit the response is significantly stronger during the latter. Here, a one standard deviation shock to net issues elicits a dynamic response of roughly –8 standard deviations in stock returns over three quarters with the effects lasting over two years. Again the 1953–81 period, represented in Panel C of Figure 6.1a, indicates that innovations in net issues of corporate equity have a negligible impact on stock market returns. The figure also shows that innovations to mutual fund flows have an even greater impact on the time path of returns in both the 1953–99 and 1982–99 periods. In the later period, a one standard deviation shock to mutual flows causes stock returns to jump up 16 units. There is evidence of price reversal and the effects are negligible after one year. However, as Panel C shows, the dynamic response of returns to shocks in mutual fund flows is significantly smaller for 1953–81 with the effects disappearing after two quarters. Likewise, innovations to foreign portfolio flows cause a large change in the time path of returns for 1982–99. The response on returns when traced through the system is slightly smaller during the 1953–99 period. Again we find evidence of price reversal and the effect peters out after five quarters. During the 1953–81 period innovations to portfolio flows have a negligible impact on S&P returns, again indicating that the relationship is driven by the period corresponding to the recent boom.

These results validate our earlier findings but it must be underscored that when we alter the ordering of the variables only the results pertaining to net issues and returns remain consistent with the flow theory of equity price determination. Given that it is possible that flows have a contemporaneous impact on returns and vice versa, neither ordering of the variables with respect to foreign portfolio flows, mutual fund flows and returns is particularly attractive. Thus, assuming that shocks to stock market returns have no contemporaneous effect on mutual and foreign portfolio flows may be an extremely strong assumption. As opponents of the VAR methodology note, imposing such 'incredible identifying restrictions' contradicts the principal purpose of the reduced form approach (Enders, 1995, p. 308). That is, 'how can a change in one variable have no effect on another variable in a simultaneous system?' (Kennedy, 1993, p. 163). Nevertheless, there is no way to circumvent imposing restrictions in order to achieve identification. We therefore give causal priority to flows in the system since bivariate and multivariate Granger causality tests (reported above) support this Cheolski decomposition.

(a) Model 2a

Panel A 1953–99

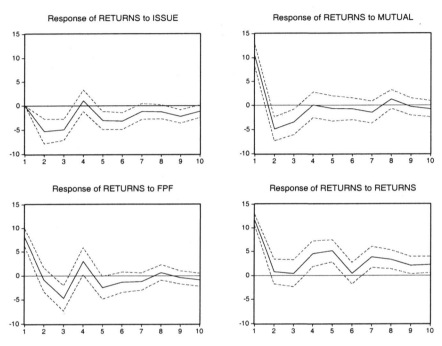

Figure 6.1: Impulse response functions

Panel B 1982–1999

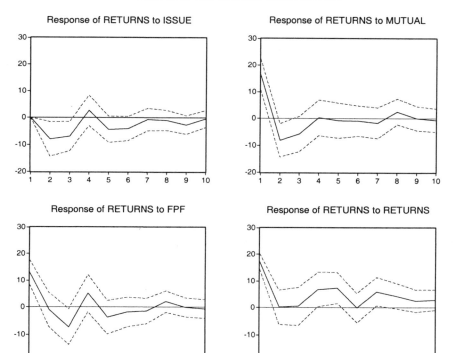

Panel C 1953–1981

Response to One S.D. Innovations ± 2 S.E.

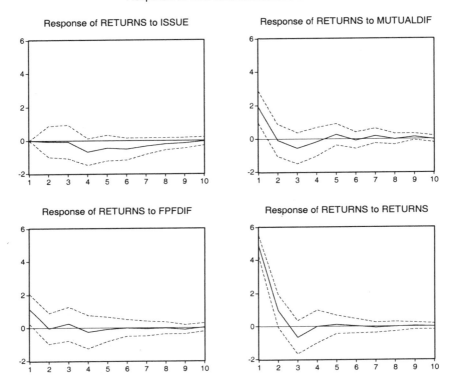

Notes: Graphs of the impulse functions for S&P returns after shocking either net issues of corporate equity (Issues), mutual fund flows (Mutual) or foreign portfolio flows (Portfolio). The impulse response is calculated from the parameters estimated by Model 2a and obtained by shocking variable *i* and tracing the impact through the VAR (4) system on returns using the Choleski decomposition ordering Mutual, Portfolio, Returns, Issues. The effects are traced over 10 quarters (two and a half years). The dashed lines represent the 90% confidence interval.

(b) Model 2b

1982–99

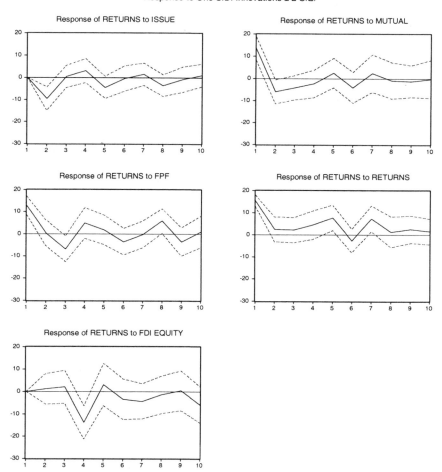

Response to One S.D. Innovations ± 2 S.E.

Notes: Graphs of the impulse functions for S&P returns after shocking either net issues of corporate equity (Issues), mutual fund flows (Mutual), foreign portfolio flows (Portfolio) or FDI equity flows (FDI Equity). The impulse response is calculated from the parameters estimated by Model 2b and obtained by shocking variable *i* and tracing the impact through the VAR (5) system on returns using the Choleski decomposition ordering Mutual, Portfolio, FDI Equity, Returns, Issues. The effects are traced over 10 quarters (two and a half years). The dashed lines represent the 90% confidence interval.

Table 6.5a, which presents the results of the variance decompositions for S&P stock market returns, yields another look at the dynamic interactions discussed above. As to be expected by our analysis via impulse response functions, the percentage of forecasting error variance in stock returns explained by the other variables in the system is substantial. Even with the restrictions we have placed on the error matrix that gives a low priority to net issues, innovations to net issues explain a significant portion of the forecasting error variance at periods three through ten (11–12 per cent) for 1953:1–1999:4 and 1982:1–1999:4. Of course, this does not pertain to the 1953:1–1981 interval where, even in period 10, innovations in net issues account for only 3.6 per cent of the variation in stock returns.

The innovation accounting technique suggests that an even larger proportion of the forecast error variance in stock returns is explained by mutual fund flows. Table 6.5a reveals that between periods 1 and 10 over 25 per cent and as much as 36 per cent of the movement in stock returns is due to innovations to mutual fund net flows during the 1982–99 and 1953–99 periods. Even during the 1953–81 period, flows from these particular institutional investors account for between 12 and 13 per cent of the variation in market returns. To the contrary, foreign portfolio flows are found to account for an insignificant amount of the 1953–81 quarterly variation in stock market returns. However, during 1953–99 and 1982–99 these flows explain a greater proportion of the movement in stock returns than net issues but less than mutual fund flows. The evidence here contradicts the findings of Tesar and Werner (1995) who find that US purchases of equity in foreign developing markets are positively associated with returns while foreign purchases of US equity are not related to the US market index. Nevertheless the same caveats apply regarding the Choelski decomposition used to identify the VAR (4) model as was previously discussed with respect to our impulse response functions.

Figure 6.1b and Table 6.5b illustrate the impulse response function and variance decomposition from the five variable VAR (3) model (Model 2b) estimated to assess the contribution of FDI equity flows to the US stock market boom. The impulse response function suggests a small positive contribution of shocks to FDI flows on changes in the time path of quarterly stock returns over three periods. However, the effect turns strongly negative in period four before petering out in periods five through nine. It is difficult to interpret the fact that net purchases of corporate equity by foreigners who own more than 10 per cent of a particular firm has such a large negative impact on stock returns in later periods. Nevertheless, vector decompositions also suggest that innovations to FDI equity flows explain a significant amount of the variation in stock returns. In fact, the inclusion of these flows increase the amount of variation explained by foreign portfolio flows while decreasing that amount explained by mutual fund net purchases.

Table 6.5 Variance decompositions

(a) Model 2a

Period	S.E.	Issue	Mutual	Portfolio	Returns
Panel A: 1953–99					
1	11.79749	0.00000	36.65772	22.97188	40.37040
2	16.21457	7.29746	38.78301	19.61799	34.30154
3	18.12994	11.06964	36.91989	22.27118	29.73929
4	18.97843	10.90466	34.17218	23.10539	31.81778
5	21.17191	11.71084	31.66475	22.52938	34.09503
6	21.54788	12.89160	31.18756	22.41082	33.51002
7	22.55208	12.48717	30.36944	21.81631	35.32708
8	22.92157	12.26350	30.14522	21.61693	35.97435
9	23.31612	12.70466	29.82591	21.38837	36.08106
10	23.65342	12.62522	29.64998	21.27166	36.45314
Panel B: 1953–81					
1	1.014528	0.000000	12.86361	4.446071	82.69032
2	1.325539	0.015388	12.48679	4.313109	83.18471
3	1.556966	0.033279	13.20372	4.399399	82.36361
4	1.655675	1.554966	13.06843	4.532943	80.84366
5	1.685927	2.198939	13.17124	4.512042	80.11778
6	1.697592	3.046524	13.07725	4.472161	79.40406
7	1.700779	3.399607	13.12320	4.459545	79.01764
8	1.702769	3.527289	13.10605	4.454639	78.91202
9	1.703860	3.591043	13.13513	4.481165	78.79266
10	1.704101	3.595754	13.13513	4.483465	78.78565
Panel C: 1982–1999					
1	7.56295	0.00000	34.96406	20.45959	44.57636
2	10.29339	7.79360	36.38690	17.65965	38.15985
3	11.61509	12.55517	34.11968	20.47116	32.85400
4	12.25152	11.95911	31.79996	21.13593	35.10500
5	13.76823	12.82968	29.16296	20.59462	37.41275
6	14.09836	14.48757	28.53989	20.45191	36.52064
7	14.85018	14.20474	27.86506	19.96891	37.96129
8	15.21723	14.10611	27.41274	19.51717	38.96398
9	15.57430	14.75575	26.95159	19.20157	39.09108
10	15.90811	14.78314	26.68156	19.07126	39.46403

Notes: The forecast error variance is computed using the VAR (3) system where Returns, Issues, Mutual and Portfolio are S&P 500 returns, net issues of corporate equity, mutual fund flows and foreign portfolio flows, respectively. The table shows the percentage of two-year forecast error variance of variable i explained by variable j.

Table 6.5 (Continued)

(b) Model 2b

Period	S.E.	Issue	Mutual	Portfolio	Returns	FDI equity
1982–99						
1	9.017841	0.000000	30.84222	28.21163	40.94615	0.000000
2	15.37637	12.69995	30.02975	22.94678	34.12706	0.196453
3	17.05175	11.55517	29.43848	26.71963	31.53099	0.755744
4	18.09840	9.715451	22.90056	22.64383	25.95391	18.78625
5	19.89388	10.57183	21.46517	20.93501	29.01943	18.00855
6	20.53965	10.16152	22.00325	21.13159	28.45751	18.24614
7	21.94987	9.695001	21.03626	19.77353	30.93517	18.56003
8	22.34572	10.26462	20.25848	21.67349	29.83272	17.97068
9	22.83045	10.15638	20.05486	22.25704	29.83204	17.69968
10	24.15248	9.959621	19.49031	21.70406	29.14434	19.70167

Notes: The forecast–error variance is computed using the VAR (3) system where Returns, Issues, Mutual, Portfolio and Fdiequity are S&P 500 returns, net issues of corporate equity, mutual fund flows, foreign portfolio flows and FDI equity flows, respectively. The table shows the percentage of two-year forecast error variance of variable i explained by variable j.

Summary

The results for the VAR modeling procedure supports the contention that the declining supply of equity is at least one of the driving forces behind the recent inflation in stock prices. We find this to be an especially robust finding since announcements regarding mergers and repurchases activity at $t - 1$ may immediately impact prices through an increased demand for the stock. This is important to note because share retirements merger activity is a significant component of the *Flow of Funds* net issues series. Thus, the results are biased towards the finding that prices appear Granger-prior to net issuance of corporate equity. Even in this likelihood and with demand-side flows included in the investigation we have found evidence of a causal relationship running from net issues to stock prices. We also gave causal priority to stock returns over net issues in the VAR system and still were not able to reject the hypothesis that net issues do not influence the time path of aggregate stock market returns. Thus, we hold the results here to be robust.

The results also suggest that pension fund and life insurance flows exhibit no significant correlation with stock market returns. However, we uncovered strong evidence of a Granger causal relationship between mutual fund, foreign portfolio and FDI equity flows and stock returns, albeit the effect of the former became insignificant when we included the equity component of FDI flows into the multivariate system. Innovation accounting techniques further revealed that shocks to these variables had strong effects on S&P returns and a significant proportion of the variance in the latter was correspondingly explained. Still, the evidence that mutual fund and portfolio flows influence the time path of stock returns was dependent on a relatively strong assumption that contemporaneous stock market returns do not impact these flows. Furthermore, impulse response functions suggested a small positive effect followed by a strong negative relationship between FDI equity flows and market returns for the 1982–99 period.

However, the VAR approach cannot lead to decisive rejection of the hypothesis that pension fund and life insurance net flows did not influence stock market valuations during the recent bull market. Neither should we place too much emphasis on the questionable results obtained from the examination of FDI equity and mutual fund flows. Why? The Granger causality and VAR analysis asks whether past values of flows predict market returns. Since prices respond quickly to flows, it is more appropriate to examine whether current (contemporaneous) values of institutional investor and foreign equity flows explain market valuations. Seen in this light, the findings of Granger causality between the demand-side variables in question and stock market returns appear robust as well, since we have evidence of a causal relationship based on past values alone. In the same vein, we cannot completely reject the claim that pension fund flows have contributed to the dramatic run-up in equity values.

What about the fundamental reasons why supply and demand changes might impact prices? The VAR technique relies crucially on timing and the use of lagged values of explanatory variables to model the evolution of the dependent variable. Unfortunately, because stock prices are forward looking, pro-cyclical variables, the unrestricted VAR procedure precludes the investigation into whether the effects of net issues and demand-side flows on stock returns are robust when measures of future economic fundamentals are included. Thus, while extremely useful for analyzing the timing patterns in and co-movements of macroeconomic variables, it cannot address whether or not the price movements were unjustified on the basis of economic fundamentals.

We could, however, by imposing restrictions and moving to a structural VAR model, investigate whether the relationship between lagged flows and net issues is robust in the presence of economy-wide fundamentals. Utilizing the VAR methodology in this manner, while sacrificing the benefits of the unrestricted reduced form approach, illustrates how the technique can be modified for investigative purposes. However, such an experiment runs contrary to the initial spirit of the VAR approach as set out by Sims (1980), designed to treat all variables *symmetrically* to scrutinize the interrelationships between economic time series. Moreover, even in this case, the structural VAR would be ill-suited for an investigation into whether contemporaneous demand-side flows impact returns in the presence of proxies for fundamentals. Such an examination is crucial because the immediate impact of flows on stock market valuations may leave little explanatory power for lagged values of the flow variables.

The need to account more appropriately for fundamentals in an examination into whether current and past values of net issuance and net purchases influence equity price dynamics lead directly to an investigation exploiting the structural model approach where both of these dilemmas are decisively eliminated.

THE STRUCTURAL MODEL APPROACH

To more thoroughly consider whether supply- and demand-driven price appreciation is warranted or unwarranted by fundamental economic considerations, contemporaneous values of the flow variables need to be included into the investigation along with contemporaneous forward-looking variables and leads of measures of expected profitability. This is beyond the scope of any investigation within the unrestricted VAR framework, which relies exclusively on past information to model the dynamic impact on stock market returns. However, through the structural model and instrumental variables approach we can control for endogenous equations bias and the fundamental forces behind equity valuations while simultaneously investigating whether the stock market boom was driven to unprecedented heights by institutional investor and foreign equity flows and the corporate sector's considerable retirement of equity.

Controlling for Fundamentals

Conventional investigations of stock price movements center directly on the standard valuation model, identifying shocks to expectations of future income flows, the share of income accruing to corporations and discount rates as the driving forces behind equity price fluctuation. In principal, any systematic force that affects the economy's pricing operator or expected dividend payments to shareholders can impact stock prices for reasons that can be considered fundamental or related to intrinsic value. Unfortunately, there is no direct measure for intrinsic values and thus no precise or direct manner in which to control for fundamentals. Therefore, ex ante observable variables must be identified which might adequately proxy for the ex post, unobservable fundamentals in the formal econometric work. Chapter 3 discusses the implications of this inevitability, noting that the attempt to control for market fundamentals via alternative measures may introduce measurement error with the results extremely sensitive to the choice of proxy, possibly under- or overstating the efficiency of the pricing mechanism.

As indicated previously, the seminal econometric works of Fama (1990, 1981), Schwert (1990), and Chen et al. (1986) utilize leads of industrial production, short-term bond yields, as well as the term structure and default (or risk) spread

(spread between low- and high-quality bond yields) to explain the fundamental variation in stock returns. Implicitly these variables are held to determine the equilibrium value of aggregate stock market valuations, or more appropriately, the fundamental news regarding future movement in dividend payouts. In Chapter 3 we also expressed our skepticism about how adequately these variables serve as measures of expected discounted cash flows to shareholders and how consistent they are with the theory of efficient capital markets. Nevertheless, these variables provide a pre-established manner in which to proxy for the information about future economic and business fundamentals in order to test the hypotheses advanced here.

One should be skeptical about the ability to proxy adequately for ex post fundamentals and the possible omission of variables vital to the characterization of stock market equilibrium. This, however, must be balanced against the potential overstating of the explanatory power stemming from the fact that the standard variables were initially selected on the basis of goodness-of-fit (Fama 1981; 1990, p. 1107). In point of fact, Chen et al. (1986) develop no 'theoretical foundation for the state variables' but suggest in conclusion that their signs are plausible (p. 395). Furthermore, possible simultaneous equations bias that arises from taking leads of real economy variables as wholly exogenous with respect to stock prices suggests that a relationship found to be suggestive of the EMH could be further overstated. Nevertheless, for consistency with the existing literature, we follow Edwards and Zhang (1998) in their study of mutual fund flows and employ these variables to proxy for the fundamental influences underlying aggregate stock market indices as well. Similarly, we follow standard procedure in the literature, analyzing market returns instead of changes in the S&P Index. Below we briefly reintroduce and summarize the variables as they are presented in the established literature. Again, Table 6.1 presents and defines these variables explicitly.

Interest rates
An obvious candidate for inclusion in a study of stock valuations is the short-term interest rate, not only because the risk-free interest rate is directly related to market prices through the standard valuation model, but also because bonds are rival assets to equity. Thus, we expect a negative relationship between bond market yields and stock returns. Additionally, interest rates are pro-cyclical and thus sensitive to measures of business cycle changes. It should be mentioned that because stock prices are also pro-cyclical this negative correlation between returns and interest rates might be significantly weakened. Nonetheless, we utilize the yield on three-month treasury bills, noted Tbill3m hereafter, to examine the impact of interest rates on stock market returns. This variable was found earlier to be non-stationary and therefore we entered it into stock return regressions in first differences.

Industrial production

Industrial production is commonly used as the aggregate proxy for future profitability and because equity values are related to changes in long-run industrial activity (Chen et al., 1986, p. 387). Fama (1981) notes that, 'the stock market is concerned with the capital investment process and uses the earliest information from the process to forecast its evolution' (p. 555). Thus, it is presumed that industrial production contains more information about fundamentals than profits. Changes in industrial production, QIP, are calculated as the first difference of the quarterly series. Since stock prices are understood to capture *future* developments in the real economy, we lead this variable by one period. Again, there is serious concern over the endogeneity of real economic variables with respect to the stock market given the wealth effect and cost of capital channels discussed in Chapter 3. Nevertheless, we do not take the leading indicator view of stock prices to task here and instead, remaining consistent with directives of the theory of efficient markets, we proceed as if IP is exogenous.[4]

Risk spread and term premium

It has been suggested that interest rate spreads are informative business cycle variables that lead turning points in real activity and capture information relevant to the evolution of the real side of the economy. Recall that Bernanke (1990) demonstrated empirically that the default spread (the difference between high- and low-quality bonds) has predictive power for several real economy variables such as industrial production, durable orders, the unemployment rate, personal income, capacity utilization and consumption. Chen et al. (1986) argue that the default spread proxies for changes in the expected risk premium and document a relationship between the contemporaneous default spread and stock returns. That is, when spreads are high market conditions are poor and inherently more risky, warranting a higher rate of return. Keim and Stambaugh's (1986) study provides evidence that confirms that bond spreads proxy for changes in risk premium. We are inclined to treat the default (or risk) spread as a proxy of systematic economy-wide risk and business conditions. Thus, the risk spread (risk) is calculated as the spread between Moody's Baa bond rate and Moody's Aaa rate.

Likewise, the term structure or yield curve is reported to 'capture cyclical variation in expected returns' or changes in the term premium (Fama, 1990; Fama and French, 1989). Estrella and Mishkin (1998) show that the slope of the yield curve impounds important business cycle information. Lower than average spreads are found to be associated with a higher possibility of recession while higher than average spreads indicate a lower than average probability of a recession. Correspondingly, Keim and Stambaugh (1986) demonstrate that the term structure of interest rates has a shallow slope around business cycle peaks and a steeper slope around business troughs. The term structure (term) is calculated as the spread between the 20-year government bond rate at time *t* and the yield on the 1-month T-bill at time *t* − 1. Both interest rate spread variables are found to bill at time $t - 1$. Both interest rate spread variables are found to be stationary processes (see Table 6.2). As we noted earlier, the use of such variables to capture the rational variation in market returns presumes the efficiency of bond markets.

Unexpected Equity Issuances and Net Purchases

Because of the time-varying nature of expected returns uncontrolled for by the aforementioned 'fundamental' variables, it could be contended that the relationship between net issues and net purchases of corporate equity and stock market returns is spurious. This extends from the fact that the flow variables may be proxying for the time variation in expected returns and should therefore be capable of forecasting returns on that basis. This concern along with the caveats expressed by Chen et al. (1986) mentioned earlier[5] leads us to extract the predictable component from each of the series to generate an unexpected series for net issues and each of the demand-side flow variables. Again, this also deals adequately with the issue that stock prices may very well predict future inflows, prompting the relationship. As indicated by the VAR model and impulse response functions, net issues show persistence, that is, the net equity series is significantly predictable. An AR (3) model is fitted to the net issues of corporate equity series, and the resulting residuals make up the derived series, unexpected net issues (*uissue*).

Accordingly we fit AR (5), AR (6) and AR (7) models to the autocorrelated series *Mutual*, *Life* and *Pubpen*, using the residuals to create the unexpected series *Umutual*, *Ulife* and *Upubpen*. Finally, *Uportfolio* and *Ufdi* were constructed from the residuals obtained from fitting AR (7) and AR (6) models to foreign portfolio flows and foreign direct equity flows, respectively. These series allow for a more rigorous test since effectively we enquire into whether net flows predict returns 'above and beyond the predictability generated by past returns' (Froot et al., 1998, p. 4). The correlations between these new variables and stock returns are reported in Table 6.6. The 1982–99 interval shows a strong positive relationship between unexpected mutual fund flows and stock market returns but an even stronger relationship between unexpected foreign equity flows (portfolio investment and FDI equity flows) and stock market returns. The table also confirms relatively weak correlation between life insurance and public pension flows. It is important to note, however, that a strong association exists between unexpected pension flows and unexpected mutual fund and foreign portfolio flows. This finding proves useful for our analysis below utilizing the instrumental variable technique.

Table 6.6 Correlation coefficients

1953–99	Umutual	Upubpen	Ulife	UPortfolio	Returns
Umutual	1.000000				
Upubpen	0.310417	1.000000			
Ulife	0.091739	0.189401	1.000000		
Uportfolio	0.311380	0.237599	0.079616	1.000000	
Returns	0.372706	0.099655	0.107776	0.491938	1.000000

1953–81	Umutual	Upubpen	Ulife	UPortfolio	Returns
Umutual	1.000000				
Upubpen	0.032609	1.000000			
Ulife	0.097323	0.066512	1.000000		
Uportfolio	0.089688	0.029034	0.012323	1.000000	
Returns	0.194752	− 0.074077	0.289311	0.193786	1.000000

1982–99	Umutual	Upubpen	Ulife	UPortfolio	Ufdi	Returns
Umutual	1.000000					
Upubpen	0.303812	1.000000				
Ulife	0.084053	0.181795	1.000000			
Uportfolio	0.315260	0.241600	0.080665	1.000000		
Ufdi	0.150527	− 0.109125	0.022180	− 0.004616	1.000000	
Returns	0.367065	0.067300	0.084119	0.530134	0.420591	1.000000

Notes: Correlation coefficients in unexpected movements between series obtained using quarterly data. See Table 6.1 for a full description of the variables.

Bivariate Results

The bivariate regressions results in Table 6.7a show that contemporaneous unexpected net issues have no explanatory power for quarterly stock returns for the 1982–99 period. However, lagged unexpected net issues are significant negative explainers of the variation in market returns. The R^2 from regressions of returns on unexpected net issues for one period lagged alone is 0.12. This result is consistent with coefficients of determination, ranging from 0.12 to 0.16, attained by Baker and Wurgler (1999). Moreover, including another lag adds an additional 6 per cent in explanatory power. The findings that contemporaneous net issues do not impact stock returns could possibly be reflective of simultaneous equation bias. Typically endogenous variables tend to influence one another in the same direction (that is money supply and GNP) and thus a regression of one on another that does not properly account for endogenous equations bias is likely to overstate the relationship. In our case the forces work in opposite directions and thus endogenous equations bias acts as measurement error to obscure the relationship between contemporaneous unexpected net issues and stock returns. However, it could also be the case that the potential impact of the variables on each other is better captured with a lag as indicated earlier by our examination of correlation coefficients. Thus, instead of estimating the relationship utilizing the two-stage least squares procedure, we circumvent the endogeneity issue by addressing whether the influence of lagged unexpected net issues is robust in the presence of economic and business cycle variables presumed to be the fundamental determinants of market returns.

There is another advantage to using lagged net issues. Brealey and Nyborg (1998) note that several studies on seasoned IPOs suggest that the announcement of new equity issues result in a small, negative change in stock prices. However, it is not clear whether the price decline is the result of 'temporary market indigestion' or simply the result of investors responding to the increase in net issues as a negative signal about firm cash flow (p. 71). Since investors are more likely to respond to the announcement immediately with some activity occurring contemporaneously, what is most likely remaining when we address the relationship between lagged net issues and returns is pure shrinking supply effects. Thus, we can more adequately assess whether shrinking supply itself has aided in the run-up in US equity values. The results of the structural VAR model support this lag structure and indicate that the relationship between net issues and returns is robust to the inclusion of proxies for fundamental variation in market return. In our multivariate tests we will control for fundamentals and demand pressures to investigate the hypothesis more rigorously.

Panels B–C of Tables 6.7a are consistent with our earlier findings obtained from the reduced form approach. Contemporaneous unexpected pension fund and life insurance flows do not explain a statistically significant portion of the variation in stock returns – the R^2s for both regressions on stock returns are zero. Although not reported, we also find that aggregate pension fund flows (public and private) explain none of the variation in stock market returns (as is to be expected given the lack of explanatory power of public pension funds). However, life insurance flows two periods lagged provide some statistically significant, albeit small, explanatory power. Given these findings we again omit these sectors from our analysis.

Table 6.7a   Bivariate OLS results I

(1982–99)	Equation: Returns$_t = b_0 + b_1X_t + b_2X_{t-1} + b_3X_{t-2} + \ldots + e_t$			
Panel A	X = Uissue			
	(1)	(2)	(3)	(4)
Constant	21.23	19.72	18.32	18.25
	(4.91)***	(4.84)***	(4.60)***	(4.52)***
Uissues$_t$	– 0.04			– 0.04
	(– 0.15)			(– 0.17)
Uissues$_{t-1}$		– 0.70	– 0.71	– 0.71
		(– 3.04)***	(– 3.18)***	(– 3.16)***
Uissues$_{t-2}$			– 0.54	– 0.53
			(– 2.39)**	(– 2.37)**
R-square	0.00	0.12	0.18	0.18
Panel B	X = Upubpen			
	(1)	(2)	(3)	
Constant	19.81	20.54	20.81	
	(4.64)***	(4.87)***	(4.89)***	
Upubpen$_t$	0.51			
	(0.55)			
Upubpen$_{t-1}$		– 0.45	– 0.44	
		(– 0.48)	(–0.64)	
Upubpen$_{t-2}$			– 0.58	
			(– 0.62)	
R-square	0.00	0.00	0.04	
Panel C	X = Ulife			
	(1)	(2)	(3)	
Constant	19.80	20.30	19.70	
	(4.67)***	(4.82)***	(4.77)***	
Ulife$_t$	0.60			
	(0.69)			
Ulife$_{t-1}$		0.09	0.22	
		(0.10)	(0.26)	
Ulife$_{t-2}$			1.67	
			(1.95)*	
R-square	0.00	0.00	0.05	

Notes: Uissues, Upubpen and Ulife denote unexpected net issues, public pension fund and life insurance flows, respectively. Numbers in parentheses are t-statistics. (***) Significant at the 1% level, (**) 5% level, (*) 10% level.

Table 6.7b   Bivariate OLS results II

(1982–99)	Equation: Returns$_t$ = b_0 + b_1X$_t$ + b_2X$_{t-1}$ + b_3X$_{t-2}$ +...+ e$_t$			
Panel A	X = Umutual			
	(1)	(2)	(3)	(4)
Constant	19.70	22.09	22.65	21.02
	(5.07)***	(5.39)***	(5.53)***	(5.85)***
Umutual$_t$	2.17			2.14
	(4.52)***			(4.75)***
Umutual$_{t-1}$		– 1.39	– 1.37	– 1.36
		(– 2.64)**	(– 2.63)**	(– 2.98)***
Umutal$_{t-2}$			–1.02	– 0.71
			(–1.47)	(– 1.53)
R-square	0.23	0.09	0.11	0.34
Panel B	X = Uportfolio			
	(1)	(2)	(3)	(4)
Constant	21.45	21.26	21.11	21.31
	(5.80)***	(4.97)***	(4.98)***	(5.80)***
Uportfolio$_t$	3.20			3.17
	(4.97)***			(4.88)***
Uportfolio$_{t-1}$		– 0.67	– 0.86	– 0.33
		(– 0.90)	(– 1.15)	(– 0.50)
Uportfolio$_{t-2}$			– 1.14	– 1.10
			(– 1.52)	(– 1.70)*
R-square	0.26	0.01	0.04	0.29
Panel C	X = Ufdi			
	(1)	(2)	(3)	(4)
Constant	21.30	21.51	21.64	21.70
	(4.15)***	(5.16)***	(5.18)***	(5.29)***
Ufdi$_t$	0.79			0.67
	(2.28)**			(1.94)*
Ufdi$_{t-1}$		0.84	0.75	0.633
		(2.39)**	(2.12)**	(1.80)*
Ufdi$_{t-2}$			0.58	0.52
			(1.49)	(1.50)
R-square	0.07	0.08	0.10	0.15

Notes: Returns denote the return on S&P 500 stocks and Umutual, Uportfolio and Ufdi denote unexpected mutual fund, foreign portfolio investor and FDI equity flows, respectively. Numbers in parentheses are t-statistics. (***) Significant at the 1% level, (**) 5% level, (*) 10% level.

Contrariwise, Panels A–C of Table 6.7b shows that contemporaneous mutual fund, portfolio investment and FDI equity flows explain a significant amount of the variation in stock returns over the 1982–99 interval. Panel A illustrates that unexpected contemporaneous mutual fund net purchases explain 23 per cent of the variation in quarterly returns. Likewise unexpected foreign portfolio equity flows at time t accounts for 26 per cent of the variation in quarterly returns (Panel B). The strength of the explanatory power of these variables may be reflective of endogenous equations bias to some degree and as such one should reserve drawing conclusions about which sector played the bigger role in the dramatic run-up in US equity values. Finally, Panel C of Table 6.7b illustrates that unexpected contemporaneous foreign direct equity flows explain roughly 7 per cent of the variation in US stock market returns. With two lags included the R^2 increases to 15 per cent.

Multivariate Results

Before we address whether contemporaneous flows are significant explainers of market returns when fundamentals are controlled for, we inspect the relationship between stock returns and the variables deemed to proxy for genuine information about future corporate profitability by EMH proponents. Following Fama (1990) and Chen et al. (1986) we estimated the model:

$$\text{Returns}_t = b_0 + b_1 \text{QIP}_{t+1} + b_2 \text{Term}_t + b_3 \text{Risk}_t + b_4 \Delta \text{Tbill3m} + \varepsilon_t \quad (6.1)$$

for the 1953–99, 1953–81 and 1982–99 time periods. The results of the multivariate regressions for each time period are presented in Panels A and B of Table 6.8a. White's test for heteroskedasticity revealed the null hypothesis could be rejected at the 1 per cent level for each of the models run on the separate samples. Consequently, the standard errors and t-statistics were corrected for heteroskedasticity using White's procedure (White, 1980). The variables are also correlated to a degree that multicollinearity may affect the variances and t-statistics corresponding to the parameter estimates. However, the OLS estimator remains the best linear, unbiased estimator and the R^2 statistic remains unaffected. Since we are interested in the collective explanatory power of the 'fundamental' variables, we are then relatively unconcerned with individual t-statistics in equation (6.1).

The regressions in each panel illustrate the explanatory power of fundamental factors for stock returns. The R^2 from the regressions on 1953:1–1999:4 data seems remarkably low (0.13). However, our finding that variables deemed to proxy for the fundamental factors underpinning stock values explain only 18 per cent and 25 per cent of the variation in quarterly returns during 1953:1–1999:4 and 1982:1–1999:4 is consistent with the findings of Fama (1990) and Schwert (1990). The former and latter successfully explain 23 per cent and 27 per cent of the variation in quarterly returns, respectively. It should be noted that more of the variation in stock returns is explained by these factors at longer horizons (yearly data). As was discussed in Chapter 3, Fama's (1990) explanation for this result is that 'measurement error' in short-horizon investigations tends to weaken the relationship between industrial production and stock returns. However, another explanation is that under- and overvaluation is even more likely to be observed by investigations utilizing high-frequency data and therefore proxies for fundamentals will exhibit less explanatory power for market returns. Nevertheless, the results suggest that 'fundamentals' do explain a significant portion of the fluctuation in US equity returns during the 1982–99 period.

There remains the question of why fundamentals explain a larger portion of the variation in stock returns in the 1982–99 and 1953–81 sub-periods than the entire sample, 1953–99. Also the parameter estimates appear to be drastically different in size. There have been dramatic changes in the US economy that might favor a structural change in the behavior of stock market returns. At least two factors immediately come to mind. One is the passage of ERISA in 1974, which liberated pension fund managers from the 'prudent man rule' and by stressing portfolio diversification, provided a green light to invest in risky stocks. As noted in Chapter 4, ERISA was psychologically relevant for all institutional investors, not just pension fund managers. Second, May Day 1975 saw the elimination of fixed commission rates and permitted institutional investors, who had come to dominate the exchange, to trade on significantly cheaper terms. In addition, the 1970s witnessed the collapse of Bretton Woods, financial market deregulation and the rise of new instruments such as options, index funds and other derivative instruments that permitted investors the ability to invest passively. Not surprisingly then, Chow's breakpoint test confirms that the null hypothesis that no structural change took place in 1974 can be rejected at the 1 per cent level of significance. Consequently, we have included the results of regression (6.1) estimated for the 1953–73 and 1974–99 periods in Table 6.8a as well.[6]

We also addressed the collective explanatory power of net issues and the demand-side flow variables for quarterly market returns during the 1953–73, 1974–99 and 1982–99 periods before moving to directly test whether these causal forces are robust when fundamentals are controlled for. Table 6.8b documents the results of four regressions, which employ different combinations of the flow variables to explain market returns. Again we were able to reject the hypothesis of no heteroskedasticity in the residuals and, therefore, the standard errors and t-statistics were again corrected using White's (1980) procedure. The results illustrate that, while fundamentals alone explained 25 per cent and 16 per cent of the quarterly variation in S&P 500 returns during the 1982–99 and 1974–99 periods, unexpected mutual fund and foreign portfolio flows and unexpected net issues of equity collectively explain 47 per cent and 48 per cent during the corresponding intervals (Panel A, regression 1a). However, during the 1953–73 period, unexpected mutual fund and foreign portfolio flows account for just 14 per cent of the variation in quarterly returns, and the null hypothesis for unexpected net issues cannot be rejected. Panel A, regression 1b, also indicates that unexpected FDI equity flows do not add additional explanatory power to market returns in the presence of the other flow variables for the 1982–99 period. This implies that FDI equity flows were proxying for more important causal forces in our bivariate investigation.

Although we previously found no evidence of a statistically significant relationship between the net purchases of any of the other institutional investors and market returns, we aggregated them to assess the collective impact on institutional investor flows on the stock market. That is, the variable Instinvest was constructed by summing the net purchases of corporate equity of insurance companies, pension funds, closed-end funds and mutual fund companies. Subsequently, we identified the resulting data-generating process as an AR (4) model and followed the usual method of extracting the predictable component from the series, constructing the new series Uinstinvest. In the like manner we constructed the series, Uforeign, aggregating foreign portfolio equity investment and FDI equity flows and extracting the predictable component using an AR (6) model. Utilizing these variables, we can address whether total institutional investor and foreign equity flows into the stock market aided in the run-up in US equity values. Given the results of the disaggregated investigation we would expect much weaker results when these variables are substituted in lieu of Umutual and Uportfolio.

Panel B of Table 6.8b presents the results of two different regressions on market returns employing the newly constructed variables. Regressions on returns utilizing unexpected institutional investor flows in the place of mutual funds flows for the various time periods are labeled 2a. These regressions revealed that the null hypothesis could be rejected for Uinstinvest at the 5 per cent level of significance for 1974–99 and 1982–99. However, as anticipated, the R^2s are lower than those achieved by regression 1a in Panel A, again emphasizing that it is mutual fund flows that drives the relationship between institutional investor flows and stock market returns. It should be noted that in substituting total institutional investor flows in the place of mutual fund flows for the 1953–73 period results in an increase in the R^2 from 14 per cent to 26 per cent. Collectively, these findings suggest that collectively institutional flows help explain the stock market boom of the 1960s; however, the 1982–99 bull market can be linked exclusively to the growth of mutual fund corporations. A telling finding, since the latter are widely held to be a measure of 'irrational' investor sentiment while pension fund managers are deemed more sophisticated investors.

Table 6.8 Preliminary Multivariate Results

(a) Returns and Fundamentals

Equation: Returns$_t$ $= b_0 + b_1 QIP_{t+1} + b_2 Term_t + b_3 Risk_t + b_4 \Delta Tbill3m_t$ (6.1)			
Panel A	1953–99	1953–81	1982–99
	(6.1)	(6.1)	(6.1)
Constant	1.33	1.80	44.43
	(0.45)	(1.63)*	(2.89)**
QIP$_{t+1}$	6.61	1.51	10.01
	(3.11)***	(2.51)***	(2.56)***
Term$_t$	− 3.92	− 0.18	− 11.60
	(− 1.62)*	(− 0.32)	(− 2.62)***
Risk$_t$	6.72	1.60	− 5.25
	(2.14)**	(2.16)**	(− 0.76)
ΔTbill3m$_t$	− 1.41	− 0.26	− 7.39
	(− 1.22)	(− 0.54)	(− 2.04)***
R^2	0.13	0.18	0.25
Panel B	1974–99	1953–73	
	(6.1)	(6.1)	
Constant	18.43	2.64	
	(1.43)	(2.64)***	
QIP$_{t+1}$	8.54	1.83	
	(2.85)***	(2.01)**	
Term$_t$	− 7.11	− 1.40	
	(− 2.25)**	(− 1.94)**	
Risk$_t$	1.89	0.24	
	(1.32)	(1.24)	
ΔTbill3m$_t$	− 3.06	− 1.01	
	(− 1.66)*	(− 1.30)	
R^2	0.16	0.14	

Notes: Returns denote the return on S&P 500 stocks and uissues denote unexpected net issues of domestic corporate equity. QIP is the quarterly change in industrial production, term is the term structure, risk is the default spread and Tbill is the three-month treasury bill rate. T-statistics are in parentheses and are adjusted for heteroskedasticity following White's procedure. (***) Significant at the 1% level, (**) 5% level, (*) 10% level. The reported R^{2}s are adjusted for the number of included regressors.

Table 6.8 (Continued)

(b) Returns and Flows

$$Returns_t = b_0 + b_1 Umutual_t + b_2 Uportfolio_t + b_3 \Delta Uissue_{t-1} \tag{1a}$$
$$Returns_t = b_0 + b_1 Umutual_t + b_2 Uportfolio_t + b_3 Ufdi_t + b_4 \Delta Uissue_{t-1} \tag{1b}$$
$$Returns_t = b_0 + b_1 Uinstinvest_t + b_2 Uportfolio_t + b_4 \Delta Uissue_{t-1} \tag{2a}$$
$$Returns_t = b_0 + b_1 Uinstinvest_t + b_2 Uforeign_t + b_4 \Delta Uissue_{t-1} \tag{2b}$$

Panel A	1953–99	1953–81	1982–99	
	(1a)	(1a)	(1a)	(1b)
Constant	6.98	15.06	18.45	18.66
	(5.67)***	(6.75)***	(5.90)***	(5.95)***
$Umutual_t$	3.14	1.80	1.72	1.57
	(1.97)**	(3.07)***	(2.88)***	(2.48)**
$Uportfolio_t$	4.40	2.14	2.17	2.08
	(1.79)*	(3.15)***	(3.16)***	(2.95)***
$Ufdi_t$				− 0.20
				(−1.58)
$\Delta Uissue_{t-1}$	− 0.55	− 0.79	− 0.75	−0.77
	(− 0.60)	(− 2.74)***	(− 2.65)***	(− 2.57)***
R^2	0.14	0.47	0.48	0.49

Panel B	1953–73	1974–99	1982–99	
	(2a)	(2a)	(2a)	(2b)
Constant	8.79	15.42	19.13	20.48
	(8.87)***	(6.67)***	(5.73)***	(5.68)***
$Uinstinvest_t$	3.57	0.52	0.48	0.45
	(3.39)***	(2.47)**	(2.17)**	(2.07)**
$Uforeign_t$				1.05
				(2.91)***
$Uportfolio_t$	4.52	2.66	2.69	
	(2.34)**	(3.92)***	(3.92)***	
$Uissue_{t-1}$	− 0.47	0.78	− 0.72	− 0.64
	(− 0.70)	(− 2.53)***	(− 2.44)	(− 3.93)
R^2	0.26	0.39	0.40	0.35

Notes: Returns denote the return on S&P 500 stocks and Uissues denote unexpected net issues of domestic corporate equity. Umutual and Uportfolio are unexpected net purchases of equity by mutual funds and foreign portfolio investors, respectively. Ufdi denotes unexpected FDI equity flows. Uinstinvest are the unexpected net purchases of all institutional investors while Uforeign = Ufdi + Uportfolio. T-statistics are in parentheses and are adjusted for heteroskedasticity following White's procedure. (***) Significant at the 1% level, (**) 5% level, (*) 10% level. The reported R^2s are adjusted for the number of included regressors.

Regression 2b in Panel B of Table 6.8b analogously shows that by aggregating FDI equity flows and foreign portfolio flows less of the variation in quarterly stock returns is explained during the 1982–1999 period. In replacing unexpected foreign portfolio flows with unexpected total foreign equity flows into the stock market (moving from regression 2a to 2b) results in additional decline in the R^2 from 40 per cent to 35 per cent (recall we began with an initial R^2 of 48 per cent). Again, these results are predictable given that finding the FDI equity flows do not offer supplementary explanatory power for market returns when net issues, mutual fund flows and foreign portfolio investment are included in the investigation. Given that we have omitted key variables (proxies for information regarding economic and business fundamentals), we will recheck these results as we move to a more complete model.

We have yet to illustrate that demand-side flows and net issues of corporate equity have moved S&P returns above levels that can be reasonable justified by the expected discounted cash flows to shareholders. Thus, to evaluate completely the book's hypotheses that net issues, institutional investor flows and foreign purchases of equity are important causal forces in run-up in US equity values independent of information regarding economy-wide fundamentals, we estimated the following independent models for the 1982–99 and 1974–99 periods:

$$\text{Returns}_t = b_0 + b_1 \text{QIP}_{t+1} + b_2 \text{Term}_t + b_3 \text{Risk}_t + b_4 \Delta \text{Tbill3m}_t \\ + b_5 \text{Uissue}_{t-1} + \varepsilon_t \tag{6.2}$$

$$\text{Returns}_t = b_0 + b_1 \text{QIP}_{t+1} + b_2 \text{Term}_t + b_3 \text{Risk}_t + b_4 \Delta \text{Tbill3m}_t \\ + b_5 \text{Umutual}_t + \varepsilon_t \tag{6.3}$$

$$\text{Returns}_t = b_0 + b_1 \text{QIP}_{t+1} + b_2 \text{Term}_t + b_3 \text{Risk}_t + b_4 \Delta \text{Tbill3m}_t \\ + b_5 \text{UPortfolio}_t + \varepsilon_t \tag{6.4}$$

$$\text{Returns}_t = b_0 + b_1 \text{QIP}_{t+1} + b_2 \text{Term}_t + b_3 \text{Risk}_t + b_4 \Delta \text{Tbill3m}_t \\ + b_5 \text{UiFdi}_t + \varepsilon_t \tag{6.5}$$

The tau-statistics are again adjusted for heteroskedasticity using White's (1980) procedure. Table 6.9 provides evidence that supply and demand forces move prices even when fundamentals are controlled for. Regression 6.2 in each panel of Table 6.9 in particular lends support to the claim that the decline in the volume of equity outstanding helps to explain the dramatic appreciation in equity values in the US. The null hypothesis that lagged unexpected net issues has no explanatory power for stock returns is rejected at 5 per cent for 1974:1–1999:4 with the proxies for fundamental value included. For the 1982:1–1999:4 period the null hypothesis is again strongly rejected and the R^2 improves from 0.25 to 0.32 when unexpected net issues are included into the regression on stock returns (Panel B).

Table 6.9 *Full multivariate results*

$$\text{Returns}_t = b_0 + b_1\text{QIP}_{t+1} + b_2\text{Term}_t + b_3\text{Risk}_t + b_4\Delta\text{Tbill3m}_t + b_5\text{Uissue}_{t-1} \qquad (6.2)$$
$$\text{Returns}_t = b_0 + b_1\text{QIP}_{t+1} + b_2\text{Term}_t + b_3\text{Risk}_t + b_4\Delta\text{Tbill3m}_t + b_5\text{Umutual}_t \qquad (6.3)$$
$$\text{Returns}_t = b_0 + b_1\text{QIP}_{t+1} + b_2\text{Term}_t + b_3\text{Risk}_t + b_4\Delta\text{Tbill3m}_t + b_5\text{Uportfolio}_t \qquad (6.4)$$
$$\text{Returns}_t = b_0 + b_1\text{QIP}_{t+1} + b_2\text{Term}_t + b_3\text{Risk}_t + b_4\Delta\text{Tbill3m}_t + b_5\text{Ufdi}_t \qquad (6.5)$$
$$\text{Returns}_t = b_0 + b_1\text{QIP}_{t+1} + b_2\text{Term}_t + b_3\text{Risk}_t + b_4\Delta\text{Tbill3m}_t + b_5\text{Uissue}_t$$
$$+ b_6\text{Umutual}_t + b_7\text{Uportfolio}_t \qquad (6.6)$$

Panel A	1974–99			1953–73		
	(6.2)	(6.3)	(6.4)	(6.2)	(6.3)	(6.4)
Constant	17.01	18.37	19.20	4.19	3.63	3.41
	(1.96)**	(1.99)**	(2.22)**	(3.51)***	(3.48)***	(3.36)***
QIP_{t+1}	7.85	7.19	7.15	1.69	1.70	1.69
	(3.52)***	(3.46)***	(2.76)***	(1.84)*	(1.81)*	(1.63)*
Term_t	− 6.04	− 7.17	− 6.44	1.98	2.25	1.85
	(− 2.16)**	(2.67)***	(− 2.16)**	(2.06)**	(2.43)**	(− 2.35)**
Risk_t	1.57	2.04	1.56	0.02	0.62	0.48
	(1.34)	(1.42)	(0.31)	(0.12)	(0.58)	(0.46)
$\Delta\text{Tbill3m}_t$	− 2.86	− 2.85	− 3.12	− 0.73	− 1.24	− 1.38
	(− 1.72)*	(− 1.64)*	(− 1.77)*	(− 0.92)	(− 1.65)*	(− 1.93)*
Uissue_{t-1}	− 0.65			− 1.28		
	(− 2.34)**			(− 1.92)*		
Umutual_t		2.08			2.63	
		(3.16)***			(2.05)**	
Uportfolio_t			2.94			4.11
			(4.07)***			(2.11)**
R^2	0.25	0.35	0.36	0.20	0.20	0.21

Table 6.9 (Continued)

Panel B	1982–99				1982–99	1974–99
	(6.2)	(6.3)	(6.4)	(6.5)	(6.6)	(6.6)
Constant	40.56	43.57	45.23	47.98	40.24	17.34
	(3.03)***	(3.17)***	(3.93)***	(3.66)***	(3.47)***	(2.33)**
QIP_{t+1}	10.53	9.23	8.75	10.14	6.60	5.75
	(3.25)***	(2.99)***	(2.39)***	(2.39)***	(2.42)**	(3.33)***
$Term_t$	– 11.60	– 13.97	– 13.97	– 11.83	– 11.65	– 5.53
	(– 2.25)**	(– 3.16)***	(– 3.16)***	(– 2.26)**	(– 3.72)***	(– 2.78)***
$Risk_t$	– 3.65	– 2.25	– 2.77	– 6.60	– 2.16	1.44
	(– 0.57)	(0.36)	(0.46)	(– 1.02)	(– 0.51)	(0.42)
$\Delta Tbill3m_t$	– 7.54	– 6.07	– 6.20	– 6.93	– 5.42	– 2.70
	(– 2.14)	(– 1.73)*	(– 1.76)*	(– 2.00)**	(– 1.72)*	(– 2.01)**
$Uissue_{t-1}$	– 0.64				– 0.58	– 0.71
	(– 3.13)***				(– 2.74)***	(– 2.91)***
$Umutual_t$		1.77			1.58	1.69
		(2.31)**			(2.49)***	(2.97)***
$Uportfolio_t$				– 2.88	2.03	1.98
				(– 3.67)**	(3.21)***	(3.03)***
$Ufdi_t$				0.49		
				(1.06)		
R^2	0.32	0.44	0.47	0.29	0.62	0.55

Notes: Returns denote the return on S&P 500 stocks and Uissues denote unexpected net issues of domestic corporate equity. QIP is the quarterly change in industrial production, Term is the term structure, Risk is the default spread and Tbill is the three-month treasury bill rate. Umutual and Uportfolio are unexpected net purchases of equity by mutual funds and foreign portfolio investors, respectively. Ufdi denotes unexpected FDI equity flows. T-statistics are in parentheses and are adjusted for heteroskedasticity following White's procedure. (***) Significant at the 1% level, (**) 5% level, (*) 10% level. The reported R^2s are adjusted for the number of included regressors.

Note well, performing this same experiment with lagged changes in aggregate dividends yielded insignificant results (not reported). These results suggest that the notion that supply changes are irrelevant for asset pricing is not consistent with the recent stock market boom and that the general efficiency of stock markets has been overstated.

The results of regressions models 6.3 and 6.4 are also presented in Table 6.9, illustrating that the inclusion of unexpected mutual fund and portfolio equity flows into regressions of stock returns on macroeconomic fundamentals leads to significant increases in the R^2s. Accordingly, both variables are found to be statistically significant at the 5 per cent level for the 1982–99 and 1974–99 periods. However, looking exclusively at 1953–73, the results indicate that the null hypothesis that unexpected mutual fund flows have no impact on stock returns cannot be rejected at the 10 per cent level. This finding is to be expected since the explosion in equity mutual funds in the United States did not begin until the mid-1980s. (As late as 1982 mutual funds held less than 7 per cent of all equity outstanding.)

Unexpected foreign direct equity flows, on the other hand, are found to be statistically insignificant explainers of equity returns once fundamentals are controlled for during the 1982–99 period in Panel B (model 6.5). Consequently, we can infer that FDI equity flows have tended to move returns in a manner consistent with fundamentals, that the impact is significantly delayed, or that relationships gauged earlier were spurious. Clearly, FDI equity flows and foreign portfolios are different and, therefore, impact the US stock market differently. Moreover, it is very difficult to interpret foreign direct equity flows into the United States since they are recorded as an inflow even when the entire transaction is done by exchange of shares without money changing hands. The inability to separate true flows from equity exchanges may lead to an underestimation of the influence these flows have on market returns. Nevertheless, aggregating both measures of foreign flows (portfolio flows and FDI equity flows) again gave weaker results than those obtained from running model 6.4 (not reported in Table 6.9) underscoring the need to separate these foreign flows.

Thus, from the OLS analysis we have established a causal significance only for net issues of corporate equity, mutual fund flows and foreign portfolio investment. Also included in Panel B of Table 6.9 is the result of a regression model, which pools these explanatory variables together. Here we assess whether the flow variables are significant collectively in explaining quarterly returns in the presence of variables that proxy for the economy-wide forces driving the fundamental ('rational') variation in stock market returns for 1974–99 and 1982–99. That is, we estimate the model:

$$\text{Returns}_t = b_0 + b_1 \text{QIP}_{t+1} + b_2 \text{Term}_t + b_3 \text{Risk}_t + b_4 \Delta \text{Tbill3m}_t$$
$$+ b_5 \text{Uissue}_{t-1} + b_6 \text{Umutual}_t + b_7 \text{Uportfolio}_t + \varepsilon_t \qquad (6.6)$$

White's tests indicated that heteroskedasticity was present and thus the t-statistics presented are corrected accordingly using White's method for obtaining heteroskedasticity-consistent standard errors. Tests for the presence of autocorrelation in the residuals were unanimously negative. Both Q (Pormanteau) and Lagrange multiplier (LM) tests revealed that the null hypothesis of no serial correlation in the residuals could not be rejected at any reasonable level of significance. Furthermore, the Jarque-Bera test of normality suggested that the residuals were normally distributed.

The results corroborate those found from employing the independent regressions on the data. Lagged, unexpected net issues, and contemporaneous unexpected mutual fund and foreign portfolio flows explain a significant portion of the variation in stock returns during the period corresponding to the unprecedented run-up in US equity values. For each of these variables the null hypothesis can be rejected at the 1 per cent significance level and collectively, along with fundamentals, explain 62 per cent of the variation in stock returns during the 1982–99 period. This should be compared to the results in Table 6.8 where fundamentals successfully explained 25 per cent of the variation in stock returns. It should be noted that the significance of net issues in explaining market returns is not proxying for the increased demand for corporate equity as it adds explanatory power even in the presence of demand-side variables and surrogates for fundamental information about future corporate profitability.

Instrumental Variables Analysis

Unfortunately, these results may not be enough to fully confirm whether foreign and mutual fund flows actually played a role in the escalation in market values independent of the prospects for future corporate profitability. This is essentially because one of the assumptions of the classical linear regression model necessary for consistent and unbiased estimators may have been violated in equations (6.3) through (6.6). In short, the right-hand-side variables, unexpected mutual fund flows and foreign portfolio equity investment may be endogenous with respect to stock market returns and therefore correlated with the error term. In this likelihood the OLS estimates will be biased and inconsistent.[7] Edwards and Zhang (1998) presume unexpected mutual fund flows to be endogenous and proceed straightaway to the instrument variable analysis without formally testing for exogeneity. Warther (1995), on the other hand, implicitly assumes unexpected fund flows to be exogenous when assessing the impact of the latter on market returns.

We, however, tested formally for the exogeneity of unexpected mutual fund and foreign portfolio flows for the 1974–99 interval. Using Engle's LM test for weak exogeneity we computed LM statistics of 0.416 and 1.04. The LM statistic is asymptotically distributed as $\chi^2(1)$ and the null hypothesis is that the variables are uncorrelated with the error term and therefore OLS provides efficient estimates of the true betas. Thus, we cannot reject the null hypothesis and the demand-side flows are weakly exogenous. The results hold when we look exclusively at the 1982–99 period as well. Moreover, recall that our Granger causality tests for the 1982–99 period also revealed that the null hypothesis that returns do not cause unexpected mutual fund or foreign portfolio flows cannot be rejected at the 10 per cent level for any reasonable lag length. Consequently, we are inclined to follow Warther (1995), treating quarterly foreign portfolio and mutual fund flows as exogenous in our system. This also validates the restrictions placed on the VAR model in order to obtain the impulse response functions and variance decompositions presented in Tables 6.5a–b and Figures 6.1a–b.

It could be argued that returns do impact flows but the effect is incorporated quickly and therefore regressions utilizing quarterly data are likely to improperly gauge the correlation. Yet Warther's (1995) meticulous study finds that 'there is no evidence that aggregate fund flows are positively related to past returns in weekly, monthly, quarterly, or yearly data' (p. 210). Similarly, Remolona et al. (1997), utilizing the instrumental variable methodology, find that short-term market returns have a weak impact on mutual fund flows. Nevertheless, in the likelihood that we have misjudged the endogeneity issue, and for comparison with Edwards and Zhang (1998), we proceeded with the instrumental variable analysis, illustrating the robust nature of our results. The outcome is consistent with our earlier findings and solidifies the book's hypotheses. Table 6.10 presents the results from the instrumental variable or two-stage least squares procedure (2SLS).

The biggest dilemma encountered in utilizing the instrumental variable approach is finding appropriate instruments for the 'endogenous' variables. We modeled unexpected mutual fund flows as a function of the change in mutual fund gross profits (ΔMfprofit), the change in gross personal savings (ΔSavings) and unexpected public pension fund flows (Upubpen). We chose the pension fund variable mainly because it was found to be highly correlated with unexpected mutual funds but relatively uncorrelated with stock returns (see Table 6.6). In turn, increases in domestic savings permit the accumulation of financial assets by households, including mutual fund shares while mutual fund profits enable fund mangers to plow more earnings into financial markets, the stock market in particularly. Collectively these variables explain roughly 17 per cent of the variation in unexpected mutual fund flows during 1982–99 and 1974–99.

As instruments for unexpected foreign portfolio flows we utilized the spread between the US prime rate less the six-month LIBOR rate (Spread), the government deficit as a percentage of GDP (Bd) and unexpected pension fund flows. The interest rate spread variable was selected since the larger the differential the more attractive the United States is as a haven for capital inflows. Likewise, budget deficits and the higher interest rate it may engender serves to increase the flow of foreign savings into US financial instruments. Because Bd left Spread with little explanatory power, we dropped the former from our consideration when multicollinearity became a problem (see below). Regressions of unexpected foreign portfolio flows on these variables for the 1974–99 and 1982–99 periods yielded R^2s of 13.2 per cent and 14.4 per cent, respectively.

To illustrate the differences between the OLS and instrumental variables technique, variations of the following structural model were estimated using the 2SLS method:

$$\text{Returns}_t = b_0 + b_1 \text{QIP}_{t+1} + b_2 \text{Term}_t + b_3 \text{Risk}_t + b_4 \Delta \text{Tbill3m}_t$$
$$+ b_5 \text{Uissue}_{t-1} + b_6 \text{Umutual}_t + b_7 \text{Uportfolio}_t + \varepsilon_t \qquad (6.7a)$$

$$\text{Umutual}_t = c_0 + c_1 \Delta \text{Mfprofit}_t + c_2 \Delta \text{Savings}_t + c_3 \text{Upubpen}_t \qquad (6.7b)$$

$$\text{UPortfolio}_t = d_0 + d_1 \text{Bd}_t + d_2 \text{Spread}_t + d_3 \text{Upubpen}_t \qquad (6.7c)$$

The first stage of the 2SLS procedure regresses each endogenous variable on all the exogenous variables in the system to obtain fitted values for Umutual and Uportfolio. In this manner all the exogenous variables are combined to 'act as the "best" instrumental variable' for the endogenous variables (Kennedy, 1993, p. 159). The second stage of 2SLS uses these estimated (fitted) values in equation (6.7a) from which we can then test the hypotheses that flows do not cause stock returns, $b_5 = 0$, $b_6 = 0$ and $b_7 = 0$. If the variables are truly endogenous the two-stage least squares method purges the system of correlation between the explanatory variables and the corresponding error terms, yielding consistent parameter estimates. If the right-hand-side variables are exogenous (and we hold this to be the case) the 2SLS estimates are biased and inefficient.

Since the instruments for unexpected mutual fund and portfolio flows are both written as a linear combination of all the exogenous variables in the system, multicollinearity is now a serious concern. In the wake of high correlation among the instruments for portfolio and mutual fund flows we are likely to accept the null hypothesis even if it is untrue. This notwithstanding, Table 6.10 illustrates that the independent results (for portfolio investment and mutual fund flows separately) are still consistent with the theory that flows move prices irrespective of fundamentals. Regression 1IV finds that the null hypothesis for unexpected mutual fund flows can be rejected for both the 1974–99 and 1982–99 periods at the 10 per cent and 5 per cent level of significance, respectively. Similarly, the null hypothesis for unexpected foreign portfolio flows can be rejected as well for both periods in question with 95 per cent confidence (Regression 2IV).

Table 6.10　Instrumental variables results

$\text{Returns}_t = b_0 + b_1\text{QIP}_{t+1} + b_2\text{Term}_t + b_3\text{Risk}_t + b_4\Delta\text{Tbill3m}_t + b_5\text{Uissue}_{t-1} + b_6\text{Umutual}_t$						(1IV)
$\text{Returns}_t = b_0 + b_1\text{QIP}_{t+1} + b_2\text{Term}_t + b_3\text{Risk}_t + b_4\Delta\text{Tbill3m}_t + b_5\text{Uissue}_{t-1} + b_6\text{Uportfolio}_t$						(2IV)
$\text{Returns}_t = b_0 + b_1\text{QIP}_{t+1} + b_2\text{Term}_t + b_3\text{Risk}_t + b_4\Delta\text{Tbill3m}_t + b_5\text{Uissue}_{t-1} + b_6\text{Umutual}_t +$						
$\qquad\qquad b_7\text{Uportfolio}_t$						(3IV)

	Panel A – 1974–99			Panel B – 1982–99		
	(1IV)	(2IV)	(3IV)	(1IV)	(2IV)	(3IV)
Constant	19.67	18.33	6.20	45.72	42.03	11.84
	(2.24)**	(2.05)**	(0.86)	(3.01)***	(3.48)***	(0.75)
QIP_{t+1}	6.47	5.66	5.08	7.23	7.04	8.92
	(3.58)***	(2.22)**	(3.14)***	(2.79)***	(1.79)*	(3.10)***
Term	– 5.62	– 5.02	– 5.09	– 11.66	– 11.43	– 8.22
	(– 2.67)***	(– 2.06)**	(– 2.62)***	(– 3.33)***	(– 3.06)***	(– 2.11)**
Risk	0.47	1.05	1.82	– 4.69	– 2.84	– 1.34
	(0.12)	(0.28)	(0.51)	(– 0.88)	(– 0.53)	(– 0.19)
$\Delta\text{Tbill3m}_t$	– 2.67	– 2.96	– 1.24	– 5.94	– 5.79	– 7.09
	(– 1.81)*	(– 1.99)**	(– 0.81)	(– 1.87)*	(– 1.52)	(– 1.94)*
Uissue_t	– 0.77	– 0.61	– 0.77	– 0.66	– 0.47	– 0.50
	(– 2.65)***	(– 2.46)**	(– 2.78)***	(– 2.70)***	(2.17)**	(2.24)**
Umutual_t	2.11		2.72	2.52		2.44
	(1.88)*		(1.99)**	(2.36)**		(1.76)*
Uportfolio_t		4.71	2.42		4.21	3.38
		(2.35)**	(2.40)**		(2.37)**	(2.32)**
R^2	0.43	0.36	0.45	0.49	0.47	0.46

Notes: Returns denote the return on S&P 500 stocks and Uissues denote unexpected net issues of domestic corporate equity. QIP is the quarterly change in industrial production, Term is the term structure, Risk is the default spread and Tbill is the three-month treasury bill rate. Umutual and Uportfolio are unexpected net purchases of equity by mutual funds and foreign portfolio investors, respectively. Instruments used: mutual fund profits, domestic savings, unexpected pension fund flows, the government deficit as a percentage of GDP (Bd) and the spread between the US prime rate and the six-month LIBOR rate. Bd was dropped when estimating model 3IV. T-statistics are in parentheses and are adjusted for heteroskedasticity following White's procedure. (***) Significant at the 1% level, (**) 5% level, (*) 10% level. The reported R^2s are adjusted for the number of included regressors.

However, when we attempted to estimate regression (6.7a) with both variables included, neither b_5 nor b_6 was statistically significant for 1974–99. For the 1982–99 period the null hypothesis for foreign portfolio flows could be rejected at the 5 per cent level but the parameter estimate for mutual fund flows was only significantly different than zero at the 13 per cent level (these results are not reported). Thus, if we were to stop the analysis here (believing mutual fund and portfolio flows to be endogenous), we might conclude that the run-up in equity values could be attributed to foreign flows and negative net issuance of corporate equity but not mutual fund flows. Yet, the failure to reject the null hypothesis for mutual fund flows reflects the multicollinearity that now affects the results due to the high degree of correlation between the fitted values of unexpected mutual and foreign portfolio flows. To illustrate this, we dropped Bd from equation (6.7c) and Savings from equation (6.7d) and re-estimated the model. The result is regression 3IV in Table 6.10, which shows that both unexpected mutual fund and portfolio flows are significantly correlated with stock market returns in both periods even in the presence of proxies for fundamental news about future profitability. (For the 1982–99 period unexpected mutual fund flows are significant at the 10 per cent level.)

This exercise illustrates that the results of the instrumental variable approach are extremely sensitive to the choice of instruments and multicollinearity so that the results should always be interpreted with caution. For example, Edwards and Zhang (1998), assuming the OLS technique to produce asymptotically biased parameter estimates, select instruments for mutual fund flows that explain just 3 per cent of the variance in the former. Not surprisingly then, with possible multicollinearity in the background, they are not able to reject the null hypothesis for the 1984–96 period and falsely conclude that mutual fund flows do not assist in explaining the recent stock market boom. Because we are able to uncover stronger instruments for our investigation we were able to avoid this pitfall. Nevertheless, our 2SLS estimators (although the results support the main thesis) are neither unbiased nor consistent in our investigation. Instead, because we found mutual fund and portfolio flows to be exogenous with respect to stock returns, the OLS produces the best parameter estimates in the class of linear estimators.

The main purpose of the exercise was to illustrate that even if we were to proceed to the instrumental variable analysis without formally testing for contemporaneous correlation we could still achieve results consistent with the OLS regression by selecting the appropriate instruments. This underscores the strength of the relationship between these demand-side flows and S&P stock market returns. It should also be appropriately noted that throughout this digression the t-statistics on net issues remain significant at or above the 5 per cent level. Thus, it cannot be said that unexpected net issues are not proxying for the growth in domestic or foreign demand. Therefore, the shrinking supply of corporate equity remains an independent explainer of the escalation in US equity values over

1982–99. The significance of net issuance for market returns raises important questions for the EMH and the Modigliani–Miller theorem, which holds that the value of the firm is independent of the manner in which it finances its capital.

Returning to OLS

The results in Table 6.9 remain relevant for our analysis and the explosion in US equity values can be partially attributed to the growth of mutual funds and thus the growth in domestic demand for corporate equity. Moreover, a slightly larger proportion of the run-up in equity values can be attributed to foreign portfolio flows into the stock market. Finally, the results are also consistent with the theory that the dramatic reduction in volume of corporate equity outstanding has moved prices to a considerable degree. Yet, it is important to note that the significance of these results critically hinge on our treatment of fundamentals, which have been proxied with variables commonly used by proponents of the EMH. However, when loaded up the regression, including leads of after-tax profits and inflation, which could be argued measures the economy's growth potential, the results remained unchanged. Also, like the EMH empirical literature detailed in Chapter 3, we did not address the potential endogeneity between industrial production and stock returns which might serve to exaggerate the role of fundamentals in the stock market boom. We conclude, then, that the relationships between net flows, net issues and stock returns are robust and have moved market valuations above and beyond that which can be justified by economic fundamentals.

Controlling for the falling risk premium
It might be concluded that the significance of flows in explaining market returns could be attributed to a fall in the risk premium owing to the rise of institutional investors. Many times even the most sophisticated empirical work is incapable of distinguishing between competing theories. However, the econometric evidence here, along with the stylized facts laid out in the previous chapter, allows us to make a strong case against the falling risk premium theory. Blanchard's (1993) risk premium story, based as it is on the increased participation of pension funds, is wholly contingent on the finding that pension fund flows impact market returns. However, the evidence documented here suggests that among institutional investors only mutual fund flows can be implicated in the surge in stock values. Again these institutional investors are widely held to be short sighted and the evidence suggests that they have a higher propensity to herd in and out of stocks than other institutional segments of the stock market.

A glimpse at the stylized facts in Chapter 5 also revealed that a good portion of the total shift in equity ownership from individual to institutional investors had already taken place by 1975 and that only mutual fund ownership of stock increases significantly during 1982–99. Thus, the falling risk premium theory is ill-equipped to explain the stock market appreciation puzzle unless one is willing to suggest that the rise of mutual funds have resulted in the lowering of the required rate of return on stocks. Recall from Chapter 4 that indeed some theorists have suggested that a fall in the equity risk premium has likely occurred because mutual funds have lowered the cost of obtaining a diversified portfolio (Diamond, 2000). Nonetheless, one has to question why investors have suddenly exploited mutual funds and this decline in cost of diversification must be balanced with the evidence that suggest mutual funds contribute to excess volatility, making expected returns less predictable.

The same is to be said about any theory that holds the significance of portfolio investment flows to proxy for a falling risk premium from increased foreign ownership. While portfolio flows have been significant, the actual proportion of US corporate equity held by foreigners has remained constant throughout the 1990s (see Chapter 5). Furthermore, while foreigners are perhaps willing to except a lower rate of return going forward owing to a shallower return–risk profile, it is unlikely that their participation in the stock market could alter the risk premium for the entire market. Thus, the theory that domestic institutional and individual investors will also accept a lower expected rate of return is quite dubious. Instead, we hold that the faith in a falling risk premium should be perceived in Minskian terms and, therefore, rooted in the same type of euphoria that gave rise to the belief in a 'new economy' and unrealistic profit expectations. Thus, we maintain that mutual fund and foreign portfolio flows have moved prices in a manner unrelated to corporate fundamentals.

For argument's sake, let it be assumed that mutual funds are a stabilizing force in the stock market and, therefore, the increase in the proportion of equity held by institutional investors can account for a portion of the rise in stock market valuations in the manner suggested by Blanchard (1993). Consistent with this line of thinking, expected returns could have then varied upwards as a result of the decline in the riskiness of stock market investing. It is straightforward to alter regression model (6.6) to examine whether the results obtained earlier are robust when we account for the growing proportion of equity held by institutional investors and the consequent (presumed) fall in the risk premium. In this manner, we estimate one final model to underscore the robust nature of our results:

$$\text{Returns}_t = b_0 + b_1 \text{QIP}_{t+1} + b_2 \text{Term}_t + b_3 \text{Risk}_t + b_4 \Delta \text{Tbill3m}_t$$
$$+ b_5 \text{Uissue}_{t-1} + b_6 \text{Umutual}_t + b_7 \text{Uportfolio}_t + b_8 \text{IO} + \varepsilon_t \qquad (6.8)$$

where IO denotes the percentage of US corporate equity outstanding held by institutional investors with all other variables the same as those in regression model (6.6).[8]

Table 6.11   Summary – OLS results

Returns$_t$ = b_0 + b_1QIP$_{t+1}$ + b_2Term$_t$ + b_3Risk$_t$ + $b_4\Delta$Tbill3m$_t$ + b_5Uissue$_{t-1}$
                                   + b_6Umutual$_t$ + b_7Uportfolio$_t$ + b_8IO   (6.8)

	Panel A – 1974–99			Panel B – 1982–99		
	(6.1)	(6.6)	(6.8)	(6.1)	(6.6)	(6.8)
Constant	18.43	17.34	– 2.48	44.43	40.24	– 5.63
	(1.43)	(2.33)**	(– 2.42)***	(2.89)**	(3.47)***	(– 1.45)
QIP$_{t+1}$	8.54	5.75	4.62	10.01	6.60	3.97
	(2.85)***	(3.33)***	(3.05)***	(2.56)***	(2.42)**	(1.65)*
Term	– 7.11	– 5.53	– 6.71	– 11.60	– 11.65	– 8.50
	(– 2.25)**	(– 2.78)***	(– 3.58)***	(– 2.62)***	(– 3.72)***	(– 3.04)**
Risk	1.89	1.44	3.81	– 5.25	– 2.16	5.79
	(1.32)	(0.42)	(1.15)	(– 0.76)	(– 0.51)	(0.97)
ΔTbill3m$_t$	– 3.06	– 2.70	– 2.65	– 7.39	– 5.42	– 3.22
	(– 1.66)*	(– 2.01)**	(– 2.66)***	(– 2.04)***	(– 1.72)*	(– 1.05)
Uissue$_t$		– 0.71	– 0.58		– 0.58	– 0.53
		(– 2.91)***	(– 3.13)***		(– 2.74)***	(3.19)***
Umutual$_t$		1.69	1.63		1.58	1.68
		(2.97)***	(2.56)***		(2.49)***	(2.41)***
Uportfolio$_t$		1.98	1.97		2.03	1.93
		(3.03)***	(3.16)***		(3.21)***	(3.05)***
IO			1.38			2.31
			(4.25)***			(2.53)***
R^2	0.16	0.55	0.63	0.25	0.62	0.65

Notes: Returns denote the return on S&P 500 stocks and Uissues denote unexpected net issues of domestic corporate equity. QIP is the quarterly change in industrial production, Term is the term structure, Risk is the default spread and Tbill is the three-month treasury bill rate. Umutual and Uportfolio are unexpected net purchases of equity by mutual funds and foreign portfolio investors, respectively. IO denotes the proportion of US corporate equity held by institutional investors. T-statistics are in parentheses and are adjusted for heteroskedasticity following White's procedure. (***) Significant at the 1% level, (**) 5% level, (*) 10% level. The reported R^2s are adjusted for the number of included regressors.

These final results are presented in Table 6.11 along with the results obtained earlier for comparison (Models (6.1) and (6.6)). We again tested for autocorrelation and normality in the residuals and were unable to reject the null hypotheses of no serial correlation or that the residuals are normally distributed. Heteroskedasticity remained a problem and as such the t-statistics are corrected in the manner discussed previously. Employing regression model (6.8) on the 1974–99 and 1982–99 periods reveals that changes in the proportion of equity held by institutional investors is positively and significantly related to stock market returns. Moreover, the inclusion of IO into the regression model leads to an increase in the amount of the variation in S&P returns explained over the periods in question. The core variables of interest, however, Uissue, Umutual, and Uportfolio maintain their explanatory power and, in fact, exhibit remarkable stability. Clearly, the results indicate that, even if we presumed that risk premium fell as the result of the stabilizing impact of the rise of institutional investors, mutual fund flows, foreign portfolio flows and the shrinking supply of equity independently explain a good portion of the run-up in US equity values.

It should be noted that the positive relationship between IO and stock market returns is also consistent with the theory that institutional investors are myopic and therefore tended to push returns to unjustifiable levels during the 1982–99 period. This theory is quite plausible, especially given that mutual fund corporations were the major forces behind the increase in the share of US corporate equity held by institutions. To the extent that returns during the 1982–99 period were 'abnormal', our findings using macro-level data are consistent with Dennis and Strickland (2000) who arrive at similar results using firm-level data. Thus, it not clear that we should simply except the variation in returns explained by IO as a proxy for the fundamental variation in stock market returns.

It should also be noted that we could not control for the possibility that investors 'discovered' that stocks are less riskier investments vis-à-vis alternative assets than had been previously realized and are therefore willing to accept a lower return going forward (Siegel, 1994, 1999). The version of the falling risk premium theory is difficult to bring to empirical court. Nevertheless, the thorough surveys conducted by Shiller (2000a, 2000b) among others indicates that investors were expected similar or higher returns in the late 1990s – evidence which conflicts with the rationale of the falling risk premium theory. There is evidence from the *1998 Survey of Consumer Finances* that investors become less risk-adverse over the 1990s and therefore were willing to take on more risk. From 1989 to 1998 the percentage of investors willing to tack above-average risk for above-average returns rose from 9 per cent to 18.8 per cent while the percentage investors unwilling to take risks fell from 47.3 per cent to 36.5 per cent.[9] Consequently, it is plausible that a small portion of the run-up could have been due to a declining risk premium stemming from this change in risk aversion.

CONCLUSION

The supply and demand theory advanced in Chapter 4 fares well when juxtaposed to the stylized facts and formal econometric analysis, thereby raising fundamental questions about the overly restrictive nature of the theory of efficient capital markets. The empirical investigation conducted here lends credence to the claim that the reduction in the amount of domestic corporate equity outstanding and the Minsky-like growth in the demand for US stock helps explain the recent run-up in US equity values. Bivariate and multivariate tests of Granger causality indicate a predictive relationship between supply, demand and stock returns. Likewise, variance decomposition and impulse response functions confirm that innovations in net issues, mutual fund flows, and foreign portfolio investment explain a significant proportion of the variance in stock prices. We also found a smaller causal role for FDI equity flows but public pension fund and life insurance flows provided no predictive content for market returns.

However, the reduced form technique was unsuited for an investigation into the role of fundamentals in asset pricing since it relies only on past data and stock prices are forward looking. The structural model approach was necessary to control for ex post economic fundamentals while explicitly testing the theory that supply and demand forces drove the bull market to levels unjustified by economic fundamentals. The results indicate that lagged unexpected net issues of equity and contemporaneous values of unexpected mutual fund and foreign portfolio flows are significant explainers of stock returns even when ex ante variables believed to be proxies for the fundamental determinants of aggregate stock market indices are included. On the other hand, FDI equity flows were not significant in explaining the US equity values once we controlled for fundamentals. Looking back at Panel B of Table 6.11 shows that regression of market returns on 'fundamentals' results in the explanation of one-fourth of the total variation in quarterly returns. However, when we included unexpected net issues, mutual and foreign portfolio flows we were able to explain 62 per cent of the variation in stock market returns. When we controlled for the proportion of equity held by institutional investors, close to two-thirds of the variation in quarterly returns were successfully explained.

Thus, the hypothesis that net flows (supply and demand forces) effectively influence prices irrespective of fundamental value is consistent with the data. The significance of corporate share issuance and demand-side flows in explaining price movements contradicts the EMH corollary that the excess demand curve for stock is horizontal. That is, the results of our macro-level investigation presented in this chapter suggest that the effective demand curve is not horizontal at the full information price. Furthermore, the results suggest that fully unpacking the run-up in US stock prices require mores than a theory of 'irrational exuberance' since supply issues are also found to factor into the bull market. While most studies focus on the demand side of the horizontal excess demand corollary, our supply-side inquiry produced results consistent with the hypothesis that shrinking supply has helped to drive US stock values to unjustifiable levels. Clearly, inflated prices cannot be viewed exclusively as an indicator of future prosperity or the outcome of investor euphoria but partially due to transitory institutional dynamics and the approval of SEC Rule 10b-18 in November 1982.

Moreover, Shiller (2000a), who accurately points to the societal preoccupation with stock market investing as an important precipitating factor in the overvaluation of the stock market, also makes an appeal for a policy of freer and more open financial markets as a solution to speculative bubbles. He argues:

> Given that speculative bubbles are heavily influenced by word-of-mouth effects, by locally perceived values and information, and by patriotic feeling, foreign investors are less likely to go along with a bubble than are local investors, and they may even trade in way that would offset it (p. 228).

Yet the results presented in this chapter indicate that foreign investor flows are highly correlated with domestic flows and played a significant role in the run-up in US equity values. These findings support Minsky's open economy version of the financial instability hypothesis, which maintains that euphoria is likely to spread across national boundaries hastening speculative bubbles. Hence, speculative bubbles are more likely to intensify in an integrated global economy. Therefore, we hold that Shiller's, *Irrational Exuberance* (2000a) tells an important part of the story but still misses two important issues equally important to the run-up in US equity values that call for more intensive study.

Another important finding is that of all institutional investors, it is mutual funds flows that are statistically significant explainers of the stock market boom. Public pension funds were significant net purchasers of corporate equity over the 1982–97 period, yet the data is inconsistent with the hypothesis that their activity helps explain the run-up in US equity values. This implies unexpected public pension fund flows conveyed no information that was not already embedded in market returns or the impact of these flows occurred over a shorter time interval (that is monthly or weekly). Nevertheless, because we found significance for mutual fund and foreign portfolio flows, it is more likely the case that pension funds were not instrumental in explaining the escalation in stock prices. Given the issues raised about the differences between mutual fund and public pension fund managers, this is a damming finding. For argument's sake we were willing to concede that pension fund flows moved returns in a manner consistent with fundamentals, either by lowering the risk premium or anticipating increased corporate profitability. Instead we found that it was mutual funds, a sector pegged as the appropriate proxy for 'irrational exuberance' that played the more significant role in the run-up making it clear that the phenomenon was indeed a bubble.

7. Boom, Bubble and Burst

Wall Street did one of its best hype jobs ever. The right devices were in place – low margin rates and lots of fast info, be it on CNBC or online. I really believed the IPO market was rigged. They were selling very few shares, making consumers hang on to them and driving up prices with the talking heads on TV. A lot of amateurs – cab drivers and schoolteachers – got hurt. Old value guys like me looked stupid for one year, but we weren't stupid, we just passed. The brokers got rich, and now they're getting laid off. It was a real bubble, and we haven't seen the end of it yet ... (Michael Price, *Fortune*, April 2, 2001)

Price was prophetic. After the bubble burst in 2000, the remainder of 2001 and the first three-quarters of 2002 saw further declines in stock prices, a rash of high profile earnings restatements (including some by Fortune 500 companies that imploded as a result) and a widespread acknowledgment that the 1990s should be reinterpreted under a more scrutinizing lens. It has become abundantly clear that there was no 'new' economy and the risk premium had not fallen enough to justify the excessive market valuations. While fundamentals were found to play an important role in the bull market, the empirical investigation indicates that 'irrational exuberance' was a large part of the 1982–2000 equity appreciation puzzle. The findings documented here support the hypotheses that foreign portfolio and mutual flows as well as equity retirements moved stock prices to levels unjustified by economy-wide fundamentals. We draw this conclusion from (1) the fact that these extrinsic ingredients showed significant explanatory power even when we controlled for fundamentals, (2) the growing literature on investor flows that suggests that mutual funds are myopic investors, contributing significantly to market volatility and price risk and correspondingly, (3) the widely held notion that foreign investors are less informed than their domestic counterparts.

Although more research on the divergent characteristics of institutional investors is necessary, the asymmetric purchasing behavior of pension funds on the one hand, and foreigners and mutual funds on the other, during the height of the boom, is a suggestive stylized fact. While pension funds (held to be more sophisticated investors) were rebalancing portfolios, mutual funds and foreign investors were rushing in headlong. To be sure, foreign investors and mutual funds purchased roughly $190 billion worth of corporate equity each, while pension funds unloaded approximately $70 billion in 2001. This behavior underscores the finding that the mutual funds moved market returns along with foreign investors while the pension funds did not – an indication that the unprecedented stock price appreciation was indeed a bubble.

While the role of foreign equity flows distinguishes the recent stock market bubble from its immediate precursor, it was the shrinking supply of corporate equity that made a distinct quantitative difference. Public corporations were net issuers of corporate equity during the run-up of the 1960s; however during the 1982–2000 bull market net issues were strongly negative. This important fact is omitted from most discussions of the stock market boom although supply is explicitly acknowledged as a factor in price movements in other asset markets, especially during times of suspected bubbles. For example, in real estate markets, explosive housing prices are often linked to supply or space shortages (for example Manhattan, and Washington, DC). It is taken as a fundamental truth in macroeconomics that the Federal Reserve Bank can influence interest rates through its control of the supply of money. However, in equity markets supply forces are typically ignored, either treated analogously to dividends or taken as constant. In the first instance it is considered a fundamental determinant and in the second case, its constancy implies stock prices are largely independent of supply.

Yet, the empirical evidence laid out here has shown that lagged supply explains a significant portion of the 1982–2000 price appreciation independent of fundamentals, contradicting the notion that supply changes are inconsequential for stock market valuations. That is, just like other financial assets supply and demand forces jointly determine stock prices. The SEC's policy stance prior to 1982 illustrates there was concern over the price manipulative possibilities of share repurchase programs and, thus, an implicit understanding that supply forces codetermined stock values. With the passage of SEC Rule 10b-18, the SEC reversed its prior policy of discouraging share repurchases, opening the door for aggressive company buybacks. The amount spent on share repurchases tripled the year following the approval of Rule 10b-18 and the number of companies initiating buybacks grew to over 80 per cent in 2000 (Grullon and Michaely, 2002). It is therefore not surprising that the unprecedented escalation in stock prices coincided with the significant reduction in the amount of corporate equity outstanding from November 1982 through 1999. The complete empirical results are consistent with the hypothesis that net flows (supply and demand forces) effectively set prices. In more precise terms, the excess demand curve for equity is not perfectly elastic at the full information price.

It is important to emphasize that the initial forces underpinning the bull market were principally fundamental (corporate profits). However, as time progressed, demand forces inspired by adaptive expectations contemporaneously with a shrinking supply of shares produced prices that by the late 1990s no longer reflected the true underlying economic condition.[1] It is also imperative to underscore that while the identified forces explain a great deal of the run-up some are more significant than others at key times, and therefore must be understood together. For example, foreigners did not significantly factor into the stock market until the 1990s. Prior to their entrance, mutual funds and share retirements drove the boom backed at first by strong corporate fundamentals. Likewise, in 1988 and 1989 when the mutual funds retreated from the stock market selling $15 billion worth of corporate equities it was the corporate sector which initiated over $100 billion in cash takeovers and $22 billion in stock buybacks resulting in a dramatic reduction in the amount of shares outstanding, that perpetuated the boom.[2] In 1993 when cash-strapped corporations issued new shares increasing the effective supply of equity and placing downward pressure on prices, it was mutual fund flows that ensured equity valuations remained strong. Collectively these forces resulted in widespread stock market overvaluation.

A popular justification for this run-up was found in the new economy concept which, as we argued in Chapter 4, is in line with the efficient market hypothesis (EMH) but largely untenable. Instead, the belief in a new economy served to quiet investor suspicions about overvaluation and was part of the euphoria predicted by Minsky's financial instability hypothesis and the consequent portfolio shifts towards equity it produces. As Galbraith noted, at the core of every 'speculative episode' is some new 'artifact or some development that captures the financial mind' (J. Pontin, *Red Herring Magazine*, September 1997). Regarding the bull markets of the past in the United States, Galbraith (1988) perceptively wrote:

> Those who dissented or doubted were held not to be abreast of the mood of the times; they did not appreciate the new world of Calvin Coolidge and Herbert Hoover or, in these last years, that of the innovative and indomitable Ronald Reagan. The vested interest in euphoria leads men and women, individuals and institutions, to believe that all will be better, that they are meant to be richer, and to dismiss as intellectually deficient what is in conflict with that conviction (pp. xii–xiii).

This quote applies adequately to the new economy concept that surfaced in the business press during the mid-1990s and the implausible dividend growth rates going forward it advocated.

In the academic literature, a slightly more credible case has been made for the falling equity risk premium theory. Correspondingly, the argument might be made that variables shown to have econometric significance in Chapter 6 are spurious. Instead some might interpret the predictability found as indicative of the time variation in expected returns due to changes in the required rate of return. Yet, we also presented evidence, based on theory, stylized facts and preexisting empirical work, that the various falling risk premium theories are insufficient in explaining the intensity of the stock market boom. The case for a falling risk premium stemming from the growing importance of institutional investors appears weak given that the latter has dominated trade since 1975. Moreover, the strong counter-arguments that contend that the rise in institutional ownership (namely mutual funds) has resulted in an increase in the riskiness inherent in stock markets make the theory more untenable. In fact, surveys suggest that institutions are more likely than individual investors to have 'bubble expectations' (Shiller, 2000b). Even so, when controlling for the increase in institutional ownership of corporate equity, the significance of the flow variables and net issuance of corporate equity remained robust.

The 'investor-learning justification' for the supposed fall in the equity risk premium (Siegel, 1999) appears just as deficient. Shiller (2000a) points out that investors have had an opportunity to 'learn' about the historical dominance of stocks over bonds well before the 1990s. Just prior to the run-up in US stock prices in the late 1920s, a best-selling book was published that touted the risk–return superiority of stocks over long holding periods. Thus, the information presented in Siegel (1994) and other texts that allegedly lead to investor learning was not an entirely 'new revelation' (pp. 192–3). Moreover, a falling risk premium and, therefore, a lower required rate of return must be consistent with investor expectations. Again, survey evidence does not corroborate the theory, suggesting instead that investors were not expecting returns on the stock market going forward low enough to validate the 1982–99 run up in equity prices (Welch, 2000; Kon–Ya and Shiller, 1998). Within Shiller's paradigm the assumed public awareness that stocks cannot lose over the long run is simply a trend in social thought that occasionally generates speculative bubbles. Within the Minskian paradigm, used to underpin the book's supply and demand theory, the underpricing of risk is a natural consequence of profit-based euphoria.

By presenting a more general theory of asset price movements and testing for the significance of net flows during the 1982–2000 boom, this book has attempted to show that the supply and demand for corporate equity cannot be overlooked in the assessment of equity price behavior. The EMH predicts random stock price movements consistent with rational expectations equilibria, thereby ruling out the possibility of extreme overvaluation. This view marginalizes supply and demand issues, attributing stock price dynamics to persistent changes in discount rates or optimal forecasts of future dividend payouts. Thus, the US stock market during the 1990s typifies the type of market outcome the overly restrictive conventional theory cannot explain.[3] Yet, the econometric significance of foreign flows and net issues also illustrates that the theory of over-exuberant domestic expectations is insufficient by itself to explain the phenomenal run-up in equity valuations during the 1982–2000 period. Nevertheless, the general theories sketched out by Keynes, Veblen, Kindleberger, Minsky, Toporowski, Shiller, and Galbraith yield considerably more mileage in unpacking US equity price dynamics during the 1982–2000 period than the EMH.

WHY THE BUBBLE BURST

It was the euphoric demand for, and shrinking supply of, corporate equity, that caused the shares of several dotcom and high-tech companies to balloon in value in their first day of trading in the late 1990s, some by as much as 400 per cent. Their prices continued to climb despite the fact that more than 80 per cent of the top 133 Internet IPOs had not shown any profits as late as the second quarter of 1999 (Perkins and Perkins, 1999). However, the bubble was not confined to the Internet sector. The price appreciation in other segments of the stock market, although not as extreme, was significant such that movements in aggregate indices over the 1990s grossly overstated the earning potential of publicly listed US corporations. More than the outcome of an efficient market, the phenomenon was reminiscent of Keynes' (1964) description of the stock market as a game of 'Snap', 'Old Maid', or 'Musical Chairs' (p. 154).

Once the bubble formed its collapse was inevitable. The US stock market bubble burst simply because the valuations were not reflective of the economy's true potential – a discrepancy investors could no longer tolerate and, corporations could not continue to support with continuous equity retirements. Contrary to the expectations generated by the stock market, profits after taxes turned down sharply from $845.4 billion in 2000 to $698.5 billion in 2001. Although mutual fund net purchases and foreign portfolio flows remained robust in 2000, these sectors could not match the $495 billion worth of equity sold by the household sector. Moreover, these flows slowed significantly in 2001 and during the first quarter of 2002. In fact, the fall in equity prices in 2001 resulted in a negative valuation adjustment that dwarfed foreign portfolio inflows that year.[4]

Nor could corporations continue to place upward pressure on prices by retiring corporate shares. Evidence suggests that the continued pace of share repurchases exhibited during the 1990s by S&P 500 companies would require the utilization of 90 per cent of their aggregate earnings. Payout ratios of this size are decapitalizing as they leave little for the financing of new investment. Without new investment firms could not produce the profits necessary to validate the lofty stock valuations. Ironically the very activity that initially helped to fuel and reinforce the bubble eventually ensured its collapse. (Like a lizard eating its own tail for nourishment.) Not surprisingly, net issues turned positive in 2001 to the tune of $83.9 billion. New issues continued to swamp buybacks and takeover activities during the first quarter of 2002, placing downward pressure on market valuations.

Before euphoria yielded to market retreat, stock market participants facilitated the establishment of an environment where expectations of future prosperity outstripped realistic assessments of corporate profitability. As the economy evolved from a state of robustness to speculative advance, expected future profitability and the ratio of debt financing rose. As a result, classic examples of the 'speculative' and 'Ponzi' units (debt-burdened firms euphorically driven by past profitability) detailed in Minsky's model of financial fragility abounded in 2000, 2001 and 2002. For example, Tyco International aggressively acquired well over 700 companies during the late 1990s into 2000 utilizing questionable accounting practices along the way to exaggerate the profitability of its activities. Tyco's stock price plummeted in 2001 once the subterfuge was uncovered. After trading for as high as $60 the stock closed under $13 at the end of July 2002 and its debt burden resulted in its debt being relegated to 'junk' status or 'near-junk' status by the major credit rating agencies.

WorldCom, the quintessential Ponzi unit described in Minsky's paradigm, grew through 60-plus debt-financed mergers and acquisitions from 1983. The market erroneously rewarded its efforts and its stock price closed at $45.31 near the peak of the market in 2000 and at $64 a year earlier. However, time revealed that underlying the stock price appreciation was a firm worth less than the book value of its debt. WorldCom officials ultimately revealed the blatantly fraudulent accounting practices it employed to stretch the bottom line in order to mask the company's true financial condition. By the July 31, 2002 bankruptcy proceedings had been initiated and its stock price had fallen to 75¢ per share. Both Tyco International and WorldCom Group are concrete examples of the fact that mergers and the related retirement of shares do not always result in increases in corporate profits, yielding dividends to shareholders.

Despite the disturbing trend in accounting irregularities recently uncovered, the bubble did not burst because of revelations of corporate malfeasance. The market had already turned downwards well before indications of the fraudulent accounting practices of Enron, Adelphia, WorldCom and others. Moreover, the Enrons and WorldComs of 2001 and 2002 did not enigmatically pop into existence. There were numerous (literally hundreds) examples of companies employing similar tactics to inflate earnings well before 2001. Domestic and international investors simply ignored the corporate improprieties of Waste Management, Rite Aid, Sunbeam and too many others, pushing the broad market higher. In 1997, top executives at the now defunct Centennial Technologies gave investors an early warning of the impending cost of financial euphoria. In this instance, the company booked millions of dollars in fictitious revenues from a non-existent product turning a $28 million loss into a $12 million profit.[5]

Moreover, some of the fraudulent accounting was a direct result of the stock market bubble either through pressuring managers to stretch General Accepted Accounting Principles or by providing the euphoric environment conducive to swindles, misrepresentation and deception. Enron Corporation, which collapsed under cleverly disguised, speculative derivative trades that dwarfed its brick-and-mortar operations, illustrates perfectly that the very climate that encourages a stock market bubble also facilitates the creation of 'bubble companies'.[6] Undoubtedly, the false prosperity theorized in Veblen's model of speculative price behavior left investors susceptible to such examples of corporate misrepresentation. Kindleberger's overview of financial manias, panics and crashes indicates that financial fraud is a predictable part of the Minsky cycle. He writes:

> The propensities to swindle and be swindled run parallel to the propensity to speculate during the boom. Crash and panic, with their motto, *suave qui peut*, induce still more to cheat in order to save themselves. And the signal for panic is often the revelation of some swindle, theft, embezzlement or fraud. (Kindleberger, 1996, p. 69)

Galbraith noting a connection between stock market bust and embezzlement notes that it is difficult to defraud a cautious public but euphoric investors are easily victimized. Either way these corporate debacles are clear signals that the financial euphoria has been overdone.

Chairman Greenspan (2002) astutely points out that the unintended consequence of SEC Rule 10b-18 was that it provided corporations with the impetus and opportunity to inflate earnings. As dividend payments gave way to share repurchases, the focus of stock price evaluation shifted from the cash dividends and dividend yields towards earnings. Whereas the value of cash dividends is straightforward there is no unambiguously correct value of earnings. Thus, Greenspan maintains that the recent rise in earnings restatements reflects the rise in the importance of earnings and the uncertainties it poses for stock valuation:

> Not surprising then, with the longer-term outlook increasingly amorphous, the level and recent growth of short-term earnings have taken on especial significance in stock price evaluation, with quarterly earnings reports subject to anticipation, rumor, and 'spin'. Such tactics, presumably, attempt to induce investors to extrapolate short-term trends into a favorable long-term view that would raise the current stock price. CEOs, under increasing pressure from the investment community to meet short-term elevated expectations, in too many instances have been drawn to accounting devices whose sole purpose is arguably to obscure potential adverse results ... (p. 3)

Nevertheless, the bubble has burst revealing corporate misdeeds and there is enough blame to be laid at many doorsteps – publicly listed companies, mutual funds, foreign investors, the media, stock analyst, investment banks, and lest we forget domestic investors themselves.

GOING FORWARD

Stock prices maintain an important informational role in developed capitalist economies, both as signal for the allocation of capital and as a leading indicator of corporate and macroeconomic performance. The logical and uneventful consequence of this informational responsibility is that if the prices arrived at by the stock market mechanism are 'wrong', the signals sent to economic agents, and about the course of the macroeconomy, are faulty. Thus, as the quote from

Shiller (2000a) at the beginning of the book emphasizes, there are tremendous consequences for a market economy when prices are detached from their more fundamental values. These implications include but are not limited to the inefficient allocation of resources and the stimulation of individual economic behavior premised on counterfeit prosperity.

During the 1990s households experienced a $15 trillion increase in net worth, the bulk of which was stock market-related. A $10,000 investment in a portfolio mimicking the Standard and Poor's (S&P) 500 in 1982 was worth $140,363 in capital gains alone by the end of 1999. Simultaneously, by 1998 consumer debt had soared to record levels and the personal savings rate had fallen below 1 per cent owing in part to stock market wealth gains and consumer's confidence about the future (Browne, 1999, p. 13). Since the wealth was premised on factors unrelated to future corporate performance as we have argued here, consumers have spent too much and not saved enough. In the corporate sector, AOL provides the most obvious example of how perverse pricing can lead to faulty and costly decision making. In 2000, AOL acquired Time Warner paying $147 billion based partially on inflated market valuations. As it turns out AOL paid $54 billion too much and was eventually forced to write down the value of it assets in order to reflect the true value of Time Warner.

Moreover, overvaluation implies a reversion in prices to more justifiable levels either abruptly or gradually. After the market reached a record high price–earnings ratio of 32.6 in 1929, the S&P Index fell 80.6 per cent over the next three years. Subsequent to reaching a price–earnings (p–e) ratio of 24.1 in 1966, S&P stock prices fell 56 per cent by 1974 not rebounding to its initial 1966 level in real terms until 1992 (Shiller, 2000a, p. 4). Japan, whose market capitalization in 1990 was larger than that of the United States despite an underlying economy that was half as small, continues to suffer through a bear market over a decade old. Not surprisingly the 44.3 p–e ratio that stood on US S&P 500 stock at the end of 1999 has fallen precipitously over the subsequent years. However, the market remained overvalued as measured by the p–e ratio that endured at the end of July 2002 (24 relative to the historical average of roughly 16). Thus, if history is any guide for the future, poor stock market performance going forward should be expected. The stock market can only come close to matching the performance of the last two decades if corporations continually retire equity and foreign and domestic funds continue to flow into the market at unprecedented rates despite the deteriorating fundamentals.

On a final note, the bubble psychology of the 1990s was not confined to stock market investing but transferred into the minds of policymakers, impacting the policy formation process. For example, many advocates for the privatization of Social Security have premised their arguments on the relative performance of the bond and stock markets and the belief that the stock market will continue to produce real rates of return around the historical average, 7 per cent. However, this ironically conflicts with the law of averages. Given the double-digit gains reaped over the 1990s, low or even negative returns are necessary to bring stock market returns back in line with the historical average. Consequently, investing a portion of the Social Security Trust Fund in the stock market under the guise of private accounts will bring disappointment and may jeopardize a long-established safety net for the elderly. While stocks are never safe, in this environment they are even more risky since they have been bid to such high levels that they can possibly lose, even over the long run.

Nevertheless, we maintain that by the first quarter of 2000 US equity values were at levels unjustified by optimal forecasts of future discounted cash flows; the general case for market efficiency has been overstated; and the future bodes poorly for the US stock market all things being equal. Collectively, investors, entrepreneurs and policymakers must re-learn that equity prices are inherently risky, influenced not only by fundamental forces but also supply changes, waves of optimism and pessimism, rumor and a host of other psychological factors. To paraphrase Strange (1998), stock markets can be viewed as the weakest linkage in the international system and should be, therefore, scrutinized periodically for signs of crisis-provoking phenomenon. In short, the manner in which financial markets work and how prices are set in speculative markets need to be more fully explored and understood.

Notes

CHAPTER 1

1. *Wall Street Journal*, March 3, 1999, p. 26.

CHAPTER 2

1. Government scrip is shorthand for 'the IOUs issued by the Continental Congress and states to wartime soldiers and suppliers' (Blume et al., 1993, pp. 21–2).
2. Not surprisingly, the EMH emerged concomitantly with the ascendance of rational expectation models in macroeconomics (Raines and Leathers, 2000, p. 37).
3. In this since (and this since only) Minsky is more Veblenian than Keynesian.
4. This does not imply that Galbraith is wrong for modeling agents as irrational.
5. James Tobin objected to Toporowski's use of the word inflation in the context of financial markets, holding inflation to refer specifically to a rise in general price level for goods and services (that is, nothing changes but prices). Accordingly, we refer to it as the flow theory of capital market price fluctuation.
6. The relatively new area of behavioral finance also attempts to inject psychology and human behavior into the realm of financial economics. See Barberis (1998) in *The Complete Finance Companion*.
7. For a thorough review of stock market anomalies see Dimson (1988).
8. For the remaining discussion we use the term 'rational' and 'irrational' in a manner consistent with efficient markets theory unless otherwise indicated.
9. This work is predated by Flood and Garber (1980), which was one of the first works to consider price bubbles within a rational expectations context.
10. Note, many of the Keynesian theories surveyed above are not premised on irrational behavior. Nonetheless, they have been interpreted as such in the mainstream literature.
11. Raines and Leathers (2000) advocate for the KVGS (Keynes, Veblen, Galbraith and Shiller) model of equity price movements, which they argue, provides a plausible alternative approach.

CHAPTER 3

1. The small literature on capital flows and equity prices is a notable exception to be surveyed briefly below. We also discuss the literature on small open economies for which foreign influences cannot be ignored.
2. See the empirical work of Cutler et al. (1990) discussed below.

3. Recall from Chapter 2 that the formal statistical representation of the EMH is the martingale model.
4. Note the default spread (DEF) is the same as the risk premium (UPR) in Chen et al. (1986).
5. As noted above both interest spread variables can send misleading signals because speculation in the bond market may lead to yields unreflective of fundamentals.
6. This 'Q-channel' is far from uncontroversial even on theoretical grounds. For example, Crotty (1990) and Bosworth (1975) note that there is no reason to expect managers to passively react to market valuations when they are closer to the production process and the operation of the firm. New Keynesian theorists cite the problem associated with asymmetric information inherent in stock markets and note firms' marked preference for internal and bank financing over the exploitation of capital markets. This immediately challenges the notion that stock prices strongly impact corporate investment demand directly (Mayer, 1990).
7. Proponents of the New Keynesian paradigm place special emphasis on this 'collateral' channel, thus stressing the indirect impact of stock price changes on investment demand. Collateral assuages the principal–agent problems of moral hazard and adverse selection that lead to market imperfections laid out in Akerlof's (1970) seminal article.
8. One of the assumptions of the CLRM is that the right-hand-side variables are uncorrelated with the error term, or more formally, $E(Xi|Ui) = 0$.
9. It appears that Shaikh has neglected the literature on the dynamic dividend discount model, which relaxes the constant dividend growth and discount rates assumption (see Chapter 4).
10. Thus the argument we developed earlier that the dividend yield approximated the role of error correcting term.
11. There are also some econometric problems with Edwards and Zhang (1998) and therefore the conclusion they draw. We address this directly in Chapter 6.
12. This is Davidson's (1999) basic point – the more liquid the market the more inefficient it will become.

CHAPTER 4

1. For example, between 1984:11 and 1989:11, real stock prices rose 1,253.2 per cent in the Philippines. In Peru the corresponding number was 743.1 per cent during the 1991:9–1996:9 period.
2. Speculative bubbles are ruled out with the assumption, $\lim_{(j \to \infty)} b_j\, p_{t+j} = 0$.
3. S. Shepard, 'The New Economy: What it Really Means', *Business Week*, November 1997, pp. 48–50.
4. Martin Wolf (2001), 'The Price of Stocks is Still High,' FT.com (*Financial Times*), October 16.
5. According to Wolff (2000), the average wealth of the bottom 40 per cent fell 76 per cent between 1983 and 1998. The poorest 10 per cent had a lower income in 1999 than in 1977 while the richest 10 per cent saw their incomes rise by 115 per cent over the same period. In 1999, the income differential in the US between the poorest and richest 20 per cent had reached levels unseen since 1945 (Paulre, 2000, p. 16).
6. Many investigators concentrate on nominal growth rates of dividends. Our nominal calculations, reported in Table 4.1, are consistent with these estimates (for example, see Jagannathan et al., 2001).

7. It should be noted that using the entire 129-year history, historical averages also yield a risk premium in the neighborhood of 4 per cent (Welch, 2000, p. 503).
8. Pratten (1993), in an extensive survey, found that institutional investors in the United Kingdom, who account for 80 per cent of stock market turnover, contributed significantly to volatility and riskiness in stock markets. First, he uncovers evidence that fund mangers consider the asset allocation practices of their competitors when composing or rebalancing portfolios, suggesting an endeavor to confirm with average or majority behavior. Furthermore, the results of the survey were consistent with the notion that fund mangers attempt to anticipate the changes in investment strategies of other fund managers to evaluate possibilities to beat market. The results of several surveys with institutional investors summarized in Shiller (2000a, 2000b), Kon Ya and Shiller (1998) and Shiller and Pound (1989) provide strong evidence that this analysis most probably applies to the United States as well.
9. Shiller (2000a) describes speculative bubbles, especially the stock market of the late 1990s, as a 'naturally occurring Ponzi processes'.
10. Veblen's model of speculative advance (or false prosperity) is also closely related to this analysis.
11. Excerpted from Chairman Greenspan's speech at the Economic Club of New York, December 6, 1999.

CHAPTER 5

1. Included in this sector are bank personal trusts and estates that were not so constrained. Collectively corporate equity and mutual fund shares made up over 70 per cent of all financial assets of this sector in 1997, 1998 and 1999.
2. Here we include money market fund shares as deposits along with demand, time and foreign deposits.
3. Percentages computed using the Federal Reserve Board's *Flow of Funds Accounts*, Table L.100.
4. *Flow of Funds Accounts*, Federal Reserve Board.
5. Investment Company Institute (2000 and 2001), *Mutual Fund Fact Book.*
6. Del Guerico and Tkac, 2000 and Investment Company Institute, 2001.
7. Investment Company Institute, 2001.
8. Researchers at the Federal Reserve Board note that this cast doubt on the accuracy of the corporate equity tables in the *Flow of Funds Accounts*. Thus, the level tables may lead to an underestimation of the amount of equity actually held by foreigners. Because the equity held by the households is calculated as a residual it then must be the case that the amount held by this sector is overstated by the same amount that the foreign sector is understated (see *Guide to the Flow of Funds Accounts*).
9. Data on the decomposition of FDI dates back only to the second quarter of 1982. Prior to this The Bureau of Economic Analysis' *Survey of Current Business* and therefore the Federal Reserve Boards' *Flow of Funds Accounts* code FDI equity as zero. We therefore do not address the relationship between FDI equity flows and stock prices prior to the 1982–2000 period.
10. Margin debt, according to the estimates of Ned Davis Research, has ballooned to $228.5 billion in 1999, up from $141 billion from the previous year.
11. Jane D'Arista (1999) in the publication *Capital Flows,* produced by the Financial Markets Center, proposes a substitution effect, which is premised on the idea that for-

eigners purchase bonds from the domestic public who then increase purchases of equity, directly or through mutual funds.

12. *Business Week*, November 1999, 'Is the US Building a Debt Bomb?'.
13. *The Wall Street Journal*, 'Portfolio Profits Boost Firms' Bottom Line But Stir Controversy', November 26.
14. The efficiency gains from merger and takeovers has been called into question by the fact that approximately one-third of all leveraged buyouts after 1985 lead to defaults on the existing debt. See Kaplan and Stein (1993) and Holmstrom and Kaplan (2001).
15. Recall from Chapter 4 that the original formulation of the Gordon equation is $P_t = D_t(1 + g)/i + \rho - g$. The equation generates from the conventional dividend discount model where the growth rate of dividends is assumed to be constant. See Myron J. Gordon (1962) and Campbell et al. (1997).
16. See the aforementioned articles for a more formal proof.
17. Here the growth rate of dividends is not assumed constant but when such an assumption is made, the dynamic and static dividend growth models are equivalent.
18. Dr. Bailey Preston (2000), 'How to Trade in Volatile Markets', http://www.Manhattanbaptist.org/Supertraders/ST10-06001.htm.
19. *Business Week*, November 1999, 'Is the US Building a Debt Bomb?'.
20. We must also entertain the possibility that stock buybacks were enabled by permanent increases in corporate profitability and therefore can persist into the future. In this case high returns can be maintained not in the form of higher dividends but in the form of capital gains.
21. One example is detailed in the January 2000 issue of *Black Enterprise*, 'Hitching a Ride: Share buybacks signal confidence in a company's future', p. 36.

CHAPTER 6

1. The S&P Index is also found to be stationary for 1953–99 and 1982–99. Total pension fund (private and public) flows and total institutional investor flows are found to be difference stationary processes. These results are not reported in Table 6.2.
2. We also employed the model on the 1989:1–1999:4 period. With the number of variables and lags included the degrees of freedom were reduced to just 28 and thus, the results should be questioned. Nevertheless, the results, not reported here, are always consistent with those from the 1982–99 period.
3. The results for the VAR in levels are not reported here but suggest stronger relationships between the causal variables investigated here and the S&P Index.
4. We do employ an alternative model, which utilizes after-tax profits (profit), but the results do not significantly alter our results and are therefore not reported. In fact utilizing profits leads to a decline in the amount of the variation of market returns explained by fundamentals. This is not surprising given that the variables chosen as proxies for fundamental value were done so primarily on the basis of goodness-of-fit (see Chapter 3).
5. 'Failure to adequately filter out expected movement in an independent variable is to introduce an errors-in-the-variables problem' (p. 386).
6. Note well, we arbitrarily separated the data the sub-periods 1953–81 and 1982–99 in our reduced form investigation without investigating the possibility of structural breaks. Consequently, the 1953–81 period combines data from two distinct eras and the Granger causality tests on this subsection of the data are therefore biased.

7. Many econometricians simply accept the asymptotic bias of OLS estimates in the presence of endogenous equations bias for several justifiable reasons. First, the OLS estimator has minimum variance over 2SLS and other alternative estimators. Second, in small samples alternative estimators are biased and OLS estimators may have a minimum square error. And finally, OLS estimates are less sensitive to data problems such as measurement error and multicollinearity than alternative estimators (Kennedy, 1993, pp. 157–8).

8. We performed the same experiment using the percentage of equity held by foreign investors to investigate a potential relationship with market returns. The results, however, were statistically insignificant.

9. The *Survey of Consumer Finances* is conducted once every three years by the Federal Reserve Board, http://www.federalreserve.gov.

CHAPTER 7

1. Inflated earnings during the late 1990s both from accounting improprieties and the general practice of not expensing stock options may have served to exaggerate the role of fundamentals. One study estimates that as a result of the failure to expense stock options, profits of the largest 100 companies were inflated by 30 per cent, 36 per cent, 56 per cent and 50 per cent in 1995, 1996, 1997 and 1998, respectively (Morrissey, 2000).

2. *Liquidity Trim Tabs* (2002), Volume 9, Number 30, August 5.

3. An efficient stock market relies heavily on a large number of infinitesimally small agents who individually cannot move equity prices; this is the sine qua non of perfect competition. With institutional investors dominating the market, the representative agents can no longer be deemed infinitesimal and thus, a consistent, euphoric balance of opinion about future profit growth among market participants is more likely to move equity prices in a manner unjustified by economic fundamentals (Gompers and Metrick, 1998; Friedman, 1996). For this reason alone, we maintain that the boom of the 1990s was drastically different from that of the 1960s when households held the bulk of all corporate equity outstanding.

4. *Capital Flows Monitor* (2002), Financial Markets Center, July 26.

5. The guilty parties fabricated the revenue by shipping empty boxes and fruit baskets to friends and old colleagues to create false sales records. A five-year prison sentence and $150 million dollar fine ensued.

6. Warren Buffet made this point in his annual report to shareholders. *Business Week* (2002), 'How Corrupt is Wall Street?', May 13.

Bibliography

Aggarwal, R. and D. Schirm (eds) (1995), *Global Portfolio Diversification: Risk Management: Risk Management, Market Microstructure and Implementation Issues*, San Diego: Academic Press, Inc.

Akerlof, G. (1970), 'The Market for Lemons: Qualitative Uncertainty and the Market Mechanism', *Quarterly Journal of Economics,* **84**, 488–500.

Allen, F., A. Bernardo and I. Welch (2000), 'A Theory of Dividends Based on Tax Clienteles', *Journal of Finance*, **55** (6), 2499–536.

Anderson, T. (1983/84), 'Some Implications of the Efficient Capital Markets Hypothesis', *Journal of Post Keynesian Economics*, Winter, 281–94.

Asprem, M. (1989), 'Stock Prices, Asset Portfolios and Macroeconomic Variables in Ten European Countries', *Journal of Banking and Finance*, **13**, 589–612.

Baker, M. and J. Wurgler (1999), 'The Equity Share in New Issues and Aggregate Stock Returns', Yale ICF Working Paper 99–07.

Balke, N. and M. Wohar (2001), 'Explaining Stock Price Movements: Is there a Case for Fundamentals?', *Economic and Financial Review*, Third Quarter, 22–34.

Balduzzi, P. (1995), 'Stock Returns, Inflation, and the "Proxy Hypothesis": A New Look at the Data', *Economic Letters*, **48**, 47–53.

Balvers R., T. Cosimano and B. McDonald (1990), 'Predicting Stock Returns in an Efficient Market', *Journal of Finance*, **45**, 1109–1128.

Barberis, N. (1998), 'Markets: The Price may not be Right', in *The Complete Finance Companion: Mastering Finance*, London: Pitman Publishing.

Barro, R. (1989), 'The Stock Market and the Macroeconomy: Implications of the October 1987 Crash', in R.Kamphius, R. Kormendi and J. Watson (eds), *Black Monday and the Future of Financial Markets*, Homewood, IL: Dow Jones Irwin.

—— (1990), 'The Stock Market and Investment', *Review of Financial Studies*, **3**, 115–32.

Barsky, R. and J. De Long (1983), 'Why does the Stock Market Fluctuate?', *Quarterly Journal of Economics*, **108**, 293–311.

—— (1989), 'Bull and Bear Markets in the Twentieth Century', NBER Working Paper 3171.

Bekaert, G. and C. Harvey (1998a), 'Capital Flows and Behavior of Emerging Market Equity Returns', National Bureau of Economics Research, Working Paper 6669.

—— (1998b), 'Dating the Integration of World Equity Markets', National Bureau of Economics Research, Working Paper 6724.

Bernanke, B. (1986), 'Alternative Explanations of the Money–income Correlation', *Carnegie Rochester Conference Series on Public Policy*, **25** (Autumn), 49–101.

—— (1990), 'On the Predictive Power of Interest Spreads', *New England Economic Review* (November–December), 51–68.

Bernanke, B. and M. Gertler (1995), 'Inside the Black Box: The Credit Channel of Monetary Policy Transmission', *Journal of Economic Perspectives*, **9** (4), 27–48.

Bernheim, B. (1991), 'Tax Policy and the Dividend Puzzle', *RAND Journal of Economics*, **22**, 455–76.

Bernstein, P.L. (1992), *Capital Ideas: The Improbable Origins of Modern Wall Street*, New York: The Free Press.

—— (1996), *Against the Gods: The Remarkable Story of Risk*, New York: John Wiley & Sons.

—— (1998a), 'Stock Market Risk in a Post Keynesian World', *Journal of Post Keynesian Economics*, **21** (1), 15–24.

—— (1998b), 'How Long can you Run – and Where are you Running?', *Journal of Post Keynesian Economics*, **20** (2), 183–189.

Binswanger, M. (1999), *Stock Markets, Speculative Bubbles and Economic Growth,* Aldershot, UK and Northampton, US: Edward Elgar Publishing.

Black, F. (1986), 'Noise', *Journal of Finance*, **93** (1), 529–43.

Blanchard, O. (1993), 'Movements in the Equity Risk Premium', *Brookings Papers on Economic Activity*, **2**, 75–118.

Blanchard, O., C. Rhee and L. Summers (1993), 'The Stock Market, Profit and Investment', *Quarterly Journal of Economics*, **108** (1), 115–136.

Blanchard, O. and M. Watson (1982), 'Bubbles, Rational Expectations and Financial Markets', in P. Wachtel (ed.), *Crisis in the Economic and Financial Structure*, Lexington, MA: Lexington Books.

Blume, M., J. Siegal and D. Rottenberg (1993), *Revolution on Wall Street: The Rise and Decline of New York Stock Exchange*, New York: W.W. Norton & Company.

Bohn, H. and L. Tesar (1996), 'US Equity Investment in Foreign Markets: Portfolio Re-balancing or Return Chasing?', *American Economic Review*, **86** (2), 77–81.

Bosworth, B. (1975), 'The Stock Market and the Economy', *Brookings Papers on Economic Activity*, **2**, 257–300.

Bowles, S., D. Gordon and T. Weisskopf (1986), 'Power and Profits: The Social Structure of Accumulation and the Profitability of the Postwar US Economy', *Review of Radical Political Economics*, **18** (1–2), 132–67.

Brainard, W. and J. Tobin (1968), 'Pitfalls in Financial Model Building', *American Economic Review*, **58** (2), 99–122.

Brealey R. (1991), 'Harry M. Markowitz's Contributions to Financial Economics', *Scandinavian Journal of Economics*, **93** (1), 7–17.

Brealey R. and K. Nyborg (1998), 'New Equity Issues and Raising Cash', in *The Complete Finance Companion: Mastering Finance*, London: Pitman Publishing.

Brennan, M. and H. Cao (1997), 'International Portfolio Investment Flows', *Journal of Finance*, **52** (5), 1851–80.

Browne, L. (1999), 'US Economic Performance: Good Fortune, Bubble, or New Era?', *New England Economic Review* (May/June), 3–20.

Bulow, J. and P. Klemperer (1994), 'Rational Frenzies and Crashes', *Journal of Political Economy*, **102** (1), 1–23.

Campbell J., A. Lo and A. MacKinlay (1997), *The Econometrics of Financial Markets*, Princeton, NJ: Princeton University Press.

Campbell J. and R. Shiller (1988), 'The Dividend–price Ratio and Expectations of Future Dividends and Discount Factors', *Review of Financial Studies*, **1**, 195–228.

—— (1998), 'Valuation Ratios and the Long Run Stock Market Outlook', *Journal of Portfolio Management*, **24** (2), 11–26.

Campbell, J. and L. Viceira (1999), 'Consumption and Portfolio Decisions when Expected Returns are Time Varying', *Quarterly Journal of Economics* (May), 11–26.

Canova, F. and G. De Nicolo (1995), 'Stock Returns and Real Activity: A Structural Approach', *European Economic Review*, **39**, 981–1015.

Capon, N., G. Fitzsimons and R. Prince (1996), 'An Individual Level Analysis of the Mutual Fund Investment Decision', *Journal of Financial Services Research*, **10**, 59–82.

Carlson, J. and K. Sargent (1997), 'The Recent Ascent of Stock Prices: Can it be Explained by Earnings Growth or Other Fundamentals?', *Federal Reserve Bank Cleveland Economic Review*, **33** (2), 2–12.

Cass, D. and K. Shell (1983), 'Do Sunspots Matter?' *Journal of Political Economy*, **91** (2), 193–227.

Chamberlain, T. and M. Gordon (1989), 'Liquidity, Profitability and Long-run Survival: Theory and Evidence on Business Investment', *Journal of Post Keynesian Economics*, **11** (4), 589–610.

Chan, K., S. Norbin and P. Lai (1997), 'Are Stock and Bond Prices Collinear in the Long Run', *International Review of Economics and Finance*, **6** (2), 193–201.

Chen, N., R. Roll and S.A. Ross (1986), 'Economic Forces and the Stock Market', *Journal of Business*, **59** (3), 383–403.

Choi, J., S. Hausar and K. Kopecky (1999), 'Does the Stock Market Predict Real Activity? Time Series Evidence from G-7 Countries', *Journal of Banking and Finance*, **23**, 1771–92.

Ciccolo, J.H. (1978), 'Money, Equity Values, and Income: Tests for Exogeneity', *Journal of Money, Credit and Banking*, **10** (1), 46–64.

Ciccolo, J.H. and G. Fromm (1980), 'q, Corporate Investment, and Balance Sheet Behavior', *Journal of Money, Credit and Banking*, **12** (2), 294–307.

Claessens, S., M. Dooley and A. Warner (1993), 'Portfolio Capital Flows: Hot or Cool?' in S. Claessens and S. Goptu (eds), *Portfolio Investment in Developing Countries*, Washington, DC: World Bank.

Clark, J. and E. Berko (1996), 'Foreign Investment Fluctuations and Emerging Market Stock Returns: The Case of Mexico', Federal Reserve Bank of New York Staff Report 24.

Clark, P. (1979), 'Investment in the 1970s: Theory, Performance, and Prediction', *Brookings Papers on Economic Activity*, **1**, 73–113.

Claus, J. and J. Thomas (1999), 'The Equity Risk Premium is Much Lower than You Think it is: Empirical Estimates from a New Approach', Manuscript, Columbia University.

Cochrane, J. (1997), 'Where is the Market Going? Uncertain Facts and Novel Theories', *Economic Perspectives*, **21** (6), 3–37.

—— (1999), 'New Facts in Finance', *Economic Perspectives*, **23** (3), 59–78.

Cole, K., J. Helwege and B. Laster (1996), 'Stock Market Valuation Indicators: Is this Time Different?', *Financial Analysts Journal*, **52**, 56–64.

Collins, J. (2000), 'Built to Flip', <http://www.fastCompany.com/online/32/builtoflip.txt>.

Cooley, T. and S. Leroy (1985), 'Atheoretical Macroeconomics: A Critique', *Journal of Monetary Economics*, **16**, 283–308.

Cootner, P. (1964), *The Random Character of Stock Market Prices*, Cambridge, MA: The MIT Press.

Cowles, A. (1933), 'Can Stock Market Forecasters Forecast?' *Econometrica*, **1** (4), 309–24.

Crotty, J. (1990), 'Owner–manager Conflict and Financial Theories of Investment Instability: A Critical Assessment Keynes, Tobin and Minsky', *Journal of Post Keynesian Economics*, **12** (4), 519–42.

—— (1993), 'Neoclassical and Keynesian Approaches to the Theory of Investment', in P. Davidson (ed.), *Can the Free Market Pick Winners?*, Armonk, NY: M.E. Sharpe.

Cuthbertson, K. (1996), *Quantitative Financial Economics: Stocks, Bonds, and Foreign Exchange*, New York: John Wiley & Sons.

Cutler, D., J. Poterba and L. Summers (1990), 'Speculative Dynamics', National Bureau of Economic Research Working Paper 3242.

D'Arista, J. (1994), *The Evolution of the US Finance, Volume II: Restructuring Institutions and Markets,* Armonk, NY: M.E. Sharpe.

—— (1999), 'International Capital Flows and the US Capital Account', *Capital Flows Monitor* (December), Washington, DC: Financial Markets Center.

—— (2001), 'The US International Investment Position at Year-end 2000', *Capital Flows Monitor* (September), Washington, DC: Financial Markets Center.

Davidson, P. (1972), *Money and the Real World*, New York: John Wiley & Sons.

—— (1999), 'The Role of Financial Markets: Efficiency Versus Liquidity and the Financial Fragility Hypothesis', Paper Presented at the Conference on Structure, Instability and the World Economy: Reflections on the Economics of Hyman P. Minsky, The Jerome Levy Economics Institute, Annandale-on-Hudson, NY, April 21–23.

Del Guerico, D. and P. Tkac (2000), 'The Determinants of the Flow of Funds of Managed Portfolios: Mutual Funds versus Pension Funds', Working Paper Series 2000–21, Federal Reserve Bank of Atlanta, November.

DeLong, J., A. Shleifer, L. Summers and R. Waldman (1990a), 'Positive Feedback Investment Strategies and Destabilizing Rational Speculation', *Journal of Finance*, **45** (2), 379–95.

—— (1990b), 'Noise Trader Risk and Financial Markets', *Journal of Political Economy*, **98** (4), 703–738.

Dennis, P. and D. Strickland (2000), 'Who Blinks in Volatile Markets, Individuals or Institutions?', Social Science Research Network Working Paper Series, <http://papers.ssrn.com>.

Diamond, P. (2000), 'What Stock Market Returns to Expect for the Future', *Social Security Bulletin*, **63** (2), 38–52.

Dickey, D. and W. Fuller (1979), 'Distribution of the Estimators for Autoregressive Time Series With a Unit Root', *Journal of the American Statistical Society*, **74**, 427–31.

Dimson, E. (ed.) (1988), *Stock Market Anomalies,* Cambridge: Cambridge University Press.

Domian, D.L. and D.A. Louton (1997), 'A Threshold Autoregressive Analysis of Stock Returns and Real Economic Activity', *International Review of Economics and Finance*, **6** (2), 167–79.

Donaldson, G. (1994), *Corporate Restructuring*, Boston: Harvard Business School Press.

Dornbusch, R. and Y. Park (1995), 'Financial Integration in a Second Best World: Are we Still Sure About our Classical Prejudices', in R. Dornbusch and Y. Park (eds), *Financial Opening: Policy Lessons for Korea*, Seoul: Korea Institute of Finance.

Dow, C. H. (1920) 'Scientific Stock Speculation', *The Magazine of Wall Street*, New York.

Edwards, F. and X. Zhang (1998), 'Mutual Funds and Stock and Bond Market Stability', *Journal of Financial Services Research*, **13** (3), 257–82.

Elias, D. (1999), *Dow 40,000: Strategies for Profiting from the Greatest Bull Market in History*, New York: McGraw-Hill.

Enders, W. (1995), *Applied Econometric Time Series*, New York: John Wiley & Sons.

Estrella, A. and F. Mishkin (1998), 'Predicting US Recessions: Financial Variables as Leading Indicators', *The Review of Economics and Statistics*, **80**, 45–61.

Fama, E. (1970), 'Efficient Capital Markets: A Review of Theory and Empirical Work', *Journal of Finance*, **25** (2), 383–417.

—— (1976), *Foundations of Finance,* NY: Basic Books.

—— (1981), 'Stock Returns, Real Activity and Money', *American Economic Review*, **71** (4), 545–65.

—— (1983), 'Stock Returns, Real Activity and Money: Reply', *American Economic Review*, **73** (3), 471–2.

—— (1990), 'Stock Returns, Expected Returns, and Real Activity', *Journal of Finance*, **45** (4), 1089–108.

—— (1991), 'Efficient Capital Markets: II', *Journal of Finance*, **46** (5), 1575–617.

Fama, E. and K. French (1988), 'Dividend Yield and Expected Stock Returns', *Journal of Financial Economics*, **22**, 3–25.

—— (1989), 'Business Conditions and Expected Returns on Stocks and Bonds', *Journal of Financial Economics*, **25**, 23–49.

—— (2000), 'Disappearing Dividends: Changing Firm Characteristics of Lower Propensity to Pay', CRSP Working Paper 509.

—— (2001), 'The Equity Premium', CRSP Working Paper 522.

Fischer, S. and R.C. Merton (1983), 'Macroeconomics and Finance: The Role of the Stock Market', *Carnegie Rochester Conference Series on Public Policy*, **XXI**, 57–108.

Flavin, M. (1983), 'Excess Volatility in the Financial Markets: A Reassessment of the Empirical Evidence', *Journal of Political Economy*, **91** (6), 929–56.

Flood, R. and P. Garber (1980), 'Market Fundamentals versus Price Level Bubbles: The First Test', *Journal of Political Economy*, **88** (4), 745–70.

Fortune, P. (1998), 'Mutual Funds, Part II: Fund Flows and Security Returns', *New England Economic Review*, January/February, 3–22.

Friedman, B. (1977), 'Financial Flow Variables and the Short-run Determination of Long-term Interest Rates,' *Journal of Political Economy*, **85** (4), 661–89.

—— (1982), 'Effects of Shifting Saving Patterns on Interest rates and Economic Activity', *Journal of Finance*, **37** (1), 37–62.

—— (1996), 'Economic Implications of Changing Share Ownership', *Journal of Portfolio Management*, **2** (3), 59–70.

Froot, K., P. O'Connell and M. Seasholes (1998), 'The Portfolio Flows of International Investors', National Bureau of Economics Research Working Paper 6687.

Froot, K., D. Scharfstein and J. Stein (1992), 'Herd on the Street: Informational Inefficiencies in a Market with Short-term Speculation', *Journal of Finance*, **47** (4), 1461–84.

Galbraith, J.K. (1988), *The Great Crash 1929*, Boston: Houghton Mifflin.

—— (1994), *A Journey Through Economic Time*, Boston: Houghton Mifflin.

Gallinger, G.W. (1994), 'Causality Tests of the Real Stock Return – Real Activity Hypothesis', *Journal of Financial Research*, **17** (2), 271–89.

Gavin, M. (1989), 'The Stock Market and Exchange Rate Dynamics', *Journal of International Money and Finance*, **8**, 181–200.

Geske, R. and R. Roll (1983), 'The Monetary and Fiscal Linkage Between Stock Returns and Inflation', *Journal of Finance*, **38** (1), 1–33.

Gjerde, O. and F. Saettem (1999), 'Causal Relations among Stock Returns and Macroeconomic Variables in a Small, Open Economy', *Journal of International Financial Markets*, **9** (1), 61–74.

Glickman, M. (1994), 'The Concept of Information, Intractable Uncertainty, and the Current State of the "Efficient markets" Theory: A Post Keynesian View', *Journal of Post Keynesian Economics*, **16** (3), 325–349.

Gompers, P. and A. Metrick (1998), 'Institutional Investor and Equity Prices', National Bureau of Economics Research Working Paper 6723.

Goodhart C. and B. Hoffman (1999), 'Monetary Policy Adjustments with Asset Price Fluctuations', Paper Presented at the Conference on Structure, Instability and the World Economy: Reflections on the Economics of Hyman P. Minsky, The Jerome Levy Economics Institute, Annandale-on-Hudson, NY, April 21–23.

Gordon, M. (1962), *The Investment, Financing, and Valuation of the Corporation*, Homewood, IL: Irwin.

Gordon, R. (2000), 'Does the "New Economy" Measure up to the Great Inventions of the Past?', National Bureau of Economics Research Working Paper 7833.

Graham, B. and D. Dodd (1934), *Security Analysis*, New York: McGraw-Hill.

Granger, C. (1969), 'Investigating Causal Relationships by Econometric Models and Cross-spectral Methods', *Econometrica*, **37**, 424–38.

—— (1986), 'Developments in the Study of Co-integrated Economic Variables', *Oxford Bulletin of Economics and Statistics*, **48**, 213–28.

Granger, C. and A. Escribano (1987), 'Limitation on the Long-run Relationship Between Prices from an Efficient Market', Discussion Paper, Economics Department, University of California, San Diego.

Granger, C. and O. Morgenstern (1963), 'Spectral Analysis of New York Stock Market Prices', in P. Cootner (ed.), *The Random Character of Stock Market Prices*, Cambridge, MA: The MIT Press.

Granger, C. and Paul Newbold (1974), 'Spurious Regression in Econometrics', *Journal of Econometrics*, **2**, 111–20.

Gray, H. and J. Gray (1994), 'Minskian Fragility in the International Financial System', in G. Dymski and R. Pollin (eds), *New Perspectives in Monetary Macroeconomics*, Ann Arbor: University of Michigan Press.

Greenspan, A. (2002), 'Remarks on Corporate Governance', Stern School of Business, New York University, New York, NY, March 26.

Grullon, G. and R. Michaely (2002), 'Dividends, Share Repurchases, and the Substitution Hypothesis, *Journal of Finance*, **57** (4), 1649–84.

Hall, R. (2000), 'E-capital: The Link Between the Stock Market and the Labor Market', *Brookings Papers on Economic Activity*, **2**, 73–118.

Hall, R. (2001), 'Struggling to Understand the Stock Market', *American Economic Review,* **91** (2), 1–11.

Hansen, L. and K. Singleton (1983), 'Stochastic Consumption, Risk Aversion, and the Temporal Behavior of Asset Returns', *Journal of Political Economy*, **91** (2), 249–65.

Harris, L. and E. Gurel (1986), 'Price and Volume Effects Associated with Changes in the S&P 500 Lists: New Evidence for the Existence of Price Pressures', *Journal of Finance*, **41** (4), 815–29.

Hayes, S., C. Salmon and S. Yadav (1998), 'Equities: What Can they Tell us About the Real Economy?' in *The Role of Asset Prices in the Formulation of Monetary Policy*, BIS Conference Paper 5, 178–95.

Heaton, J. and D. Lucas (1999), 'Stock Prices and Fundamentals', in B. Bernanke and J. Rotemberg (eds), *Macroeconomics Annual*, Cambridge, MA: The MIT Press.

Hendricks, D., J. Patel and R. Zeckhauser (1994), 'Investment Flows and Performance: Evidence From Mutual Funds, Cross-Border Investments, and New Issues', in R. Sato et al. (eds), *Japan, Europe and International Financial Markets: Analytical and Empirical Perspectives*, Cambridge: Cambridge University Press.

Hobijn B. and B. Jovanovic (2000), 'Information Technology Revolution and the Stock Market: Evidence', National Bureau of Economics Research Working Paper 7684.

Holmstrom, B. and S. Kaplan (2001), 'Corporate Governance and Merger Activity in the United States: Making Sense of the 1980s and 1990s', *Journal of Economic Perspectives*, **15** (2), 121–44.

Houthakker, H.S. and P.J. Williamson (1996), *The Economics of Financial Markets*, Oxford: Oxford University Press.

Hsiao, C. (1979), 'Causality Tests in Econometrics', *Journal of Economic Dynamics and Control*, **1**, 321–46.

Hussey, R. (1992), 'Nonparametric Evidence on Asymmetry in Business Cycles Using Aggregate Employment Time Series', *Journal of Econometrics*, **51**, 217–31.

Ibbotson Associates (2000), *Stocks, Bonds, Bills and Inflation – 2000 Yearbook*, Chicago: Ibbotson Associates, Inc.

International Monetary Fund (2000*), World Economic Outlook: Asset Prices and the Business Cycle*, May.

Investment Company Institute (1999, 2000, 2001), *Mutual Fund Fact Book*, Washington, DC.

Ippolito, R. (1992), 'Consumer Reaction to Measures of Poor Quality: Evidence from the Mutual Fund Industry', *Journal of Law and Economics*, **35**, 45–70.

Jagannathan, M., C. Stephens and M. Weisbach (2000), 'Financial Flexibility and the Choice Between Dividends and Stock Repurchases', *Journal of Financial Economics*, **57** (3), 355–84.

Jagannathan, R., E. McGrattan and A. Scherbina (2001), 'The Declining US Equity Premium', *Federal Reserve Bank of Minneapolis Quarterly Review*, **24** (4), 3–19.

James, C. et al. (1985), 'A VARMA Analysis of the Causal Relations among Stock Returns, Real Output, and Nominal Interest Rates', *Journal of Finance*, **40** (5), 1375–84.

Jegadeesh, N. (1990), 'Evidence of Predictability Behavior of Security Returns', *Journal of Finance*, **45** (3), 881–98.

John, K. and J. Williams (1985), 'Dividends, Dilution, and Taxes: A Signaling Equilibrium', *Journal of Finance*, **40**, 1053–70.

Johnson, L.D. and B. Pazderka (1995), *The Economic and Social Benefits of Stock Markets: It's No Gamble*, Canada: The Fraser Institute.

Jorgenson, D. (1963), 'Capital Theory and Investment Behavior', *American Economic Review*, **53** (2), 247–59.

Jovanovic, B. and P. Rousseau (2000), 'Accounting for Stock Market Growth: 1885–1998', Manuscript, New York University.

Kansas, D. (1996), 'Taking Stock', *Wall Street Journal*, May 28, R1.

Kaplan, S. and J. Stein (1993), 'The Evolution of Buyout Pricing and Financial Structure in the 1980s', *Quarterly Journal of Economics*, **108** (2), 313–58.

Kaul, G. (1987), 'Stock Returns and Inflation: The Role of the Monetary Sector', *Journal of Financial Economics*, **18**, 253–76.

Keim, D. and R. Stambaugh (1986), 'Predicting Returns in the Stock and Bond Markets', *Journal of Financial Economics*, **17**, 357–90.

Kendell, M. (1953), 'The Analysis of Economic Time-series, Part I: Prices', in P. Cootner (ed.), *The Random Character of Stock Market Prices*, Cambridge, MA: The MIT Press.

Kennedy, P. (1993), *A Guide to Econometrics*, Cambridge, MA: The MIT Press.

Keynes, J.M. (1930), *A Treatise on Money*, reprinted as *The Collected Writings of J. M. Keynes*, V and VI, London: Macmillan, 1971.

—— [1936] (1964), *The General Theory of Employment, Interest and Money*, London: Harcourt Brace & Company.

Kindleberger, C.P. [1978] [1989] (1996), *Manias, Panics, and Crashes: A History of Financial Crises*, New York: Basic Books.

Kon-Ya, T. and R. Shiller (1998), 'Results of Surveys about Stock Market Speculation', <http://www.econ.yale.edu/~shiller/investor.hmtl>.

Krugman, P. (1997), 'How Fast Can the US Economy Grow?' *Harvard Business Review*, **75** (July–August), 123–9.

Lamdin, D. (2000), 'New Results on Stock Prices and Fundamental Value', Social Science Research Network Working Paper Series, <http://papers.ssrn.com.>

Lee, B. (1992), 'Causal Relations among Stock Returns, Interest Rates, Real Activity, and Inflation', *Journal of Finance*, **47** (4), 1591–603.

Lee, I. (1998), 'Market Crashes and Informational Avalanches', *Review of Economic Studies*, **65**, 741–59.

Lehmann, B. (1991), 'Asset Prices and Intrinsic Value', *Journal of Monetary Economics*, **28**, 485–500.

Leroy, S.F. (1989), 'Efficient Capital Markets and Martingales', *Journal of Economic Literature*, **27** (4), 1583–621.

Leroy, S.F. and R. Porter (1981) 'The Present-value Relations: Tests Based on Implied Variance Bounds', *Econometrica*, **49** (3), 555–74.

Lewis, M. (1989), *Liar's Poker*, New York: Penguin Books Ltd.

Liang, J. and S. Sharpe (1999), 'Share Repurchase and Employee Stock Options and their Implications for S&P 500 Share Retirements and Expected Returns', Board of Governors of the Federal Reserve System, *Finance and Economics Discussion Paper* Series, 99/59 (November).

Ludvigson, S. and C. Steindel (1998), 'How Important is the Stock Market Effect on Consumption?', Federal Reserve Bank of New York Research Paper 9821.

Mankiw, N. and S. Zeldes (1991), 'The Consumption of Stockholders and Non-stockholders', *Journal of Financial Economics*, **29** (1), 97–112.

Mayer, C. (1990), 'Financial Systems, Corporate Finance, and Economic Development', in R. Glenn Hubbard (ed.), *Asymmetric Information, Corporate Finance, and Investment*, Chicago: University of Chicago Press.

Mayfield, E. (1999), 'Estimating the Market Risk Premium', Social Science Research Network Working Paper, <www.ssrn.com>.

McCauley, R., J. Rudd and F. Iacono (1999), *Dodging Bullets: Changing US Corporate Capital Structure in the 1980s and 1990s*, Cambridge, MA: The MIT Press.

Mehra, R. and E. Prescott (1985), 'The Equity Premium: A Puzzle', *Journal of Monetary Economics*, **15**, 145–61.

Merton C. (1980), 'On Estimating the Expected Return on the Market: An Exploratory Investigation', *Journal of Financial Economics*, **8**, 323–61.

Miller, M. (1991), *Financial Innovations and Market Volatility*, Cambridge: Blackwell.

Mills, T. (1990), *Time Series Techniques for Economists*, Cambridge: Cambridge University Press.

Minsky, H.P. (1975), *John Maynard Keynes*, London: Macmillan.

—— (1982), *Can It Happen Again*, New York: Sharpe.

—— (1986), *Stabilizing an Unstable Economy*, New Haven, CT: Yale University Press.

—— (1995), 'Financial Factors in the Economics of Capitalism', *Journal of Financial Research*, **9**, 197–208.

Mishkin, F. (1977), 'What Depressed the Consumer? The Household Balance Sheet and the 1973–1975 Recession', *Brookings Papers on Economic Activity*, **1**, 123–64.

Modigliani F. and R. Cohn (1982), 'Inflation and the Stock Market', in M. Sarnat and G. Szego (eds), *Saving, Investment, and Capital Markets in an Inflationary Economy*, Cambridge, MA: Ballinger Publishing Company.

Modigliani, F. and M. Miller (1958), 'The Cost of Capital, Corporation Finance and the Theory of Investment', *American Economic Review*, **48** (3), 261–97.

Morck, R., A. Shleifer and R.W. Vishny (1990), 'The Stock Market and Investment: Is the Market a Sideshow?', *Brookings Papers on Economic Activity*, **2**, 157–215.

Morrissey, M. (2000), 'Background Report: Employee Stock Options', Washington, DC: Financial Markets Center.

Moyer, R. and A. Patel (1997), 'The Equity Market Risk Premium: A Critical Look at Alternative Ex Ante Estimates', Babcock Graduate School of Management Working Paper, Wake Forest University.

Mullins, M. and S. Wadhwani (1989). 'The Effect of the Stock Market on Investment: A Comparative Study', *European Economic Review*, **33** (5), May.

Neftci, S. (1984), 'Are Time Series Asymmetric over the Business Cycle?', *Journal of Political Economy*, **92**, 307–28.

Obstfeld, M. (1998), 'The Global Capital Market: Benefactor or Menace', National Bureau of Economics Research Working Paper 6559.

Otoo, M. (1999), 'Consumer Sentiment and the Stock Market', Board of Governors of the Federal Reserve System, Division of Research and Statistics and Monetary Affairs, Working Paper 1999–60.

Pagan, A. (1987), 'Three Econometric Methodologies: A Critical Appraisal', *Journal of Economic Surveys*, **1**, 3–24.

Parenteau, F. and F. Veneroso (1999), 'Deriving Irrationally Exuberant Equity Conditions from Adaptive Expectations', Paper Presented at the Conference on Structure, Instability and the World Economy: Reflections on the Economics of Hyman P. Minsky, The Jerome Levy Economics Institute, Annandale-on-Hudson, NY, April 21–23.

Pastor L. and R. Stambaugh (1998), 'The Equity Risk Premium and Structural Breaks', Warton School Working Paper, University of Pennsylvania.

Paulre, B. (2000), 'Is the New Economy a Useful Concept?', National CNRS ISYS Working Paper 8595, September.

Perkins, A. and M. Perkins (1999), *The Internet Bubble*, New York: HarperBusiness Press.

Pesaran, M. and A. Timmermann, (1995), 'Predictability of Stock Returns: Robustness and Economic Significance', *Journal of Finance*, **50** (4), 1201–28.

Phillips, P. and P. Perron (1988), 'Testing for a Unit Root in Times Series Regression', *Biometrica*, **75**, 335–46.

Pontin, J. (1997), 'There is no New Economy', *The Red Herring Magazine*, September.

Portes, R. and H. Rey (1999), 'The Determinants of Cross Border Equity Flows', National Bureau of Economics Research Working Paper 7336.

Poterba, J. (2000), 'Stock Market Wealth and Consumption', *Journal of Economic Perspectives*, **14** (2), 99–118.

Poterba, J. and A. Samwick (1995), 'Stock Ownership Patterns, Stock Market Fluctuations, and Consumption', *Brookings Papers on Economic Activity*, **2**, 295–357.

Poterba, J. and L. Summers (1988), 'Mean Reversion in Stock Prices: Evidence and Implications', *Journal of Financial Economics*, **22**, 26–59.

Pratten, C. (1993), *The Stock Market*, Cambridge: Press Syndicate of the University of Cambridge.

Raines, J.P. and C.G. Leathers (1996), 'Veblenian Stock Markets and the Efficient Market Hypothesis', *Journal of Post Keynesian Economics*, **19** (1), 137–151.

—— (2000), *Economists and the Stock Market: Speculative Theories of Stock Market Fluctuations*, Aldershot, UK and Northampton, US: Edward Elgar.

Ram, R. and D.E. Spencer (1983), 'Stock Returns, Real Activity and Money: Comment', *American Economic Review*, **73** (3), 463–70.

Remolona, E., P. Kleiman and D. Gruenstein (1997), 'Market Returns and Mutual Fund Flows'', *FRBNY Economic Policy Review*, July, 33–52.

Ritter, J. and R. Warr (2001), 'The Decline of Inflation and the Bull Market of 1982 to 1999', *Journal of Financial and Quantitative Analysis*, **37** (1), <www.bear.cba. ufl. edu/ritter>.

Robertson, D. and S. Wright (1998), 'The Good News and Band News about Long Run Stock Market Returns, Social Science Research Network Working Paper Series, <http://papers.ssrn.com>.

Romer, D. (1993), 'Rational Asset-price Movements Without News', *American Economic Review*, December, 1112–30.

Rothman, P. (1991), 'Further Evidence on the Asymmetric Behavior of Unemployment Rates over the Business Cycle', *Journal of Macroeconomics*, **13**, 291–98.

Samuelson, P. (1965), 'Proof that Properly Anticipated Prices Fluctuate Randomly', *Industrial Management Review*, **6**, 41–9.

Saunders, E., Jr. (1993), 'Stock Prices and Wall Street Weather', *American Economic Review*, **83**, 1337–45.

Scholes, M. (1972), 'The Market for Securities: Substitution versus Price Pressure and the Effects of Information on Share Prices', *Journal of Business*, **45**, 179–211.

Schwert, W.G. (1990) 'Stock Returns and Real Activity: A Century of Evidence', *Journal of Finance*, **45** (4), 1237–57.

Scott, L. (1991), 'Financial Market Volatility: A Survey', *IMF Staff Papers*, **38** (3).

Sensenbrenner, G. (1991), 'Aggregate Investment, the Stock Market and the Q Model', *European Economic Review*, **35**, 769–832.

Shah, H. (1989), 'Stock Returns and Anticipated Aggregated Real Activity', Unpublished PhD Thesis, Graduate School of Business, University of Chicago.

Shaikh, A.M. (1995), 'The Stock Market and the Corporate Sector: A Profit Based Approach', Jerome Levy Economics Institute Working Paper 146.

Shapiro, C. and H. Varian (1999), *Information Rules*, Cambridge, MA: Harvard Business School Press.

Sharpe, S. (2000), 'Reexamining Stock Valuation and Inflation: The Implications of Analyst's Earnings Forecasts', Unpublished Federal Reserve Board Working Paper.

Shiller, R. (1981), 'Do Stock Prices Move Too Much to be Justified by Subsequent Changes in Dividends?', *American Economic Review*, **71** (3), 421–36.

—— (1984), 'Stock Prices and Social Dynamics', *Brookings Papers on Economic Activity*, **2**, 457–510.

—— (1989), *Market Volatility*, Cambridge: The MIT Press.

—— (1990), 'Market Volatility and Investor Behavior', *American Economic Review*, **80**, 58–62.

—— (2000a), *Irrational Exuberance*, Princeton, NJ: Princeton University Press.

—— (2000b), 'Measuring Bubble Expectations and Investor Confidence', *Journal of Psychology and Markets*, **1** (1), 49–60.

Shiller R. and J. Pound (1989), 'Survey Evidence of Diffusion of Interest Among Institutional Investors', *Journal of Economic Behavior and Organization*, **12**, 47–66.

Shleifer, A. (1986), 'Do Demand Curves for Stocks Slope Down', *Journal of Finance*, **41**, 579–90.

Shleifer, A. and L. Summers (1990), 'The Noise Trader Approach to Finance', *Journal of Economic Perspectives*, **4** (2), 19–33.

Siegel, J. (1994), *Stocks for the Long Run*, Burr Ridge, IL: Irwin Professional.

—— (1998), 'Risk and Return: Start with the Building Blocks', in *The Complete Finance Companion: Mastering Finance*, London: Pitman Publishing.

—— (1999), 'The Shrinking Equity Premium: Historical Facts and Future Forecasts', *Journal of Portfolio Management*, **26** (Fall), 10–17.

Sims, C.A. (1972), 'Money, Income, and Causality', *American Economic Review*, **62**, 540–52.

—— (1980), 'Macroeconomics and Reality', *Econometrica*, **48**, 1–49.

Sirri, E. and P. Tufano (1993), 'Buying and Selling Mutual Funds: Flows, Performance, Fees, and Services', Harvard Business School Working Paper, Cambridge, MA.

Sokalska, M. (1997), 'Equity Price Dynamics', University of Cambridge Department of Applied Economics Working Paper, Amalgamated Series: 97/30.

Standard and Poor's Corporation (1999), *Standard and Poor's Stock Market Encyclopedia*, Spring Edition.

Starr-McCluer, M. (1998), 'Stock Market Wealth and Consumer Patterns', Board of Governors of the Federal Reserve System, Division of Research and Statistics and Monetary Affairs, Working Paper 1998–20.

Stigler, G. (1964), 'Public Regulation of the Securities Market', *Journal of Business*, April, 11742.

Strange, S. (1986), *Casino Capitalism*, Oxford: Blackwell.

—— (1998), *Mad Money: When Markets Outgrow Governments*, Ann Arbor, MI: The University of Michigan Press.

Stulz, R. (1999a), 'International Portfolio Flows and Security Markets', in M. Feldstein (ed.), *International Capital Flows*, Chicago: The University of Chicago Press.

—— (1999b), 'Globalization of Equity Markets and the Cost of Capital', National Bureau of Economics Research Working Paper 7021.

Summers, L. (1981), 'Taxation and Corporate Investment: A Q-theory Approach', *Brookings Papers on Economic Activity*, I, 67–127.

Summers, L. (1991), 'The Scientific Illusion in Empirical Macroeconomics', *Scandinavian Journal of Economics*, 93 (2), 129–48.

Summers, L. and V. Summers (1989), 'When Financial Markets Work Too Well: A Cautious Case for a Securities Transactions Tax', *Journal of Financial Services*, 3, 163–88.

Taylor, L. (1994), 'Financial Fragility: Is an Etiology at Hand', in G. Dymski and R. Pollin (eds), *New Perspectives in Monetary Economics*, Ann Arbor: The University of Michigan Press.

Taylor, L. and S.A. O'Connell (1985), 'A Minsky Crisis', *Quarterly Journal of Economics*, 100 (Supplement), 875–85.

Taylor, M. and H. Allen (1992), 'The Use of Technical Analysis in the Foreign Exchange Market', *Journal of International Money and Finance*, 11, 304–14.

Tease, W. (1993), 'The Stock·Market and Investment', *OECD Economic Studies*, 20, 42–63.

Tesar, L. (1999), 'The Role of Equity Markets in International Capital Flows', in M. Feldstein (ed.), *International Capital Flows*, Chicago: The University of Chicago Press.

Tesar, L. and I. Werner (1993), 'US Equity Investment in Emerging Stock Markets' in S. Claessens and S. Goptu (eds), *Portfolio Investment in Developing Countries*, Washington, DC: World Bank.

—— (1995), 'Home Bias and High Turnover', *Journal of International Money and Finance*, 14, 467–92.

Thaler, R. (1998), 'Giving Markets a Human Dimension', in *The Complete Finance Companion: Mastering Finance*, London: Pitman Publishing.

Tobin, J. (1969), 'A General Equilibrium Approach to Monetary Theory', *Journal of Money, Credit and Banking*, 1, 15–29.

—— (1970), 'Money and Income: Post Hoc Ergo Propter Hoc?' *Quarterly Journal of Economics*, 84 (2), 301–17.

Toporowski, J. (1999a), 'Monetary Policy in an Era of Capital Market Inflation', Jerome Levy Economics Institute Working Paper 279.

—— (1999b), *The End of Finance: Capital Market Inflation, Financial Derivatives and Pension Fund Capitalism*, London: Routledge.

Veblen, T. (1904), *The Theory of Business Enterprise*, New York: Charles Scribner's Sons.

Von Furstenberg, G. (1977), 'Corporate Investment: Does Market Valuation Matter in the Aggregate', *Brookings Papers on Economic Activity*, **2**, 397–407.

Wadhwani, S. (1999), 'The US Stock Market and the Global Economic Crisis', *National Institute Review*, January, 86–105.

Warther, V. (1995), 'Aggregate Mutual Fund Flows and the Impact on Stock Prices', *Journal of Financial Economics*, **39**, 209–35.

Wasserfallen, W. (1989), 'Macroeconomics News and the Stock Market: Evidence from Europe', *Journal of Banking and Finance*, **13**, 613–26.

Welch, I. (2000), 'Views of Financial Economists on the Equity Premium and on Professional Controversies', *Journal of Business*, **73** (4), 501–37.

Wermers, R. (1999), 'Mutual Fund Herding and the Impact on Stock Prices', *Journal of Finance*, **54**, 581–622.

White, H. (1980), 'A Heteroskedasticity-consistent Covariance Matrix and a Direct Test for Heteroskedasticity', *Econometrica*, **48**, 817–38.

Williams, J.B. (1938), *The Theory of Investment Value*, Cambridge: Harvard University Press.

Wolff, E. (2000), 'Recent Trends in Wealth Ownership, 1983–98', Jerome Levy Economics Institute Working Paper 3000 (April).

Working, H. (1960), 'Note on the Correlation of First Differences of Averages in a Random Chain', in P. Cootner (ed.), *The Random Character of Stock Market Prices*, Cambridge, MA: The MIT Press.

Zandi, M. (1999), 'Wealth Worries', *Regional Financial Review*, August, 1–8.

Index

Akaike's Information Criterion 154, 165
AOL 2, 211
arbitrage pricing theory 22

beauty contest 27, 43, 96
behavioral finance 25, 33, 43, 213
Bernstein 13, 15, 35–37, 86
bond yields 8, 46–47, 49, 149, 176
Bretton Woods 135, 185
Buffet 2
bull market 2, 4–7, 10, 15, 66, 74, 76,
    78, 81, 90, 98, 100, 105, 112, 114,
    117, 120-121, 124, 127, 131, 135,
    137, 140, 153, 161-2, 175, 186, 202,
    204-6

capital flows 5, 7–8, 31, 70–72, 101,
    131, 135, 137, 148–9
capital market inflation 36–7, 43–4, 66,
    105
See also Toporowski
capital asset pricing model (CAPM) 22
corporate equity (supply)
    equity retirements 2, 7, 98, 109, 160,
        164, 204, 208
    initial public offerings (IPOs) 124,
        137, 181, 204, 208
    leveraged buyouts (LBOs) 1, 97,
        102–104, 137
    mergers 98, 102, 104–6, 137, 139,
        143, 146–7, 153, 160, 174, 209, 216
    net issuance 8, 10, 37, 137, 139, 142,
        146, 150, 153, 157, 160–162, 164–5,
        174, 176, 197–8, 207
    share repurchases 1, 7, 76, 104–5,
        138, 142–7, 153, 205, 208, 210
corporate profits 6, 16, 28, 48, 91, 98–9,
    100, 106, 108, 127, 129, 132, 134,
    138–9, 141–3, 146, 151, 164, 205,
    209
cost of capital 14, 55, 178

Cowles 17, 19
crash 2, 12, 23, 25, 31, 33, 36–7, 42, 97,
    210

D'Arista 104–5, 131, 137
Davidson 35–7, 43, 91
default spread 49–51, 52, 54, 59, 178,
    187, 191, 196, 200
depression 13, 74, 100
derivatives 14, 100, 185, 209
Dickey–Fuller tests 58, 155–7
discount rates 6, 46–7, 50, 54, 64, 75,
    96, 106, 127, 137, 144, 176, 207
diversification 4, 85, 101–102, 106,
    114, 125, 185, 199
dividend
    growth 3–4, 67, 74–83, 88–9, 98,
        100, 107, 144, 146–7, 206
    payouts 4, 10, 64, 75, 91, 144, 177,
        207
    yield 3, 46–8, 50–54, 67, 75, 82, 105,
        149–150, 210

earnings restatements 2, 28, 97, 204,
    210
e-capital 78
econometrics (reduced form)
    Box–Jenkins 154
    Granger causality 8, 10, 59, 61, 70,
        137, 149, 154, 157–8, 160–167, 175,
        194, 202
    impulse response function 62, 150,
        163–4, 166, 168, 172, 175, 179, 194,
        202
    See also innovation accounting
    innovation accounting 8, 10, 60,
        163–4, 166, 172
    variance decomposition 60, 62, 140,
        163–4, 166, 172–3, 194, 202
    See also innovation accounting

vector autoregressive technique 8, 59–62, 137, 149–150, 154, 163–7, 170–76, 179, 181, 194
vector moving average 163
econometrics (structural model)
  instrumental variable technique 8, 70, 137, 179, 194–5, 197
  ordinary least squares 58–9, 62, 150, 154, 182–4, 192–3, 195, 197–8, 200
Edwards and Zhang 70, 84, 149, 152, 154, 161, 177, 193–4, 197
Enron 2, 28, 31, 209
equity premium puzzle 82
ERISA 102, 106, 117, 185
exchange rates 63–4
expectations
  adaptive expectations 27, 30–31, 93, 95, 205
  euphoric expectations 10, 30, 99, 102, 108
  rational expectations 15, 17–18, 22–4, 28–9, 31, 40, 42, 51, 55, 58, 68, 90, 94, 207, 213
  excess demand curve 68, 108-9, 149, 202, 205
Fama 18, 21–3, 28, 34, 36, 38, 42, 46–55, 57–9, 67, 76, 80–81, 83, 91, 143, 150, 152–3, 176–8, 184
foreign direct investment 133–4, 136, 150–53, 155–6, 159–60, 162, 165–6, 171–2, 174–5, 179, 183–4, 186, 188–9, 191–2, 202
financial crisis 1, 7, 79, 101, 106
financial felony 32, 97
flow of funds methodology 8, 149
flow theory 7, 10, 38, 76, 90, 92–3, 95, 98, 105, 107, 109, 126–7, 131, 148, 167, 213
France 63, 67, 101
fundamental uncertainty 5, 9, 16, 27–30, 91, 93, 95, 97

Galbraith 14–15, 31–4, 65, 206–7, 210, 213
Germany 63, 67, 101
globalization 62, 77, 79, 99
goodness-of-fit 52–3, 64, 177
Graham and Dodd 16–17, 55
greenmail 103
Greenspan 99, 104, 108, 210

Hall 3, 25, 78
horizontalist perspective 68
See also excess demand curve

Ibbotson Associates 82
industrial production 46, 48–9, 51–2, 54–5, 59–60, 63–4, 67, 70, 151–3, 155, 157, 164, 176, 178, 185, 187, 191, 196, 198, 200
Industrial Revolution 79
international flows *See* capital flows
irrational exuberance 5, 6, 33, 54, 74, 76, 108–9, 123, 148, 202–4
See also Shiller
irrationality 19, 25, 31, 39, 40-41, 45, 53, 65, 90-91

Japan 101, 211
junk bonds 97, 102–4, 106, 146

Keynes 9, 13–14, 25–9, 31–2, 34–6, 42–4, 55, 56, 66–7, 90, 93, 95–6, 98, 147, 207, 208
Kindleberger 25, 31–2, 43, 97, 207, 210

Leroy 17, 19–23, 39, 41, 51, 65
liquidity preference 26, 35, 43

market efficiency
  efficient capital markets 6–7, 10, 14, 19, 21, 23, 40, 47, 52, 64, 69, 74, 76, 81, 106, 148, 177, 202
  efficient markets hypothesis (EMH) 3–6, 10, 16, 18, 20, 22–5, 28, 34, 35, 37–41, 43, 46, 48–9, 51, 53, 55, 57–61, 64–9, 76, 78–9, 83, 90, 92, 95, 107–8, 127, 144, 147, 177, 184, 198, 202, 206–7, 213
  joint hypothesis 9–10, 22, 59, 63, 157
  perfect competition 15, 18–20
market participants
  foreign sector 79, 109–10, 112, 116, 126–7, 132, 134–5, 139
  households 57, 79, 84, 109–10, 112–16, 120, 122–3, 127–8, 194, 211
  individual investors 5, 53, 70, 84–5, 94, 101, 106, 132, 147, 199, 207
  institutional investors 5, 7, 10, 31, 32–3, 72, 84–5, 98, 102, 104–6, 114, 116, 120, 123–5, 127, 132, 136, 152–

3, 162, 172, 185–6, 188, 198–9, 200–204, 206
life insurance companies 116, 120, 125–30, 132, 150, 152–4, 157, 161–2, 165, 174–5, 179, 181–2, 202
mutual funds 5, 15, 69–70, 84–5, 90, 105, 110, 114, 116–17, 120, 122–30, 132, 134, 147, 161–2, 186, 188, 191–2, 194, 196, 198–200, 203–4, 206–7, 210
pension funds 70, 85, 102, 110–11, 116–17, 122–30, 132, 134, 138, 142, 152–3, 162, 181, 186, 198, 203–5
market volatility 83–4, 123, 204
Markowitz 101
Marshall 12, 19–20
May Day 102, 185
Microsoft 142
Miller 26, 38, 103, 198
Minsky 9, 26, 30–32, 34, 43, 56, 67, 74, 90, 93–8, 100, 102–3, 105, 202–3, 206–7, 209–10, 213
Minsky model
  financial fragility 9, 26, 30, 93–4, 102, 105, 125, 147, 209
  financial instability 30, 93–94, 203, 206
  Ponzi units 37, 94, 96, 103, 131, 145, 208–9
Modigliani 38, 91, 103, 198
mutual fund shares 69-70, 113-17, 123-4, 194, 215

new economy 2, 4, 10, 74, 76, 77–9, 84, 88, 100, 105–6, 145, 199, 206
noise trading 9, 25, 39, 41–3, 69, 72, 95
non-equilibrium 36–7

Phillips–Perron tests *See* Dickey–Fuller tests
portfolio flows 71, 131, 134, 136, 150, 152, 154, 162, 164–7, 170–75, 179, 185, 189, 192–5, 197–9, 201–3, 208
present value *See* Valuation model
prices
  full information price 68, 108, 202, 205
  fundamental value 16–18, 20–21, 24, 29, 35–6, 38, 40, 43, 55, 64, 68, 88,

90, 92, 108, 144, 146, 149–50, 189, 202
intrinsic values 5, 17, 20, 23, 29, 34, 38, 41, 46–7, 176
martingale 18, 20–22, 41, 51, 65
overvaluation 3, 16, 26, 29, 31, 36, 38, 47–8, 58, 78, 90–91, 97–8, 185, 203, 206–7, 211
price–earnings 3, 6, 39, 105, 211
random walk 18–19, 20–21

rational bubbles 25, 39, 40–43
Reagan 44, 134, 206
required rate of return 4, 16, 46, 50, 53, 73, 75–6, 81–2, 84, 86, 88–9, 125, 199, 206–7
recession 30, 50, 74, 99, 101, 106, 178
risk premium 4–5, 10, 18, 50, 54, 64, 70, 72, 74–6, 81–4, 85, 88–90, 95, 100, 106, 125, 129, 132, 137, 143–4, 146, 148, 178, 198–9, 201, 203–4, 206–7
Roosevelt 13
Rule (10b-18) 5 105–6, 138, 160, 203, 205, 210

Samuelson 20–3, 38, 42, 55
Scholes 68–9
SEC *See* Rule 10b-18
Shiller 1, 5–6, 9, 15, 25, 32–4, 37, 41–3, 47, 53–4, 65, 67, 75–6, 80, 87–8, 90, 92, 95, 99–101, 109, 142, 144, 201, 203, 207, 211
Siegel 83–4, 86, 100, 201, 207
Sims 8, 58–9, 62, 162–4, 175
simultaneous equations bias 55, 57, 177
social psychology 33
social security 1, 211
South Sea Bubble 25
speculative markets and theory 9, 24–6, 28, 32, 34–5, 37–8, 41–3, 64, 66, 70, 90, 92, 95, 108, 147, 150, 212
speculative bubbles 1, 6, 27, 33, 38, 40-41, 53, 70, 90, 92, 94–5, 97, 109, 203, 205, 207
stock market anomalies 39, 213
stock options 6, 104, 139, 142, 146, 160
Summers 8, 23, 42, 56, 59, 61–2, 65, 67
surveys 32, 201, 207

term spread *See* Term structure
term structure 49–52, 54, 64, 70, 153,
  157, 176, 178, 187, 191, 196, 200
Tobin's q 3, 56
Toporowski 12 36–7, 38, 43, 66, 92,
  105, 207, 213
tulipmania 25
Tyco 209

United Kingdom 63, 101, 215

valuation models
  dividend discount model 17, 74, 89,
  92, 95–6, 143, 145
  Gordon growth 75, 82, 88–9, 98,
  143–4
  simple valuation model 16
  standard valuation model 17–18, 21,
  24, 28, 30, 35, 38, 45–7, 67, 90–3,
  144–5, 176–7
variance-bounds tests 45, 65, 66
Veblen 9, 26, 29, 30, 32, 34, 43–4, 67,
  90, 93, 98, 207, 209

Wall Street 13, 28, 82, 96, 204, 213
Walras 12, 19
Warther 69–70, 123, 149, 154, 193, 194
wealth effect 60, 63, 113, 178
WorldCom 2, 31, 146–7, 209

yield curve 50, 52, 54, 63, 178

NEW DIRECTIONS IN MODERN ECONOMICS

Post-Keynesian Monetary Economics
New Approaches to Financial Modelling
Edited by Philip Arestis

Keynes's Principle of Effective Demand
Edward J. Amadeo

New Directions in Post-Keynesian Economics
Edited by John Pheby

Theory and Policy in Political Economy
Essays in Pricing, Distribution and Growth
Edited by Philip Arestis and Yiannis Kitromilides

Keynes's Third Alternative?
The Neo-Ricardian Keynesians and the Post Keynesians
Amitava Krishna Dutt and Edward J. Amadeo

Wages and Profits in the Capitalist Economy
The Impact of Monopolistic Power on Macroeconomic Performance
in the USA and UK
Andrew Henley

Prices, Profits and Financial Structures
A Post-Keynesian Approach to Competition
Gokhan Capoglu

International Perspectives on Profitability and Accumulation
Edited by Fred Moseley and Edward N. Wolff

Mr Keynes and the Post Keynesians
Principles of Macroeconomics for a Monetary Production Economy
Fernando J. Cardim de Carvalho

The Economic Surplus in Advanced Economies
Edited by John B. Davis

Foundations of Post-Keynesian Economic Analysis
Marc Lavoie

The Post-Keynesian Approach to Economics
An Alternative Analysis of Economic Theory and Policy
Philip Arestis

Income Distribution in a Corporate Economy
Russell Rimmer

The Economics of the Profit Rate
Competition, Crises and Historical Tendencies in Capitalism
Gérard Duménil and Dominique Lévy

Corporatism and Economic Performance
A Comparative Analysis of Market Economies
Andrew Henley and Euclid Tsakalotos

Competition, Technology and Money
Classical and Post-Keynesian Perspectives
Edited by Mark A. Glick

Investment Cycles in Capitalist Economies
A Kaleckian Behavioural Contribution
Jerry Courvisanos

Does Financial Deregulation Work?
A Critique of Free Market Approaches
Bruce Coggins

Pricing Theory in Post Keynesian Economics
A Realist Approach
Paul Downward

The Economics of Intangible Investment
Elizabeth Webster

Globalization and the Erosion of National Financial Systems
Is Declining Autonomy Inevitable?
Marc Schaberg

Explaining Prices in the Global Economy
A Post-Keynesian Model
Henk-Jan Brinkman

Capitalism, Socialism, and Radical Political Economy
Essays in Honor of Howard J. Sherman
Edited by Robert Pollin

Financial Liberalisation and Intervention
A New Analysis of Credit Rationing
Santonu Basu

Why the Bubble Burst
US Stock Market Performance since 1982
Lawrance Lee Evans, Jr.